THE
SEARCHERS

ALSO BY KENNETH MACKSEY

Battle
Guderian: Panzer General
Tank versus Tank
Invasion
Military Errors of World War Two
Without Enigma

THE SEARCHERS

Radio Intercept in Two World Wars

KENNETH MACKSEY

CASSELL

Cassell Military Paperbacks

Cassell
Wellington House, 125 Strand, London WC2R 0BB

British Library Cataloguing-in-Publication Data:
A catalogue record for this book is available from the British Library

ISBN 0-304-36651-X

Printed and bound in Great Britain by
Cox & Wyman Ltd, Reading, Berks

CONTENTS

PREFACE

Shortly before he died, Ronald Lewin, classical scholar, soldier, one time head of the BBC Home Service, historian and author (above all of *Ultra goes to War* and *The Other Ultra*) came to say goodbye. In our last conversation, when he dwelt on Ultra, he said that somebody should write about the Y Service, without whose interception of radio transmissions the British Ultra intelligence system would not have worked. Already, indeed, he was acutely aware that his *Ultra goes to War* was flawed because he had all but failed to mention it; and probably he knew too that his larger coverage of its importance in *The Other Ultra* did not fully do it justice. Moreover, by then he was much more knowledgeable about its activities from Sir Harry Hinsley's monumental *British Intelligence in the Second World War* and Aileen Clayton's *The Enemy is Listening*.

Several years passed, a period in which public knowledge of the Ultra Secret was advanced, but mainly with emphasis on the cryptanalytical side of the story and little more than cursory mention of Y. In the meantime Harry Hinsley had publicly remarked that 'the effect of Enigma has been exaggerated' and that 'Ultra was not a war winner but a war shortener'. These were the thoughts of a man who really understood the subject and which prompted me to write *Without Enigma* in an attempt to rectify an imbalance of history – something which Hinsley believed impossible.

Researching that book reminded me of Ronald's conviction that the tens of thousands of those who worked (on both sides) in Y deserved better recognition, especially because, whenever I casually asked publishers, historians and other knowledgeable people what the Y Services meant to them, the answer was far more often than not in the negative.

So one day I visited the Public Record Office in search of clues to provide insight into the story of the British Y Service. As usual, the excellent staff of that wonderful storehouse of history gave their enthusiastic attention and, with help from the computer, suggested investigation of HW3 as a starting point. That exciting day it was hard slogging without much reward until shortly before closing time. Then occurred one of those rare moments when, with hope nearly exhausted, I struck gold in HW3/93, a piece entitled *History of Military Sigint with special reference to Interception and to War Office and Overseas Staff.*

A quick glance told me that I was looking at the Contents list of a draft book of many chapters and appendices dealing with that subject and much more besides on a world-wide basis in two World Wars. For it not only covered the German and Italian aspects of those subjects but also dealt with the less well known but every bit as important Japanese side. I then discovered that it had been written immediately after the war by Nigel de Grey. But all I knew about him at that moment was that he had worked in Room 40 at the Admiralty in World War One and that he had decoded the famous Zimmermann telegram which, in 1917, brought America into that conflict; and also, coincidentally, that his son Roger had taught me tank tactics at Sandhurst during World War Two!

Only later, after I had had the entire manuscript photocopied, did I learn that Nigel de Grey (who died in 1951) had been Deputy Director of the Government Code and Cipher School (GC and CS) at Bletchley Park and, therefore, was ideally placed to give a unique view of events and personalities who worked in that now famous establishment.

Without hesitation I resolved to do as Ronald had wished. Since then I have felt his presence and that of the leading personalities (unknown to me) whose works I have chiefly consulted in writing this book. There is, of course, a carefully selected bibliography; but the authors upon whom I have chiefly drawn, who worked at GC and CS and who are now dead, are Sir Harry Hinsley, Nigel de Grey and Aileen Clayton. I trust I have done them justice in company with the horde of remarkable searchers with whom they collaborated in hastening the celebrations of victory in 1945.

Finally I must convey my profound thanks to those relatives and friends who helped me put this story together, especially to Captain (Rtd) Peter Oldridge RN who thoroughly applied his expertise in electronics, communications and history when reading the manuscript.

Kenneth Macksey

2003

THE WAY AHEAD

This book deals chiefly with the acquisition of signals generated by electromagnetic means – that is, telegraphic, telephonic and radio (or what once was called 'wireless'). In consequence it is related closely to the techniques of disguising those signals by means of codes and ciphers designed to ensure that their security remains intact against all attempts to read them illicitly.

But the emphasis in these pages focuses on how those signals were intercepted – not about codebreaking, which has been so much in vogue since early in the 1970s when the secret story of Ultra and Magic in World War Two was made public. Here the aim is to tell the tale of the Y and Radio Intercept Services and how their dedicated searchers managed to provide the cryptanalysts with messages to decrypt, but who also themselves played vital roles in codebreaking on their own account.

These were mostly high-grade people who, to a large extent, remain unsung heroes: men and women with headphones clamped to their ears who, often for hours on end, sometimes in uncomfortable and dangerous places, searched the radio bands in order to overhear the enemy. Such achievements were made possible by the brilliantly clever inventors and technologists who delved on the frontiers of knowledge to make new discoveries possible in order to keep a step ahead of an enemy engaged in similar pursuits. It is, therefore, the story of a band of brothers and sisters who have been thrust into the shadows by the brilliant cryptanalysts who tended to prove that no code remains unbroken for much longer than two years: and who have publicised themselves as expertly as they broke the contents of hundreds of different ciphers belonging to many different nationalities.

In addition to the books mentioned in the Bibliography I have consulted many documents of which the draft copy of Nigel de Grey's unpublished *History of Military Sigint*, with its special reference to Interception, is by far the most important. If this book is dedicated to anybody it is to him for his immense services to Britain and her allies in two world wars.

THE PRACTICE OF message interception in peace and war dates from the prehistoric time when it became feasible to transmit information and orders in writing. Simultaneously, therefore, primitive encoding also entailed the need to decode. Couriers bearing vital information travelled at risk of being waylaid and their messages stolen. Ships would be boarded at sea and their despatches seized if the crew was too slow throwing overboard such important papers as they were carrying. Carrier pigeons might be brought down by hawks; flag or light signals could be observed and understood. Spies, especially in wartime, needed to pass to their masters such information as they had gained without being detected.

Yet, until the day when it became possible in wartime to relay messages swiftly, it was almost impossible to arrange for them to reach their destination in time to be of tactical value. Even the signals that were passed rapidly, nation-wide by semaphore stations during the French Revolutionary Wars, could not be other than of strategic value. It took the contributions of the scientific geniuses of the nineteenth century, above all Michael Faraday, to open the doors to the all-embracing electromagnetic revolution: an event which, in 1843, inspired the British Admiralty to ask him to construct an electric, cable telegraphic link between London and Plymouth, eventually installed in 1852.

From 1850 onward extensive telegraphic networks (the equivalent in microcosm of the present day Internet) grew rapidly into webs that transmitted messages over wire which were encoded in Samuel Morse's internationally adopted dot and dash code. For example, in 1854 a system using cables rigged on poles or laid on the seabed linked London and Paris to the battlefront against Russia in the Crimea.

Right from the start it was realised that the telegraph was insecure because its wires could so easily be 'tapped'. Quite soon this subversive practice became very common in government and commercial circles as well as in a military context. Many of the first ciphers sent by telegraph were simple and easily broken; although perfectly effective if they imposed sufficient delay to prevent a predatory interceptor gaining advantage. One cipher in particular, known as the work of Blaise de Vigeniere, for over 250 years had been rated unbreakable. That is until 1846 (or thereabouts), when Charles Babbage, the celebrated mathematician and inventor of the first mechanical computer, won a bet by breaking it – an intellectual feat which underlined the principle that the more a cipher is used the more likely is its vulnerability to decryption, signalling a triumph which, in this event and not for the last time, persuaded the British military, on the eve of a war, to prohibit disclosure of its details.

Not until 1861, in the Civil War between the disunited states of America, was the necessity recognised to take strong protective measures against breaches of signal security. In that vast and widespread modern war, during which so much depended logistically upon the combination of steam-powered railways and ships, along with command and control via telegraphic communications, the need to protect by ciphers the ever more complicated transmission of confidential orders and reports became paramount.

Despite these precautions, however, a mass of highly important intelligence was gleaned from traditional sources, as for example, information from cavalry patrols operating behind the enemy lines, or from captured couriers and spies. Only occasionally did wire tapping yield important, timely intelligence; and, for the reasons listed below, remain valid to the present day.

1. The act of interception was not easy or safe because the majority of poled wires followed busy railway tracks which, because of their importance, were in constant use and kept under guard. It was a bold tapper who, monkey-like, perched on a pole-top taking notes, hoping to go undetected by a searching patrol.

2. The difficulty and time taken to transmit the intercepted message to a collecting centre.

3. The time taken to decipher and, perhaps translate, a message and pass it to the appropriate operational headquarters.

4. The time needed to issue orders (possibly themselves enciphered) for action.

The chances of accomplishing all this to satisfy tactical demands in a fast-evolving situation were usually at a premium. At best only strategic requirements were likely to be satisfied. Yet fundamental lessons for the future were learned in America. There always would be a need for crypt-analysts. There was also a requirement for telegraphic silence to conceal the existence of secret operations. On the grand scale, in this respect, it is worth mentioning a sometimes forgotten aspect of General William Sherman's celebrated march to the sea from Atlanta in 1864. Not only did he destroy the railway behind him as he advanced to prevent his enemy threatening his rear and logistic lines of communication. He simultaneously cut the extended lines of signal communication that the enemy might have acquired in the search for intelligence, as well as saving manpower to guard those lines if they had been left intact.

As the nineteenth century progressed, communications technology rapidly advanced. During the Siege of Paris in 1870–1, brave Frenchmen and messages were flown out in balloon baskets – despite unavailing attempts by the Germans to shoot them down. Soon were invented duplex telegraph systems and Wheatstone mechanically driven perforated tape transmission machines which vastly increased capacity on line and, by the introduction of repeaters, improvements to boost signal strengths. These things, along with that significant milestone, the laying of the first of many transatlantic cables in 1866, steadily gave confidence to non-technical people that there was a lot more to come in the electromagnetic field. Indeed the next vitally important step was taken in 1877 with the granting of a patent to Alexander Graham Bell for a telephone, thus setting in motion that vital stage of communication, personal conversation, and, by extension, its potential interception.

Marvellous as were these devices, there remained for solution what many people regarded as a dream to overcome that main impediment to simple signal communications, namely their dependence upon wire as the inflexible carrier of messages.

1. Signal Intelligence Organisation, UK, January 1941
Chain of command, 1941

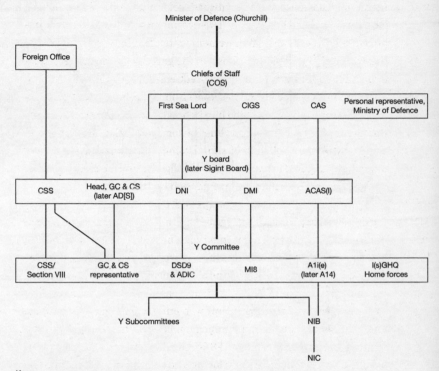

Key:

CIGS	Chief of Imperial General Staff	ACAS(I)	Assistant Chief of Air Staff (Intelligence)
CAS	Chief of Air Staff	DSD	Director Staff Duties
CSS	Chiefs of Staff Secretariat	AI	Air intelligence
GC & CS	Government code and Cipher School	NI	Naval intelligence
AD[S]	Assistant Director, Services	MI	Military intelligence
DNI	Director of Naval Intelligence		

Source: PRO HW 3/96

2. Radio intercept routes to and through GC and CS, c.1943

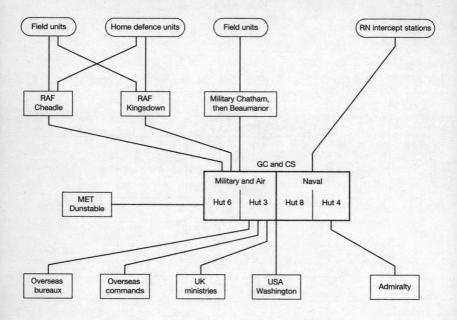

3. Allied intercept stations and main Axis transmitters, Mediterranean and Middle East, c.1942

Tripoli Allied intercept stations
Vienna Axis stations transmitting Enigma

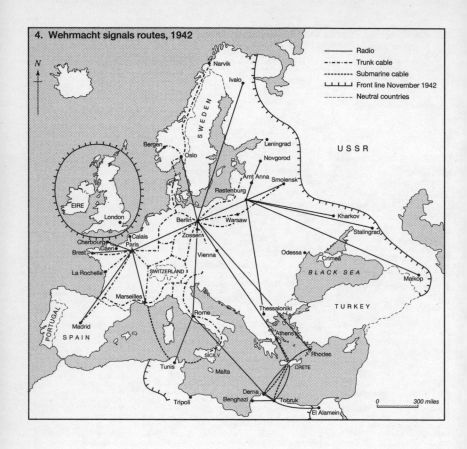

4. Wehrmacht signals routes, 1942

5. Middle East Y Organisation, 1942–5

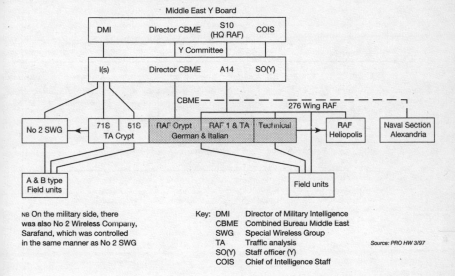

NB On the military side, there
was also No 2 Wireless Company,
Sarafand, which was controlled
in the same manner as No 2 SWG

Key: DMI   Director of Military Intelligence
      CBME   Combined Bureau Middle East
      SWG   Special Wireless Group
      TA   Traffic analysis
      SO(Y)   Staff officer (Y)
      COIS   Chief of Intelligence Staff

Source: PRO HW 3/97

6. Organisation of Hut 3, GC and CS, August 1943

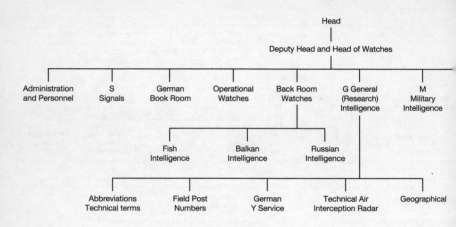

7. Organisation of Air Section, GC and CS, July 1944

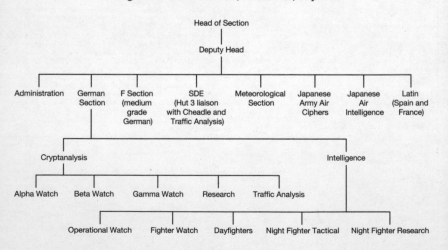

Source: PRO HW 3/99

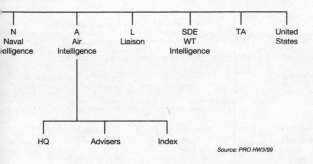

N Naval Intelligence	A Air Intelligence	L Liaison	SDE WT Intelligence	TA	United States

HQ   Advisers   Index

Source: PRO HW3/99

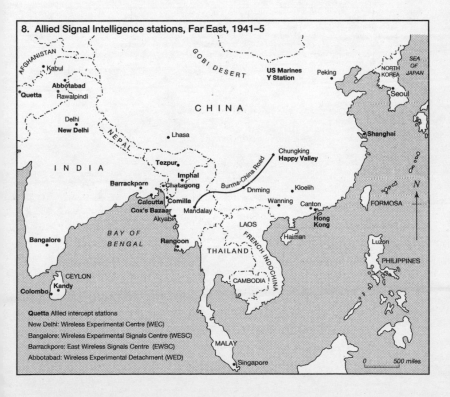

8. Allied Signal Intelligence stations, Far East, 1941–5

Quetta Allied intercept stations
New Delhi: Wireless Experimental Centre (WEC)
Bangalore: Wireless Experimental Signals Centre (WESC)
Barrackpore: East Wireless Signals Centre (EWSC)
Abbotabad: Wireless Experimental Detachment (WED)

9. Signal Intelligence Organisation, SEAC and India, April 1944

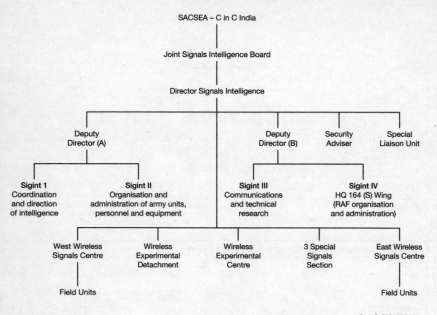

Source: PRO HW 3/102

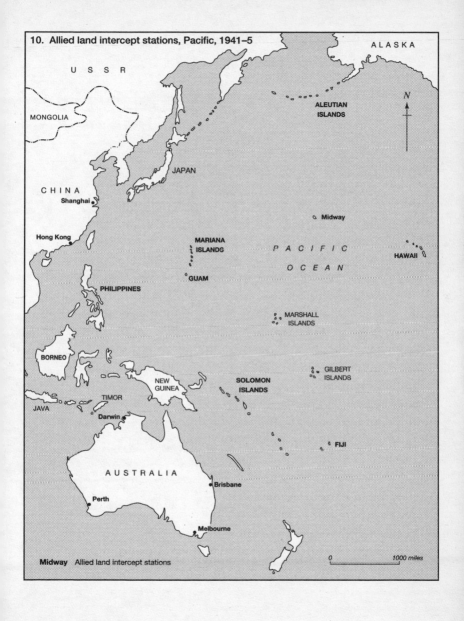

10. Allied land intercept stations, Pacific, 1941–5

ALASKA

USSR

MONGOLIA

ALEUTIAN
ISLANDS

N

JAPAN

CHINA

Shanghai

Midway

Hong Kong

MARIANA
ISLANDS

PACIFIC

HAWAII

OCEAN

GUAM

PHILIPPINES

MARSHALL
ISLANDS

BORNEO

GILBERT
ISLANDS

NEW
GUINEA

SOLOMON
ISLANDS

TIMOR

JAVA

Darwin

AUSTRALIA

FIJI

Perth

Brisbane

Melbourne

Midway Allied land intercept stations

0   1000 miles

CHAPTER ONE

THE BIRTH OF RADIO

In 1868 Henry Jackson, the thirteen-year-old son of a Yorkshire farmer, joined the Royal Navy and even as a cadet began to reveal his acute scientific bent. Such a trait was anything but common in the senior service in those days, even though steam-powered ironclads were rapidly replacing the old and obsolete sail-driven wooden walls. Come 1890, with the rank of a commander who had specialised in signalling, and had taken part in the Zulu War, he had been posted to HMS *Vernon*, the torpedo school. There, in a forward-looking, practical technical environment, he had conceived the idea of transmitting 'wireless' messages from ship to ship for tactical purposes. Not until 1895, however, after five unrewarding years of experiment with so-called Herzian waves (as described by Heinrich Herz) did he come across the existence and potential of 'coherers', as envisaged by Dr Jagadis Chunder Bose.

A coherer, as developed by Jackson, was a tube of metal filings between two metal plugs. Tapping the coherer which he fitted at one end of his ship HMS *Defiance*, berthed in Portsmouth in 1896, generated a two-inch spark of sufficient strength to transmit an electromagnetic pulse to the other end of the ship where it rang a bell. A few days later he repeated the experiment in a ship-to-ship transmission over a distance of three miles to HMS *Source*.

That same momentous year the up-and-coming Jackson was promoted captain and, at a communications conference in the War Office, met Signor Guglielmo Marconi, to discover that they were working on parallel lines. It mattered not that Marconi's aim was the commercial promotion of long-distance wireless communication over land and sea, and Jackson was intent on improving the navy's communications service. Together their immediate collaboration was rapidly to bear fruit of tremendous potential. By 1900, when Jackson was commanding a torpedo depot ship, he had designed a wireless transmitter that was superior to Marconi's. Nevertheless it was Marconi's set that the Admiralty adopted – at

Jackson's unselfish instigation – ensuring that the combat-worthiness of ships of the Royal Navy would be vastly enhanced in the near future. So too were the fleets of Russia and Japan, whose ships were soon engaged in a war that was started without declaration by the Japanese on 8 February 1904 and which reached its naval climax on 27 May 1905.

Ironically the Russo-Japanese War had been decided before that significantly dramatic event. Russia's Far East Fleet already had been virtually destroyed at Port Arthur and her army routed in Manchuria. Peace negotiations were impending. But already en route from the west was the Russian Baltic Fleet, tasked to restore the naval balance of power and Russian prestige in the east. The fight in the Straits of Tsushima between the powerful, battle-experienced Japanese fleet and the weary, mechanically weakened and poorly trained Russian fleet at the end of a long voyage round the Cape of Good Hope and from Singapore, was virtually a foregone conclusion. Fully aware of the expected time of the Russians arrival and kept informed of its approach from agents at a last coaling at Shanghai, Admiral Togo was even better informed by cruisers which shadowed and reported by wireless; and he was also obligingly helped by information supplied by intercepts of Admiral Rozhdestvensky's wireless messages reporting his state and intended course for Vladivostok.

It would be wrong to credit those wireless intercepts as the main reason for the virtually complete destruction of the Russian vessels. But they certainly helped, demonstrating additionally that a new era in naval warfare had dawned. With it was born the menace of a new world power of ingenuity and enterprise.

BEGINNING IN 1899, in collaboration with Jackson (acting for the Admiralty), the Army and the General Post Office (GPO), Marconi carried out a series of wireless trials on Salisbury Plain, on the Isle of Wight and to a tug at sea with 'damped' spark sets served by antennae (also known as aerials). From a distance of one mile, transmissions were increased progressively until messages could be received reliably at sea and, in 1901, across the Atlantic – a range of nearly 3,000 miles – using a 75 kw transmitter. The latter exciting event not only guaranteed the future of wireless and Marconi's company, but indicated that, somehow or other, electro-magnetic waves (which were known to be straight and, therefore, blocked by the earth's curvature) were being reflected back to earth by something unknown in the upper atmosphere. It was this phenomenon, recognised by Jackson in his influential 1902 paper, that inspired an Englishman, Oliver Heaviside, and an American, Arthur Kennelly, to hypothesise, that same year, that an ionised layer was causing the reflection. Although it was not until the 1920s that their thesis was scientifically proven correct, the practical exploitation of Marconi's successful experiments using low frequency, long waves was established beyond doubt as the basis for all future long-range transmissions and their audible reception.

At last a world-wide, free-for-all listeners, communication system, without dependence on an inflexible cable network, was feasible. It was now practical to transmit messages at sea, from a land vehicle and even from a basket suspended beneath a balloon (although, when the latter arrangement was tried out by Royal Engineers in the closing stages of the Boer War in South Africa, the results were discouraging).

Progress was world-wide, and recognised in 1903 by the holding of an International Wireless Telegraphy Conference at Berlin to help defuse a row over the liner *Deutschland* and the exclusive rights of wireless use by companies. The dispute had broken out between the German liner and the Marconi Company when the latter accidentally 'jammed' the former's inferior German-manufactured Telefunken set. The conference was attended by the most highly industrialised countries – Germany, Britain, Austria-Hungary, Spain, Italy, Russia and the USA.

There was undeniably a need for such meetings in the face of the dramatic growth of a system and industry which knew no frontiers. Already it was apparent that national interests were involved, given a means of communication which was open to all, and in which eaves-dropping, besides jamming, was inevitable and had to be controlled. The next conference was held in Madrid in 1906 to ratify the proposals of 1903, to broaden international co-operation and, among other things, to establish routine procedures to deal with emergencies at sea, including use of the letters SOS in morse code to raise the alarm on designated frequencies that were being monitored – thus legalising a form of interception. Furthermore, although almost incidentally, the word 'radiotelegraphy' was used for the first time, leading gradually to the obsolescence of 'wireless'. Henceforth, therefore, the word 'radio' will be used in this book.

New ideas abounded, driven by the competitive demands of profit and power to generate a mass of imaginative concepts. Shipping companies realised that they could not do without morse radio manned by trained operators. Navies and armies, above all the former, broadened their interests and gave ever deeper thought to the implications of the future as it slowly dawned, after the Wright brothers made the first manned flight in a heavier-than-air machine in 1903, that the day was nigh when men were going to fight in flying machines.

In 1904 it was discovered that the position of a transmitter could be located by Direction Finding (DF) – a technique of cross-intersection by listening receiver stations that had obvious intelligence applications. The following year morse signals were exchanged with a balloon, in 1909 with an airship and in 1910 with a heavier-than-air flying machine. The sets in use – heavy and clumsy and of the damped spark type – were already being threatened with facilities that eventually would make them obsolete. In 1904 Dr John Fleming (working closely with Marconi), invented the 'electron tube', vacuum diode so-called thermionic valve which made coherers and decoherers obsolescent. The advent of this valve promised to make future transmitters and receivers much more efficient – and incidentally coined the word 'electronics'. It now but required a way of transmitting speech to produce a wire-less radio telephone. This would be brought within reach in 1908 after Valdemar Poulson demonstrated his 'singing arc' system.

Rapid advances were also being made in the crucial design of antennae for the reliable transmission and reception of signals. Associated with this research and development was the phenomenon of atmospheric effects such as already had been touched on by Jackson in his celebrated 1902 paper. At that time he had defined, from close observations and investigation, the consequences of electrical disturbance, the effects of different times of day (dawn, daylight, sunset and night), screening by land mass, and the mutual jamming interference of two radio waves on the same frequency arriving at the same point with varying phase differences. Any of these, he had pointed out, could induce significant fading of a signal which, as already envisaged, could be overcome or mitigated by different antenna lengths, directional bearing and layout of rods or wire suspended above ground.

Hardly realised by the great military nations, the balance of weapon power on the seas and the battlefields was changing fundamentally. Surface warships, dominated by huge batteries of guns in heavily armoured battleships, were under serious threat by submarines whose locomotive torpedoes would strike subtly and devastatingly below the waterline. On land, the combination of artillery, machine-guns and barbed wire would neutralise the brave horsed cavalry and massed infantry. And overhead, rapidly improving types of aircraft were demonstrating their ability to spy beyond the horizon and on the other side of the hill, as well as drop bombs and, in due course, indulge in battles of their own waged by so-called fighter machines.

Few men of vision anticipated the effects of these new factors. Notable exceptions to that intellectual short-sightedness, however, were enthusiastic communicators like Henry Jackson who, in 1913 was holding the rank of admiral and the key appointment of chief of Admiralty War Staff. Even if the lessons of the land battles in Manchuria, with the appalling lessons inflicted by the latest weapons on men and horses in the open, were overlooked, those of Tsushima, held by naval and General Staff officers, were not. Looking ahead to the sort of conflict which might occur in a major European war, the planners took very seriously the likely impact on strategy and tactics of radio as a supplementary, perhaps crucial, system to the proven telegraph and telephone networks. Yet they were far from being prepared for the eventuality.

In August 1914 those plans were put into effect with telling, even if bizarre, results.

CHAPTER TWO

THE FIRST RADIO CONFLICT

Towards the end of July 1914, in an atmosphere of rapidly mounting political tension in Europe and the outbreak of war between Austria-Hungary and Serbia, a Marconi Co delegation was enjoying a friendly visit to their old German rivals, the Telefunken Co. An exchange of views and a tour of factories and research establishments culminated on 29 July with a visit to the latest, state-of-the-art, 200Kw transmitting station at Nauen, with its massive antennae. Immediately the Marconi people left to catch the night boat home, the German Army moved in, as it did on all other transmitters, to operate them on a war footing.

In Britain, France, Russia and Japan, in accordance with pre-war planning, similar moves were afoot on the eve of their virtually unstoppable general mobilisation. In Britain fourteen radio intercept stations were manned and, among the first messages heard in clear were logged orders sent by Nauen telling German merchant ships to run for home or neutral ports. But other messages which were encoded could not be read because prior plans for decrypting them had not been laid. Indeed, not until the formal declaration of war on 4 August, did the British Admiralty's Director of Naval Intelligence (DNI), Rear Admiral Henry Oliver, ask a cryptanalyst, by name Sir Alfred Ewing (who happened to be Director of Naval Education) to set up a new codebreaking department which, in due course, was installed in Room 40 in the Admiralty.

At the same time, in conjunction with her allies, Britain was systematically cutting every German telegraphic cable in reach, including her main link with the USA which, on 5 August, was raised by grapnel from the sea bed and broken by the cable ship *Telconia*. This isolated the Central Powers from telegraphic link with the outside world unless they could arrange use of the cables belonging to neutral nations, not all of whom were friendly. It left Germany dependent on the powerful radio transmitters which were principally intended for keeping her in touch with warships still at sea and with her colonies scattered around the world.

For the Germans in particular this was a disastrous blow, made more catastrophic as, over the ensuing three months, all but one of the overseas stations (that located in East Africa, which survived until May 1915) were captured or demolished. This meant that for the remainder of a four years' war, Germany would depend greatly on radio for reasonably safe passage of propaganda: and, in the main through neutral cable links, the sending of encrypted, essential diplomatic and military traffic. It was a situation that made the Central Powers prey to enemy cryptanalysts of steadily developing skill.

On land, too, army interceptor units were at work everywhere, their operators searching the radio frequencies for vital intelligence which would disclose the strategic intentions of their enemies – Russians versus Germans, French (with a single British set to begin with) versus Germans and so on – as the Russians invaded Germany and Austria-Hungary and the Germans struck massively through Belgium and Luxembourg in their advance to the heart of France.

On the Eastern Front occurred the first decisive and dramatic triumph of the interceptors, a reward for the sharing of radio information between the Germans and Austro-Hungarians. Indeed, since 1909 the latter had been monitoring foreign radio traffic and, since 1911, carrying out research into Serbian and Italian ciphers; and from 1913 those of Russia. On this long front were located powerful transmitter/receivers, as well as intercept units, in several strategic, fortified towns. In the field there were well-equipped, horse-drawn radio detachments connected by wire to those interceptor units, and the assistance they were receiving from the Russians was priceless beyond measure.

The Russians, whose codes had yet to be broken by their enemies, were in considerable confusion, particularly in the north where their First and Second Armies were advancing into East Prussia against a perilously outnumbered German Eighth Army. Russian radio training and discipline were extremely lax. For a start their transmissions were being unintentionally jammed by private traffic which had not been forbidden. To make matters fatally worse, however, operators at transmitter stations had to ask receivers which code they were using, and in the interest of haste were transmitting some place names and officers' names in clear, mixed with recognisable destinations in code. All enquiries were sent in clear and cipher messages were so phrased and constructed as to further simplify the tasks of enemy cryptanalysts.

On 20 August a battlefield crisis arose for German Eighth Army, one that persuaded its commander and chief of staff that a general retreat was essential. Temporarily this was resisted by two senior members of the staff who saw no need for panic since it was emerging from radio intercepts that both Russian armies were in command and logistic difficulties. But already Eighth Army commander's reports to the German Chief of Staff, General Helmuth von Moltke, gave an impression that he had lost his nerve. Without hesitation Moltke replaced both that commander and his chief of staff with Generals Paul von Hindenburg and Erich Ludendorff, who, upon arrival at their new headquarters on the 23rd, found that the seeds of victory had already been sown by senior staff officers – a victory made certain by intelligence of unprecedented quality.

For during the night 24/25 August radio interceptors at Königsberg had picked up a signal in clear from the commander of First Russian Army laying down the objectives, routes and identities of formations committed to an axis of advance which indicated that his army posed no immediate threat to Eighth Army. And a few hours later on the 25th, GHQ Eighth Army's interceptors, despite atmospheric interference, monitored a badly translated message indicating that a large gap had opened up between First and Second Russian Armies. The information was soon confirmed by zeppelin and aircraft reconnaissance. Thus two appalling radio security lapses, revealing in full the Russians' intentions, made it safe for Eighth Army to screen First Army with light forces while concentrating in strength to envelop and destroy Second Army in what became famous as the Battle of Tannenburg – an event which saved Prussia from invasion and from which the Russian Army never really recovered.

As Tannenburg was being celebrated, however, Signals Intelligence (SIGINT to use the modern abbreviation) on the West Front was not nearly so helpful for the Germans. This was almost entirely their own fault long before they launched the celebrated (though von Moltke-modified)

Schlieffen Plan that was intended to envelop the French Army by means of a wide swing of a heavy right wing directed through Belgium, via Brussels and Mons, to the west of Paris. On paper it looked magnificent, the product of Great German General Staff war-gaming and planning. Unfortunately it overlooked three important factors. One, the unexpected and undetected presence of a small, well-trained British Army extending the French left wing to Mons. Two, a gross underestimate of logistic matters which, through the enemy's cutting of railway tracks and due to insufficient motor transport, caused deprivation of supplies to exhausted marching troops and horses. And three – arguably the most damaging adverse factor of all – the breakdown of signal communications which contributed hugely to the collapse of reporting, command and control.

Historically, the members of the Great German General Staff had been addicted to Combat Arms snobbery to the nigh exclusion of lesser branches of the service such as Engineers, Logistics and Signals. In the case of the Schlieffen Plan the Chief Signals Officer had not been fully consulted and therefore was unprepared to cope with the effects of systematic, hostile cutting of telegraph and telephone wires. To make matters worse, the radio system they had been ordered to provide for central command and control of the widespread advancing armies, was not up to the job.

The moment Luxembourg was overrun, Moltke's General Headquarters was moved there to make use of the existing civilian lines, supplemented by a powerful army transmitter and receiver station netted to field radio stations moving with the headquarters of armies, corps and cavalry divisions. In theory this radio network was admirable and the General Staff placed much reliance upon it. In practice, the signals plan fell far short of expectations. To begin with the land wire routs failed because the unprepared Signals Corps was unable to restore enough broken cables routs due to ignorance of the Belgian and French wire network and shortage of sufficient materials to make repairs. This threw a far greater work load than anticipated on the radio network which, unhappily, also failed to come up to expectations.

Any busy radio network dedicated to disciplined, orderly processing of traffic depends upon the existence of a central station which imposes control. For reasons best known to themselves, the German Army did not subscribe to this method, preferring to have out-stations call GHQ as required. This permitted a sort of free-for-all whereby out-stations in the field had priority and came on and off the air as they chose. In next to no time, as the armies advanced, something like anarchy reigned. Out-stations could not get through to GHQ even with the most urgent reports. Accidental jamming was rife. Likewise GHQ, due to this chaos, was often delayed in transmitting vital orders and instructions. And to compound these pernicious faults, the well-prepared codebreaking department of the French Army's Second Bureau (Intelligence) swiftly penetrated the German Army codes and was able to read almost everything on the enemy's net.

For example, during the retreat from Mons to the River Marne, the orders radioed to a German cavalry formation to strike decisively at the flank of the retreating Franco-British armies were listened to, translated and decoded by the French. Thus, just in time, they were made fully aware of the threat through intercept – and mightily relieved to hear later by the same means that the move would be prevented because the horses needed reshoeing. Radio intercept also kept the French adequately informed about the steadily worsening logistic state of the advancing Germans and the chaos beginning to cripple their command and control system. Crucially, too, intercept provided reliable and timely knowledge that First Army, which formed the strong right wing, was vulnerable to outflanking.

This knowledge, confirmed by other sources of battlefield intelligence, laid the foundations of General Joffre's famous victory at the Battle of the Marne. By rapidly forming a new army to the west of that flank, the French C-in-C forced General von Kluck, commander of First Army, to indulge in erratic changes of axis as he attempted to avoid envelopment from his right while endeavouring to co-operate with Second Army by grappling with the fast-retreating French and British to his front. In Luxembourg Moltke became desperately anxious as he recognised an approaching disaster from an apparently worsening situation he could neither define nor adequately correct. No longer able, for lack of facts, to analyse the problem or send rational orders by wire or radio, he resorted to the desperate measure of sending Lieutenant Colonel Hentsch, a General Staff officer, to visit each army in turn so as to assess the situation and discover if any sort of retreat had already started. In that event, Hentsch was authorised to order a general retreat. On 8 September he found such gloom at HQ Second Army as to conclude that a retreat was inevitable. As became the case next day, before he reached First Army, when it was discovered that six Anglo-French columns were entering the yawning gap between First and Second Armies.

Much credit for Joffre's victory on the Marne belonged to the French intelligence staffs who made excellent use of the SIGINT provided inadvertently by German incompetence and miscalculation. But these were early days in the intercept game of World War One when most things that went wrong could be laid at the door of ignorance, poor training and shortages of sufficiently well-educated people in embryonic intercept and intelligence organisations. For example, Colonel François Cartier of the French cryptanalytic department had only six overworked and exhausted experts on his staff in August and only seven intercept units to search for enemy transmissions as they disclosed themselves. But at least the French were better served than the German Army which, pre-war, had hardly bothered with interception or codebreaking, and whose overhearing of the crucial Russian signals in clear prior to Tannenburg was the accidental outcome of casual listening by signallers with nothing better to do.

Britain, like France, also was convinced of the need for SIGINT and initially afflicted by manpower shortage to man Royal Navy ships, airships and listening stations on land as well as for Army field intercept units. To cope with this foreseen but impossible-to-miscalculate situation, many more trained radio operators and listeners were needed. There were all sorts of conflicting factors involved, such as the banning by government of use of radio by merchant ships at sea which was imposed on 3 August, along with the closing down of amateur transmitters; plus the Admiralty's taking control of the Marconi factory and lesser radio manufacturing concerns. Then came the insistence that the General Post Office (GPO) should be made responsible for running of major Marconi facilities and, at the same time, the commissioning of Marconi's Hall Street experimental station to form and run a number of intercept units.

High priority was given to the provision of trained manpower and this was met by a number of measures, some of which were self-defeating. For example, when the Royal Navy virtually press-ganged operators from merchant ships into the service, it created a crippling problem because the Merchant Navy, by law, had to embark operators in all vessels in excess of 1,600 tonnes. In dealing with this the Marconi Company played a key role, undertaking to recruit and train 2,000 operators in schools set up in its own classrooms and in rooms in King's College and Birkbeck College. At the same time it encouraged the amateur radio enthusiasts it had been fostering pre-war to enrol for instruction and qualifying examinations.

At incredible speed, men and radio receivers to meet the requirements of intercept units placed along the coastlines to monitor the German fleet were assembled and tasked to supply information in the Admiralty. Simultaneously the initial, very modest demands of the Army were tackled, although when the British Expeditionary Force went to France in mid-August it took with it only one field unit, largely because senior officers were suffering from what might be called 'the Incredulity Syndrome'. Only a handful could visualise even a supplementary role for radio as an adjunct to telephone and telegraph. Yet within four weeks, and just in time for the Battle of the Marne, that lonely lorry-borne transmitter/receiver station had been joined by another nine units as the nucleus of what would become special intercept WT Company of the Signals Branch of the Royal Engineers. This sub-unit was the first of many to come, destined to play a significant role in the short phase of mobile war that ended in October as trench warfare set in.

Already radio intercept was not only proving its value even to the sceptics but also was energetically expanding its strategic and tactical role. In this respect the Army played the leading part by recognising before the war the value of a state-of-the-art DF set developed by H. J. Round of Marconi. Using a by no means wholly reliable 'C' type, high amplification valve, incorporated in a Bellini-Tosi set, he demonstrated that two sets working in tandem could fix a transmitter's location within reasonable limits. At once Military Intelligence in the War Office seconded Round and ordered him to carry out a practical demonstration against the Germans in France (where the front had stabilised into a continuous line of fortified trenches from the North Sea to Switzerland). Two sets were set up, one near St-Omer and the other at Abbeville to form a base line, and from 1 January onward proved highly successful in fixing not only the location of enemy ground transmitters but also those in moving Zeppelins – provided the targeted transmitter helped by sending for sufficient time, as often happened. The result was the formation on 2 January of the British Army's first Wireless Signal Company and the deployment at once of a network of DF stations along the length of the front.

A highly impressed Admiralty was quick to copy the junior service, ordering numerous DF sets to be located along the coastline not only to fix the position of warships at sea and in port but also that of Zeppelins as, in 1915, they opened a campaign of bombing raids against England, including London. In due course they also installed DF equipment in ships.

Meanwhile Ewing's codebreakers in the Admiralty had struck lucky in their thwarted attempts to crack the German naval code. Early in September the light cruiser *Magdeburg* had been wrecked in the Baltic. Clutched to the body of an officer pulled from the sea by the Russians a few hours later, was found a bag containing highly secret cipher and signal books and squared charts of the North Sea and Heligoland Bight. On 13 October these priceless assets were delivered by the Russians to First Lord, Winston Churchill, and First Sea Lord, Admiral Prince Louis of Battenburg. It took three weeks for the inexperienced British cryptanalysts to break the complex code books; but from that moment they laid bare the secret of every encoded message intercepted by the eager searchers at the listening stations.

At the end of 1914 more highly confidential enemy documents were raised from deep waters to augment the increase in volume and value of decoded messages yielded by the German Navy. For that nation's Navy, unlike her Army, had from an early stage created its own listening organisation (B-Dienst) and, since 1907, had been studying industriously and profitably Royal Navy radio nets. Now, apart from a raid by five battle-cruisers on 15 December to bombard targets on the English east coast, her fleet lay safely in port as searchers and cryptanalysts redoubled efforts to discover British intentions.

Likewise, so busy and important did Ewing's department become, that in mid-November it was deemed essential to occupy a larger office adjacent to the Admiralty's Operations Room. Its new home was Room 40 of the Old Admiralty Building, graced by a small berth alongside for the duty officer. This establishment would later be named IS 25 (for Section 25 of the Naval Intelligence Division) and, when moved again to larger premises, continued to be known and later achieve fame as Room 40.

Indeed, as Turkey entered the war and the Mediterranean and Middle East became war zones, the British government felt compelled to order the Marconi Company to construct in haste a project which it had earlier delayed by procrastination. That was an Empire-wide radio network with thirteen long-range stations located at Ascension Island, the Falkland Islands, Bathurst, Ceylon, Durban, Demerara, Seychelles, Singapore, St John's, Aden, Hong Kong, Mauritius and Port Nolloth, in addition to existing stations at Malta and Egypt. The project, of course, was intended to carry confidential, diplomatic and military encoded traffic which, inevitably, would attract the keenest attention of enemy and neutral searchers.

Thus, within five months of the outbreak of war, the Russians were well aware of the importance of radio intercept, and beginning to put their house in order; the Germans were taking the matter seriously but without realising how seriously compromised were their Army and Navy codes; the British were fully committed and in the lead with the basic techniques and technology; and the French were well attuned to this branch of intelligence-gathering even if, as it happened, ill-equipped to make the best of their insight.

For while the French lacked DF and therefore, unlike the British, were unable accurately to place on the ground the transmitters they heard, they were innovators in what was to become known as Traffic Analysis

(TA). By recording call signs, sometimes the names of officers, volume of traffic and who was calling whom, they gradually learned how to assemble the enemy's order of battle and organisations to assist the Second Bureau in reading the enemy deployment and, sometimes, his intentions.

Occasionally, too, mistakes perpetrated by senders gave insight and helped break codes. The fact that the captain of the cruiser *Magdeburg* did not ensure that his codes were dumped before the ship foundered was a glaring example of how vulnerable codes were. Indeed, it should have been recognised at that time and from history that there was no such thing as an unbreakable code. And not infrequently it was the searchers themselves at intercept units who made an important contribution by identification of an enemy operator through recognising his touch on the morse key.

So, come 1915, the radio struggle had moved to its next more sophisticated phase on land, sea, in the air and on the diplomatic front.

CHAPTER THREE

SHAPING A NEW SYSTEM

Although unrecognised by the major contestants of World War One at the start of 1915, there already existed clear indications of what was impending for the vital future of radio intercept. On land the trench barrier in the West tended to limit its scope, yet it was found to be useful in locating enemy units and, through TA, formulating the outline, even the details, of orders of battle. Additionally and more significantly, it had become plain that since the transmissions from the heavy radio sets of the day in airships and Zeppelins could be monitored and located by DF in flight, there was no reason in the minds of inventors why the concept of lighter weight sets being carried in aeroplanes should be rejected. Therefore the existing technique of monitoring and plotting by DF the transmissions from lighter-than-air machines would prove as widespread from heavier-than-air machines above the front line as was becoming everyday practice in the location of static units below.

On the Eastern Front, where mobile warfare was still possible and practised at an exorbitant price, it followed that radio intercept was as valuable as it had been in 1914. There, too, the intercept contest which had started almost accidentally prior to Tannenberg became hotter as the Russians tightened their procedures (although without ever reaching a serviceable standard) and the German Army belatedly embraced the need for signals security and SIGINT in the prosecution of land warfare.

At sea, as already mentioned, reservations about the value of SIGINT had vanished once the lessons of Tsushima had been digested. From the start of hostilities each contender correctly assumed that the enemy was listening, although until the *Magdeburg* codes were recovered, nobody could penetrate the naval codes in use. Nor, until later in 1915 when the Round/Bellini-Tosi DF system came into British use, could the position of transmitters be located with any precision. Even so it was a salutary lesson to the Germans that when their battle-cruisers were on their way to bombard Scarborough and the Hartlepools in December 1914, they detected the Admiralty's accurate, though fragmentary, report of the event to the British fleet within ninety minutes of the sending of a few give-away signals by the German ships.

At about this time Winston Churchill appointed the dynamic and highly innovative Captain William Reginald Hall (known as Blinker due to a facial twitch) to replace Oliver as DNI. Certainly the nascent organisation needed pulling together. The plethora of information gathered by the steadily increasing number of intercept stations was neither being handled efficiently nor securely in the Admiralty. Ewing's small code-breaking department, populated by all manner of civilian scholars, cryptanalysts and German-speaking interpreters, was not integrated with the professional naval officers manning the key Operations Division. Meanwhile those same officers, in their anxiety to make the best of whatever information reached them, did not always sift the chaff from the wheat: there was, indeed, a tendency to obscure really important intelligence when passing a mass of messages to the Grand Fleet. Without delay Hall concentrated in Room 40 the functions of radio intercept, deciphering and translation: and he appointed Captain H. W. Hope to synthesise and interpret, for onward transmission to those who most needed to know, only those matters that were operationally important.

At the same time Hall threw his immense energy into the expansion of the Navy's interception units. These would increase to fifty, provided with the latest radio receivers and DF equipments. But the DF sets were not yet ready on 23 January 1915 when intercepted, decoded signals indicated that the enemy battle-cruisers were again putting to sea under precise instructions 'to reconnoitre the Dogger Bank'. There was, therefore, only just sufficient time for Captain Hope to synthesise the enemy intentions, augmented by their own intuition, and for the officers of the Operations Division to order Vice Admiral Sir David Beatty's battle-cruisers to sea to engage.

Bearing in mind that the Germans were already aware that the British were rapidly interpreting their signals, it may seem incredible that they permitted this interception to take place at all. After all, the High Seas Fleet lay in the River Jade, only a few miles from Wilhelmshaven, so there was no need for them to send orders by radio. Obligingly for the British, however, they stuck to routine and simply reduced the power of all transmissions to ships in home waters, in the belief that these could not be picked up in Britain. Unfortunately for them they were unaware that Round's amplifying, soft C valve made possible reception of even those low-power transmissions – with consequences of far greater significance beyond those of the ensuing Battle of Dogger Bank.

The clash of battle-cruisers, with the loss of a German armoured cruiser, severe damage to two battle-cruisers and a narrow escape from disaster for the remainder of the German squadron (due very largely to British signalling errors), severely shook German confidence. Unwilling to risk their outnumbered High Seas Fleet (the fleet-in-being), they turned to the institution on 18 February 1915 of commerce warfare by submarines (U-boats) against enemy merchant ships on 'all the waters surrounding Great Britain and Ireland'. In that public declaration of intent they also gave warning to neutrals that they could not guarantee the safety of passengers and cargoes carried in their ships entering those waters.

With only twenty operational U-boats immediately available, this policy of desperation, destructive of shipping as it might be, could hardly be rated as a decisive instrument of blockade. Quite the opposite, in fact, since it was a measure which lost Germany support among uncommitted or friendly nations. Such sentiments were exacerbated when on 7 May the British liner *Lusitania* was sunk by a U-boat with the loss of 1,198 lives, among them 128 American citizens, some very prominent. Predictably there was a colossal outcry with demands from influential Americans for war with Germany. This President Woodrow Wilson resisted. On the other hand he left the Germans in no doubt that their nigh unrestricted sinking of merchant ships without warning would lead to very serious consequences.

This warning did not bring an immediate halt to the campaign, but it did force the Germans to change rules of engagement by instructing captains to be more careful in attacks on passenger liners and all ships flying the Stars and Stripes. Inevitably sinkings continued, but fell away in the autumn as counter-measures began to have a limited effect. The

crucial business of sinking large numbers of U-boats, however, was poor
and very much because there was no way of locating them. In 1915 only
twenty were sunk in a period when sixty-one joined the fleet.

In anti-submarine warfare radio intercept and DF was far less profitable than on land and in the air against Zeppelins, even though radios had
been installed in U-boats since 1908. The British searchers' difficulties
were exacerbated by the initial shortcomings of the U-boats' transmitting sets with vertical, twin-rod antennae which at best gave a mere fifty
to sixty miles range. And although the fitting of horizontal antennae
increased range significantly, these too left much to be desired by the Germans when transmitting on the surface at night (as tactically they had
to do) mainly due to the inhibiting phenomenon of night conditions. In
consequence radio intercept and DF (which also was impaired by so-called
'Night Error') were of only limited value in locating U-boats. Moreover,
the U-boats had problems when receiving from the shore and found also
that a crude acoustic system to enable underwater communications with
other U-boats was largely useless. This made it virtually impossible for
boats to intercommunicate whenever they attempted to operate in concert
and naturally thwarted the searchers' intercept efforts.

Under the driving force of Hall, encouraged by an expert signals
enthusiast First Sea Lord, Room 40 flourished. It quickly grew to over a
hundred specially qualified men and women who broke codes alongside
naval officers, and who were moved into larger premises – while retaining
its original title. For in April 1915 Admiral Sir Henry Jackson had become
First Sea Lord and he was the last person to be sceptical of the value of
radio intercept, or of radio as a means of amplifying the powers of tactical, as well as strategic, command and control.

That year, however, it was the land campaigns which attracted by
far the most attention and expenditure of effort in an expanding war.
From March to October the Western Front consumed vast resources of
men and material as the French and British tried without avail to breach
the trench line. In April Germany and Austria inflicted a crushing defeat
on the Russians in Gorlice and advanced deeply eastwards, though without bringing Russia to her knees. In May Italy entered the war on the

Allied side and engaged in a prolonged mountain warfare campaign against Austria. At the same time the British and French landed at Gallipoli in what turned into an abortive and extremely costly attempt to force the Dardanelles, reach Constantinople and open lines of supply to Russia.

Needless to say, intercept services levied extra demands on all fronts now that their roles and potential were better recognised. Nor was it only upon radio that their attention was entirely focused. As a major example, there was the use by the Germans at an early stage of a device which enabled them to tap by induction the thousands of miles of telephone lines which, on the Western Front, spread outwards from headquarters in rear to companies and even platoons and artillery observers in the front-line trenches. Only gradually did the Allies detect the menace of this threat to their security and in due course begin the manufacture of the very expensive and ever-in-short-supply Fullerphone (developed by Major A. C. Fuller who had been a pioneer of radio since 1906 when a young officer).

In March 1916 the Germans switched their attention to the West in an endeavour to 'bleed white' the French Army at Verdun with concentrated heavy artillery fire. At the same time their Navy was instructed to seek action with the Royal Navy by luring it piecemeal into an ambush by the High Seas Fleet. Intercept by both sides at Verdun was intense but, by this time, virtually routine. The forthcoming Battle of Jutland was quite another matter.

Since Dogger Bank in January 1915 there had been several occasions when SIGINT warned Room 40 that major German warships were putting to sea. On each occasion the C-in-C Grand Fleet, Admiral Sir John Jellicoe, had been given timely warning and had been able to take precautionary, pre-emptive measures. It was the appointment of Vice Admiral Reinhard Scheer to command the High Seas Fleet in February 1916 which effectually put an end to its timorous inactivity. On the 10th he sent out light cruisers and destroyers, watched over by Zeppelins, to the Texel, but without making contact with his enemy. Three weeks later he tried another small-scale, abortive venture; and on 25 March a sortie by battle-cruisers under Vice-Admiral Franz von Hipper, also without bringing on a fight. But the next foray on 25 April of a battle-cruiser raid and bombardment of east coast towns did at last produce contact in an exchange of fire, though with nothing like the significant result hoped for – not least due to lack of thrust by the German captains when they had the chance.

In fact, the most significant factor on each of these occasions was the nearby presence, unseen by Scheer and Hipper, of major Royal Navy units already at sea. It was a situation made possible by British radio intercept and DF which always detected and correctly recognised what Sheer was attempting. So, the known departure of U-boats to keep watch and ward in the northern sector of the North Sea on 17 May, followed on 30 May by a signal ordering the High Seas Fleet to prepare for sea, and then a flurry of other transmissions (mostly undeciphered by Room 40) was convincing evidence to Jackson that the High Seas Fleet was coming out. Moreover, a change of five degrees in the DF reading of a controlling German ship, showing that she had moved out of harbour, indicated that a sortie was imminent. At once he ordered the entire Grand Fleet to sea; and so slick was Jellicoe's response that his battleships, Beatty's battle-cruisers and their supporting cruisers and destroyers actually were on their way two hours before Scheer and Hipper set forth. Unlike their enemy, however, the British were maintaining strict radio silence to ensure that the heavily outnumbered Germans were totally unaware of their peril.

After an initial head-on clash between the battle-cruisers, Beatty deliberately lured Hipper, followed by Scheer's battleships, into the arms of Jellicoe's battleships. At dusk Scheer made unavailing attempts to prevent Jellicoe from interposing between the High Seas Fleet and the safety of its minefields and ports. At nightfall, therefore, the Germans were in acute danger of being overwhelmed at first light in open waters at the entrance to the Skaggerak – a reasonably certain fate had not Jellicoe lost confidence in the reliability of SIGINT and instead put his trust in the inaccurate reports from his scouting cruisers. Yet the effects of this example of the 'Incredulity Factor' by Jellicoe might have been mitigated but for poor communications and judgement in the Admiralty between Admiral Jackson, the Operations Division and Room 40 (brought on by defective organisation), exacerbated by the demands of security. This confusion was compounded by yet another example of incredulity when, at midnight, Jellicoe chose to ignore an authoritative Admiralty signal that gave the real position and course for home of the High Seas Fleet.

In consequence, Jellicoe, long out of contact with the enemy and literally in the dark, spent the night under the false assumption that Scheer was heading for the southern entrance to the Jade instead of the northern one via the Horns Reef. This deprived him of his stated aim to defeat and annihilate the enemy at dawn, although in unchallenged possession of the North Sea. It left Scheer in safety with a badly damaged High Seas Fleet, which also had been served badly by Intelligence and would never again seriously attempt to challenge the Royal Navy.

THIRTY DAYS AFTER Jutland at the start of the Battle of the Somme the sound use of intercepted enemy signals would pay a rich dividend for the Germans. For the past seven days they had been subjected to a furious, though by no means sufficiently damaging, artillery bombardment of their front to the north of Albert and at any moment were expecting the British to advance in mass. Their infantry and machine-guns sheltered in deep dugouts but would find it helpful to know the exact time of that event. On the evening of 30 June, the answer was supplied. German searchers tapping British front-line telephone talk were delighted to hear somebody relaying a message of encouragement from a general to his troops on the following morning – and giving the exact time when they would go over the top!

The outcome on that sector and others was inevitable. As precisely foretold, the British barrage on the forward German trenches lifted, giving the cue for the German artillery to bring down defensive fire on the waiting British in their trenches, and for them to clamber to the surface and set up their machine-guns with plenty of time to mow down the lines of khaki infantry who exposed themselves in enfilade for slaughter. On a day when the assailants lost in dead, wounded and missing nearly 60,000 men, there were many places where the British hardly got beyond the start line. No doubt without that warning by telephone the result would have been much the same; there was much at fault in the British planning and execution of their biggest offensive to date in the process known as attrition. Nevertheless, assured of loss of strategic secrecy as was inevitable with that sort of attritional method, there was no excuse for forfeiture of tactical surprise through a lapse in security created by a known source of signals interception.

Yet attritional losses to the French at Verdun and the British on the Somme (in a prolonged offensive continuing into October) did not by any means leave the Germans unscathed. Come the autumn they too were exhausted and in need of a radical change in political policy and military strategy, besides rebuilding of the Army. The appointment of Generals Hindenburg and Ludendorff, the trusted victors of many offensives on the Eastern Front, was intended to enforce those changes. In a drastic change of emphasis, the famous duo decided to adopt a defensive strategy on land in the West, while they endeavoured to rebuild the strength and morale of the Army; to attempt to knock a weakened Russia out of the war; and to revive the blockade of Britain with unrestricted U-boat warfare.

As the bitter winter of 1916–17 unfolded its secrets, Captain Hall in the Admiralty and Colonel Cartier of the Second Bureau in Paris cemented their collaboration at meetings of great portent.

AS TIME WENT BY, Blinker Hall spread his net wider to embrace subjects which extended far beyond naval intelligence. He began working closely with the Secret Service and also with Basil Thompson, Assistant Commissioner of the Metropolitan Police. Naturally these activities caused concern as well as interest at the proud Foreign Office because his intercept service was reading German coded, cable diplomatic messages to Mexico via Spain and Sweden and onwards to affect the USA. But the Foreign Office, unlike the armed service ministries, lacked an intelligence department and depended for information upon its own and foreign embassies. Like it or not, they needed Hall to fill this gap. Simultaneously he broke into communications to Turkey and beyond through the Middle East to Persia and India, helping substantially to thwart schemes designed to stir up trouble in that part of the world, including Afghanistan. At home, meanwhile, the Home Office was assisted in tracking down spies and enemy agents in Britain, including Sir Roger Casement, the Irish activist who was aiding German saboteurs of British ships in the USA and involved in a German-sponsored rebellion in Ireland. But the Cabinet reposed implicit trust in Hall's judgement and integrity and allowed him a remarkable freedom of action in the use and discreet disclosure of intercepted messages and other intelligence material.

Germany decided to recommence unrestricted U-boat warfare on 19 January 1917. This was to involve Hall in far greater matters than the urgent business of tracking submarines – which remained as difficult as ever so long as Admiral Jackson's recent successor as First Sea Lord, Admiral Jellicoe, resisted suggestions that ships should be made to sail in controlled, escorted convoys and not independently as they chose.

In taking the fatal step, the Germans had weighed the risks, notably the impact on America and the danger that President Wilson might reverse his post-*Lusitania* policy and opt for war. Seven days after making the decision, and seeking to distract the Americans from declaring war, the pro-U-boat, hawkish German Foreign Minister, Arthur Zimmermann, telegraphed the German ambassador in Mexico, via the German ambassador in Washington, stating that unrestricted submarine war would commence on 1 February and proposing an alliance and support to enable Mexico to recapture her lost territories of Texas, New Mexico and Arizona. He also suggested that the Mexicans might 'invite the immediate adherence of Japan'. Zimmermann was indeed informed that the Mexican government, which recently had indulged in a minor war against the USA, continued to be pro-German. What he did not know was that his elaborately encoded telegrams (sent circuitously via Spain and the American government (!) as well as with Swedish connivance via Buenos Aires) had been tapped in both almost identical versions by the British, whose team of cryptanalysts of Room 40, led by an RNAS officer named Nigel de Grey, quickly decoded them.

Hall, who realised the power of the threat to the USA and the likelihood of attempts to debunk it by the anti-war faction there, played for time before going public, holding his hand until he obtained an actual copy of the Spanish version. Not until 22 February did he, with Foreign Office approval, tell the Americans, who, in any case, were now fully aware that the new U-boat campaign was in full swing. It took a week's diplomacy to convince the Americans of the truth of the matter. Procrastination by all nations involved in the matter was rife – and thoroughly discredited when, most unexpectedly, came Zimmermann's admission of guilt.

On 6 April a highly indignant President, Congress and people went to war to ensure Germany's subsequent defeat.

The only striking difference between the latest U-boat campaign and its predecessor was in the number of boats that were operationally at sea. In 1915 it had been about twenty: in 1917, despite possession of 160, it had increased to forty-six – many of them larger and more sophisticated than those of pre-war construction. Apart from that, the strategy and tactics by both sides remained much as before.

The Allies, lacking adequate means of detection and only hopefully dependent on the newly produced depth charge, relied largely for destruction of boats upon chance surface encounters and the net and mine barrages that were laid and defended in narrow waters, especially in the Straits of Dover which was the short cut to the Bay of Biscay and Atlantic whence most commercial traffic approached the British Isles. The Germans meanwhile were wedded to an established doctrine which permitted U-boat captains to act on their own intuition, without regard for instructions from the commander of the U-boat Flotilla, the very experienced and clever Commodore Hermann Bauer.

When Bauer attempted to make his boats take the Straits of Dover route, some commanders declined, preferring to take the ten days' longer and safer passage round Scotland. And when he endeavoured to have the big, 1,400 ton cargo cruiser *Deutschland* (used for running the blockade with valuable materials from the USA) turned into a command centre at sea of a U-boat group, the response from Scheer's staff was lukewarm. Bauer, of course, was far ahead of his time in visualising a boat equipped with radio for use by himself or deputy to control what, in the next war, became known as a 'wolf pack'. *Deutschland* and her successors, staffed by specially trained radio operators with receivers to intercept and DF transmissions from nearby warships and merchant vessels, was intended to be positioned in the Western Approaches and to guide boats to their targets. But the project was stillborn and Bauer was replaced in June 1917.

Needless to say, the British intercept stations gave priority to U-boat traffic and in this they were immensely helped by French discoveries. Earlier in the war it was invaluable when Lieutenant Paul Bassières broke the German U-boat code, and when Captain Georges Painvin overcame a stubborn four-letter naval code. These discoveries Colonel Cartier shared with Hall and suggested that they should combine in the task of naval and political codebreaking. But the latter, fearful of compromising the *Magdeburg* codes and others which were vital to British survival as a maritime nation, did not reciprocate.

Regardless of the background intrigues and unimaginative strategy and tactics committed by both sides, the latest German naval campaign won considerable success from the outset at meagre cost in boats sunk. Enemy shipping losses through February to May were extremely heavy. But there was an improvement in May shortly after Jellicoe had virtually been forced to adopt the convoy system, although even then, with the agreement of the US Navy, he was unconvinced of its merits and so postponed a wholesale implementation. It was much later in the year, with improved escorting techniques, the relatively easier passage of large convoys and a rise in U-boat losses, that a significant fall in sinkings was recorded. By this time Jellicoe had been replaced and the Germans were beginning to appreciate that they were well short of sinking a decisive quantity of tonnage.

Claims have been made that radio intercept was a principal factor in winning the battle against U-boats. This is not easy to substantiate since DF stations found it difficult both to locate a U-boat and almost impossible to track it unless it was extremely careless; and this was most unlikely since the Germans at last had rumbled the need for radio silence to attain surprise. Furthermore independently operating boats were never deliberately hunted before they disclosed their presence – and usually achieved that disclosure only when lucky enough to meet a convoy by chance. At that point it was hard-pressed to make a successful attack (mostly in daytime) without being harried and sunk. There were, in fact, enormous slices of luck in the haphazard encounters between opponents once the dense convoy system replaced the widespread, unescorted stream of independent vessels. Indeed, there is evidence that the assistance of aerial reconnaissance by airships and seaplanes was rated very highly as a means to locate U-boats on the surface. In fact there was at least one U-boat captain, by name Karl Dönitz, who was perfectly aware of the factor of chance impeding the solitary U-boat, and who one day would develop Bauer's wolf pack system – and come to bewail lack of adequate air reconnaissance to find convoys for his grouped U-boats to ravage.

Certainly in the closing stages of the war the aviation factor was becoming so important that it could no longer be sidelined; yet it was by no means infallible. One reason for its defects was the delayed arrival of a serviceable, light-weight (20lb) radio set in 1918. Another was the need for a speech facility (RT) as a far quicker and more positive method of communication instead of morse. These, as will be seen, were about to enter service. But, as in some respects with anti-submarine warfare, the value of radio intercept was limited due to the relatively meagre use of radio. True, the Zeppelins which tried to reconnoitre over sea and land, or make bombing raids on cities, could be tracked if they unwisely transmitted long enough to attract DF. However, this was unusual, just as it was unprofitable for ground-based intercept units to monitor spotting machines that crossed the static front lines.

Combat beneath the waves and in the air above had much need of radio. So too did its intercept for intelligence acquisition. Always there would be demands for much more effective ways of coping with rapidly advancing technology.

As for war on land, the pattern of radio intercept remained much as it had settled by the end of 1916. TA continued to provide useful intelligence of what was in the frontal areas' attritional battles, but without helping much to discover major enemy intentions or tactical moves. For example, the easily anticipated transfer of massive German forces to the west, when Russia collapsed and pulled out of the war, was principally registered by neutral observers and by agents behind the lines who gathered and reported information about the quantity, nature and direction of railway traffic. Therefore, although the vast Hindenburg offensive, which was launched in March 1918, came as no surprise, its frontage, direction and weight did, rolling back the shattered British and French armies until, to the astonishment of many intelligence officers, it came to a premature halt due to its own logistic inertia and the sheer exhaustion of men and beasts.

In November 1917 at Cambrai, however, the British had scored a surprise tactical victory which broke the mould and pointed to the future. That day, behind an artillery concentration of 1,000 guns, some 400 tanks rolled forward to overrun the strongest German sector, the much vaunted Siegfried Line, in a matter of hours. The fact that it too soon ran out of momentum and forfeited strategic impact was incidental to the point that, apart from the indiscretion of some prisoners of war, the Germans were totally unaware of what was impending. Concealment of the nightly shifting of troops to their assembly areas, the isolation of the front from journalists, and a total security black-out, all contributed to the radical originality of the plan of attack. The surprise was enhanced by ensuring that radio and telephone communications were also strictly controlled to give an impression of normality behind the British lines.

What came to be known as the Cambrai key was turned again and again that summer as each succeeding phase of the wilting Hindenburg offensive ran its course to breakdown. At the psychological moment, usually gauged by the routine decay of the advance, a surprise counter-stroke would stop and roll the Germans back. Then on 8 August came the Allied counter-offensive with over 500 tanks near Amiens which so shook the Germans that, to the astonishment of the Allies, they felt the need to seek an armistice. Again surprise was mutual – the Germans by reason of an event they had not expected, the Allies because their Intelligence organisation (which so often in the past had been over-optimistic) was succumbing to the 'Incredulity Factor' and had not penetrated to the heart of their enemy's state of morale.

CHAPTER FOUR

A NEW FREEMASONRY

Not one nation that was seriously involved with the research and development of radio communications had avoided participation in World War One. All those which did had depended almost entirely upon private firms to produce the state-of-the-art equipment which their armed services demanded, including a mass of trained men and women to operate and maintain them. Therefore, as the guns fell silent and the need to carry on that work, including the search of foreign frequencies for vital intelligence, was reduced, the great majority became militarily redundant. In many cases they joined firms like Marconi and Telefunken which originally had supplied the essential experts to serve in the armed forces and who now were engaged in putting the communications business on a peacetime footing. And those firms, intent on commercial survival and expansion, often freely exchanged information and ideas with potential competitors. So, in a real spirit of freemasonry, nation spoke unto nation as a world-wide network of new and powerful transmitters was constructed for basic civil and military communications as well as the broadcasting of news and entertainment.

It was a revolutionary technological environment into which the radio firms entered with gusto. During the war years the emphasis had been fixed upon making best use of and improvements to existing systems. Beyond any doubt the most important steps forward were aimed at raising the performance, versatility and reliability of thermionic valves. These brought within reach a whole range of vastly more powerful electronic equipment, quite apart from basic transmitters and receivers. Among this new equipment was the lighter-weight Marconi RT set which started coming into production in 1918 to facilitate conversations between aircraft and ground stations to great tactical advantage. At the war's end 600 were installed in British aircraft, capable of speaking to 1,000 ground stations. This not only gave the newly formed RAF an instant advantage in control of aircraft in flight but also opened a way to a new dimension in radio intercept for acquisition of tactical intelligence about an enemy.

Far more revolutionary, of course, were those new applications of electronics which had been deferred by the war's priorities and now stood ripe for dynamic development. Of these Guglielmo Marconi's earlier 1916 experiments in the higher frequency bands, as a means to relieve congestion on those lower ones in use, had come to nothing. It was C. S. Franklin who soon restored the project to prominence by concentrating power by a reflector into a 'beam'. This paved the way to Marconi sending a message to Australia in 1918 and the development of systems which enormously improved long-range radio as public broadcasting started in 1920 on both sides of the Atlantic. These innovations were prime in challenging professional and amateur enthusiasts alike in their investigations of the ether, not only to train the next generation of operators dedicated to cope with increasingly complicated methods of radio intercept, but also scientifically to establish the nature and dimensions of the ionosphere which had been noticed by Heaviside and Kennelly.

Far more revolutionary yet was a revived interest into television, which had entered the field of feasibility with Fleming's invention of the thermionic valve and had been given a boost by A. A. Campbell Swinton in 1911. The breakthrough came in 1923 with V. K. Zworykin's iconoscope – an electronic camera tube based on what, in due course, would be known as the cathode ray tube (CRT). From this tube would emerge within the next decade a host of military uses, including the concept of radar to detect ships at sea, which was first seriously put forward by Marconi in 1922.

There also was the teleprinter that promised to accelerate as well as improve the potential security of telegraphic communication. With its capability, initially, of carrying high-speed printing on wire in the 1920s (manufactured in the USA, Britain and Germany), it possessed considerable military significance. For when adapted for radio by the Siemens Company, employing the International Teleprinter Code, it clearly pointed a new way ahead. Secretly encoded, non-morse teleprinter traffic was bound to pose tremendous challenges to the searchers.

There was nothing new about encoding machines. Thomas Jefferson, later President of the USA, had, for example, invented one at the end of the eighteenth century. After World War One there were many patented types on the market, of which only those adopted by the principal participants involved in the coming World War Two (Japan, Germany, Italy, Britain, Russia and the USA) need be dealt with in this book. In the aftermath of World War One, with its rash of public disclosures about British penetrations of enemy codes, the sheer necessity for possession of codes that were foolproof against breaking by traditional, intellectual hand and hit-and-miss methods – and by luck – became paramount. The advent and record of these machines in service will be described in due chronology. At this point it is essential to record that their role and effect were integral to the systems within which they functioned, as well as those they sought to baffle. Furthermore it is also necessary to reiterate that there was very little difference between the numerous types and performances of radios which came into service in the 1920s and beyond. The freemasonry of the industry insured against that. Virtually all the technical innovations already mentioned were in general use. Few significant technical marches were stolen prior to the technically tumultuous war years of the 1940s. The fundamental causes of disparity between nations were the way the various equipment was co-ordinated and employed. These were the reasons why Germany became supreme in the communications business at the outbreak of global war in 1939.

Defeat in 1918, humiliation and drastic, selective disarmament compelled Germany to adopt in the post-war years very special and often strikingly original measures in order to devise a semblance of defence measures which did not overtly contravene the Treaty of Versailles of 1919. To begin with, the newly created Reichswehr (limited in size to 100,000 men) set itself to study what had gone wrong, what was required to put things right in the immediate and distant future, and what weapon systems were required to satisfy the almost insoluble requirements of defence. Forbidden such offensive weapon systems as submarines, warships of more than 10,000 tonnes, heavy artillery, tanks, poison gas and war planes, Germany was compelled to experiment secretly at home and abroad with the proscribed weapons and develop only those futuristic types which had been overlooked at Versailles. Of the latter there were two quite promising substitutes: rockets in lieu of heavy artillery and highly developed, ultra-secure signal systems for sophisticated control of highly mobile and efficient land, sea and air forces designed to compensate for shortage of numbers.

Versailles had also laid down the disbandment of that extremely professional think-tank of German militarism, the Great General Staff. As a substitute for the elite General Staff Corps the Germans created an organisation called the Truppenamt. It comprised ex-General Staff officers of the highest calibre and experience. Using well-tried war-gaming techniques, they settled down to formulate an army of the future that included a theoretical air arm. At the same time a navy that had but few ships (the bulk of the High Seas Fleet having been surrendered to the victorious Allies) also looked ahead, though without concocting many radical notions – except to ensure that in the future there would be unbreakable systems of codes to make securely practical the control of operations by radio. It was essential, the sailors realised, to avert a recurrence of the insecurity through radio intercept which so disastrously had undermined their operations in the previous conflict.

Similarly, strong feeling about future, secure signal systems conditioned the studies and schemes of army officers. Although there were some emotional public pronouncements by certain generals that lack of tanks had, besides the stab in the back from the home front, cost Germany the war, there was a much clearer vision than that of pre-1914 of the need for excellent signals procedures and equipment. It certainly helped that the tendency to ignore the advice of Inspectors of Signals in the planning of operations was abandoned. Better still was the vitality imparted from 1919 onwards by the genius of Captain Erich Fellgiebel and his select band of forward-looking signals specialists.

Fellgiebel was born in 1886, joined a telegraph battalion in 1904, attended the Military Technical Academy in 1907 and became an instructor at the Telegraph School in 1913. In 1914 he commanded a radio station in a cavalry corps and from 1916 to October 1919 filled various staff positions at corps headquarters. As one of those retained in the

100,000-man army, he was posted in 1919 to the Truppenamt where, until 1923, he played an important role in shaping evolving signal communications and Intelligence policy. A two-year spell as company commander in a Nachrichten battalion (meaning Signals and Intelligence) led in 1925 to more staff jobs until 1929 when he returned to the Reichswehr Ministry for two years as a major in the Abwehr, dealing with secret Intelligence and Security.

Fellgiebel thus was involved, deeply and practically, in the crucial studies which, in 1926, culminated in the bold, radical decision to abandon all existing communications equipment (which was hopelessly unreliable and obsolete) and replace it with standardised families of telephone, morse-telegraph, non-morse teleprinter and undamped, purpose-built radios (WT and RT) using thermionic valves. These were purchased for specific tasks required by all Arms. They operated in the Low Frequency (LF) band (30–300 KHz (to adopt modern terminology)), High Frequency (HF) band (3–30 MHz) and Very High Frequency (VHF) band (30–300 MHz). All equipment would be notable for rugged, unit construction linked by plug and socket strips which permitted quick dismantling, servicing and repair. They were simple to operate and clearly labelled. When in service at the renewed outbreak of war in 1939 these equipments, along with the excellent spiral, quad telephone cable had no peer in any other army. Moreover the radio sets were seemingly made completely secure by the adoption of an encoding machine called Enigma. This electro-mechanical machine, the size of a typewriter, with its vast choice (after further development) of some 150 million key settings, first came into service with the Navy in 1926 and with the Army in 1928.

The part that this equipment and Fellgiebel would play in the subsequent evolution of radio communications and intercept will be described in context, as will be the activities of those nations which had to combat the Germans and their allies. In 1926, however, upon the adoption of Enigma machines by the German Navy, most other major nations were far less worried about the crippled Germans than about other nations.

The Americans, complacently satisfied with a policy of isolation from the rest of the world (especially from Europe and its warlike politics), were more concerned about an emerging threat on the other side of the Pacific where the Japanese were exhibiting belligerent ambitions to spread their influence through the exercise of sea power with a modernised, enlarged navy and army. The US Navy, therefore, took a lead in Intelligence affairs, especially that of SIGINT, to keep tabs on the Japanese.

America was singularly fortunate in 1924 when Lieutenant Laurence Safford was put in charge of the new research desk in the Navy's Code and Signal Section. At once this clever, dynamic young officer set about creating for the Navy a much needed communications organisation founded on radio intercept and cryptanalysis. Within a few months he had assembled a team of bright young men dedicated to penetrating the Japanese Navy's signals organisation. A year later, with a clear policy agreed by his superiors, Safford was instrumental in setting up an intercept station on the island of Guam. As these searchers of the ether learned their trade, a steadily increasing volume of information about a potent threat to peace was acquired and sent to Washington for decoding, translation and evaluation. So valuable was the material gathered from Guam that, in 1927, to draw closer to the Japanese heartland, two more listening stations were activated – one in the Philippines and the other in the American consulate in Shanghai. Such was the success of Safford's brain child that, in 1928, mobile listening stations were installed in warships sent to cruise within reception range of the Japanese Fleet on manoeuvres to overhear and study its methods and technology. Fourteen years later Commander Safford was in command of an organisation 700 experts strong on the eve of war.

The decade after the Great War to end all wars for all time was anything but the utopia envisaged by the men of Versailles. It included the Russian Civil War which spilled over into an attempted, but repulsed, invasion by the Russian Communists of Germany via Poland in 1919; a French occupation of the German Ruhrland to enforce the terms of the Versailles Treaty, at the same time as, with Spanish collaboration, she was engaged in protracted hostilities against dissidents in their North African colonies; and recurrent unrest with Arabs in her Syrian colony in 1919–20. Then there was severe friction in post-war Turkey involving the Albanians, the Greeks, the French and the British.

The British had their hands well and truly full with a war against Afghanistan in 1919, along with subsequent associated tribal troubles on the North West Frontier of India; a fierce, major revolt in Ireland leading to the division of that country; various outbreaks of unrest with Arabs in Mesopotamia (Iraq), and in the Protectorate of Palestine; and tensions on the periphery of China which, between 1920 and 1926, lapsed into the turmoil of a struggle between rival war lords.

None of these outbreaks of violence of various intensities, often involving contenders with only moderate technical means, drew much upon radio intercept for acquisition of Intelligence, for the simple reason that few of the participants possessed or employed even unenciphered radio. Nevertheless, the major powers were careful to monitor transmissions in clear from the more sophisticated nations, including Japan, Russia, the USA, France, Britain, Turkey and Greece.

Post-war, like the Germans, Britain and her principal allies gave careful thought to the lessons learned and the changes which would have to be made for the future. Predictably France, as the major land power, largely opted for the status quo; and so too did the USA. Concerning the most revolutionary combat arms – armoured fighting vehicles and radio communications – both these nations relegated tanks to a subsidiary, infantry support role and retained horsed cavalry and marching infantry, supported by massed artillery, as the arms of decision. Both, however, gave full support to development of signals technology and Radio Intelligence (RI), as the Americans called radio intercept. This was hardly surprising since both had long profited in efficiency from the benefits bestowed by a Signals Corps.

Paradoxically it was the traditionally conservative British Navy and Army which embraced radical changes via the three most modern and vital Arms. In 1918 they had formed the first independent air force – the RAF. In 1923 the Army was alone in adopting the concept of armoured fighting vehicles in the independent role by forming a Tank Corps, and in the process almost halved the number of horsed cavalry regiments.

And in 1920, long after every other nation of substance had founded a Signals Corps, Britain turned the Signals Branch of the Royal Engineers into the Royal Corps of Signals. A common denominator is the fact that these three new corps attracted vastly more men of higher quality (compared with the other less technical Arms and Services) who earnestly desired to work with modern equipment in a challenging job that would train them subsequently for well-paid civilian employment.

Early in 1919 this seemingly astonishing military levity in public fitted neatly in place when twenty-five officers who had worked in Room 40 and in Military Intelligence (MI) were merged by a Cabinet decision to break entirely new ground by forming what was called the Government Code and Cipher School (GC and CS). The title was invented by Sir Victor Forbes of the Foreign Office Communications Department and, in 1921, came under Admiral Hugh Sinclair, who had been DNI. Those talented officers included cryptanalysts who had been in the RNAS and RFC (and therefore now were members of the new-born RAF). As a group they comprised, in recognition of the need for collaboration in a crucial task, the first ever tri-Service organisation – a truly amazing advance towards the future, even though it was placed initially under the Admiralty for administration.

These were years of severe financial retrenchment. The Admiralty, belatedly coming to realise that radio monitoring stations would be required by GC and CS, axed three of the four SI Shore Wireless stations still in service. At about the same time the Army established an intercept station in an old fort at Chatham and the RAF erected one at Waddington.

Three years later, however, the Foreign Office awoke to the fact that, whereas military radio traffic was meagre, diplomatic interception had grown steadily since April 1919 when a small Admiralty party, led by Commander Alastair Denniston of Room 40, had joined the French in Paris to intercept and decode, with some success, the latest ciphers in use by the German mission during the Peace Conference. At the same time, monitoring of Soviet Russian traffic (which in 1919 was not encoded) began and gradually multiplied. Interception of Japanese diplomatic traffic was also tackled but, for the ensuing ten years, the cryptographic effort was almost non-existent, due mainly to the language difficulty and a dire shortage of staff – of whom Mr Hobart Hampden and Sir Harold Parlett alone were truly expert.

Nevertheless, in 1922 Lord Curzon claimed the GC and CS was working mainly for the Foreign Office and therefore should come under its administration and funding. The Admiralty, strapped for cash, did not demur.

The next major step forward was taken in 1923 when the Cabinet accepted crucial advice for a series of departmental amalgamations. Henceforward the head of the Secret Intelligence Service (SIS) (who was known as C after the first letter of the original head's surname) would come under the Foreign Office for administration and funding, and would take under control GC and CS, with Admiral Sinclair in charge of them both. At about the same time the RAF joined GC and CS; and another new interservice organisation, to be known as the Y Service, also came into being under GC and CS, tasked to co-ordinate radio intercept.

Surprisingly the three armed services raised no serious objections to these arrangements, maybe because there was so little military traffic to intercept. What mostly concerned them were the procedures and deployments which might have to be adopted if war broke out. How, they asked, could such an important function – which was deemed far superior to espionage with all its vagaries for the gathering of intelligence – be controlled and by whom and where in time of war? It worried experienced officers that insufficient thought had been given to the fact that the three services would be involved at all levels of command and that each, as a matter of course, would demand special requirements and that its priorities would be different to the others. In the lackadaisical mood of those days, this problem was kicked around for three years until, at last, it was decided that, while the tri-service GC and CS would retain responsibility for cryptanalysis, separate rules of operation must be formulated to suit each service.

In 1927 the DNI arranged with C (Admiral Sinclair) that, on the outbreak of war, the entire naval section with GC and CS would return to the Admiralty and might even be sent abroad. But in due course this impractical arrangement was changed to retain the section in place, except in the possibility of war in the Far East alone. The Army, meanwhile, in 1926 had devised rules which would enable its field units to be responsible for intercepting the enemy's field radio nets and for the collection of all information obtainable from that source for MI. As the junior service, the RAF's Air Intelligence (AI) seems to have raised no substantial objections, possibly because Home Defence was its principal role (apart from support for the Navy and Army in foreign parts), and very likely because, at that time, there was no recognisable enemy at large in western Europe. So the RAF taught its Signals Branch Field units how to listen in to imaginary enemy airborne and ground units, just in case the need arose.

Concern over the conflicting circumstances that might arise between departmental interests and the overriding need for joint-service SIGINT had already led in 1924 to GC and CS 'at the request of the Fighting Services and with the consent of the Foreign Office', to establish a Cryptography and Interception Committee to guide the work and settle priorities. It cannot be claimed that this committee set the world on fire. Its members, drawn from GC and CS and the Service Ministries' Signals and Intelligence branches, rarely met. It is recorded that there was no continuity and that 'of the fifty officers who attended during the next fourteen years, only ten attended more than one meeting'. But what it did achieve with concrete results was the formation of a standing sub-committee which met regularly. Called the Y Service Sub-Committee, it was tasked to allocate radio intercept facilities on an Empire-wide basis. By the 1930s an inflexible system had evolved whereby the War Office took responsibility for work in the Middle East, the Admiralty for the Far East and the Air Ministry for Home Defence.

Army Y took on the lion's share of work. The Royal Signals had formed No. 2 Wireless Company at Sarafand in Palestine in 1923, ostensibly for employment in India but, as time passed, largely for use in the Middle East. Soon the Signals Corps would establish the Wireless Experimental Station in England, a field unit in Malta, a fixed wireless station in England in 1926 and, later, a DF network along with No. 4 Company at Aldershot. Allied to the training of these units went the development of tactical interception in the field and what was called Illicit Wireless

Interception – roughly speaking, the detection of crime in collaboration with the Scotland Yard station at Denmark Hill, which had been taken over by Sinclair about 1923.

Scotland Yard was searching mainly for diplomatic and illicit traffic, but it also had its ears cocked for what was known as clandestine material, such as the mass of unusual and unknown transmissions (all in cipher except for 'operators' chat'), which was detected in London in 1930 and was all of the international amateur type. It emerged, through study and DF, that this was part of a world-wide Comintern network controlled from Moscow. Quite soon a team led by Mr H. C. Kenworthy located a house in the suburbs by means of TA, DF and cryptography. These were specialists at work when there was a shortage of military manpower and facilities that were filled by Navy Y and RAF Y – as will be seen.

In June 1932 the Y Service was stretched, to say the least. The Admiralty was responsible for the Far East. The Army (No. 2 WT Company Palestine) was responsible for the Near East, including Arabia, Persia, Turkey and South Russia; and C-in-C India (with stations in north-west India and Burma) for countries adjacent to India. Traffic in Europe and America and long-distance traffic in general was dealt with by stations in England as follows: Admiralty: two Y stations; War Office: one Y station; Air Ministry: one Y station.

Men who joined any of the listening teams were of high calibre and often recruited from the thousands of amateurs who, once restrictions were lifted in 1919, were free to indulge in the hobby of practice and experiment with home radio. Many, using the latest valves, made significant contributions to the development of public broadcasting. Then there were the enthusiasts who joined the Armed Forces Signal Services in order to expand their hobby into a professional career. For when the radio ban was removed by governments in 1919, amateurs were permitted only to use either an overcrowded, narrow, medium-frequency band or higher frequency bands that were currently considered unsuitable for long-range transmissions. This handicap was soon overcome by amateurs in the USA who, using the latest, home-made sets, antennae and techniques, sent messages over distances in excess of 3,000 miles with low-power 1 KW sets tuned to 1.3 KHz.

CHAPTER FIVE

PROGRESS TO CALAMITY

Arguably World War Two began long before Germany invaded Poland on 1 September 1939. Back in 1926 a major conflict which would continue almost without pause until 1945, had started in China where Communists fought Nationalists and a mixed community of Europeans, Americans and Japanese looked on in anxiety from their International Settlement in Shanghai. Then in the summer of 1927 the Japanese army became involved in clashes which magnified into battles leading to the Japanese occupation of Manchuria and an invasion of Shanghai in 1932, the occupation of Jehol in Inner Mongolia in 1933 and further expansion into northern China in 1934. In 1937, outright war broke out. This major conflict began with a large-scale Japanese invasion of the Chinese hinterland which involved attacks on British and American gunboats on the River Yangtze. In 1939 the campaign was diversified by two months of fierce fighting between Japanese and Russians in Outer Mongolia, on the eve of the invasion of Poland by Germany.

Needless to say, neither the Americans nor the British took the Yangtze incident lying down. The Japanese were 'persuaded' to apologise and pay compensation for the lives lost and the damage done. Covertly their radio communications were intercepted with increasing vigilance and not a little success in the breaking of their codes. Likewise the Japanese, for their part, were strongly monitoring unfriendly transmissions. Thus these hidden listeners and cryptanalysts searching for intelligence were the first aggressive harbingers of World War Two.

Ironically, the escalation to world war which started in the Far East was accompanied by fervent attempts to disarm in Europe in the midst of the catastrophic financial depression which began with the 1929 Wall Street crash. Of the future Axis Powers, Italy, under the dictatorship of Benito Mussolini, launched a large naval programme in 1930, expanded her Army and Air Force and invaded Abyssinia in 1935 – a year before becoming an active participant on the Fascist side in the Spanish Civil

War. Meanwhile Germany, downcast by high unemployment and a yearning for a saviour to restore her prestige as a world power, voted Adolf Hitler and his Nazi Party into power in 1933 and immediately developed into a virtual military dictatorship.

The League of Nations was faced with the spectre of Germany withdrawing immediately from its councils and secretly planning to rearm; denouncing the Versailles Treaty and publicly announcing rearmament; forming an Air Force in 1935; reoccupying the demilitarised Rhineland; siding with Italy and the Fascists in the Spanish Civil War; and joining Japan in the signing of an anti-Communist pact in 1936. Britain herself began tentative rearmament in 1935, to be copied by France in 1936. Disarmament talks collapsed.

Thus, all at once, Britain more than any of the other European powers, found herself facing troubles from all directions – a dilemma which irresistibly threw an ever-increasing load on the Y Service as it attempted to cope with numerous calls upon its limited resources. Abruptly the neat division of labour on an arms footing that had been settled by 1930 fell apart. Like it or not, the three services were compelled to share the load on an inter-service basis.

So, in 1937, naval personnel in GC and CS found themselves working on non-naval Japanese ciphers in London while their naval ciphers were being tackled in Hong Kong; RAF Y was listening to Italian colonial traffic between Rome, north Africa and the Dodecanese; Navy Y was eavesdropping on Italian Air Force messages; while the Army's No. 2 WT Coy, still based at Sarafand, had a detachment in Malta, and a field unit in Aden that was intercepting Italian Air Force traffic in East Africa. All this was happening at a turning-point in history when it was felt, in accordance with a Cabinet opinion of March 1934, that Germany should be regarded as the main potential enemy threat; whereupon the monitoring of German communications and attempts to break their new machine codes that were in increasing use commenced in earnest.

The task was hard but not entirely unrewarding. German military signal communications under the new regime steadily became very strictly controlled and remarkably secure. It was no coincidence that the man who was most responsible for that was Erich Fellgiebel who, as Oberstleutnant (Lt Col) became Chief of Staff to the Inspector of the Nachrichten Truppen shortly after Hitler became Reich Chancellor. A year later he was promoted to Colonel and made Inspector of that inspired organisation – the first signals-trained officer ever to hold such a key appointment. For, as was commonly believed in the Reichswehr and the rapidly expanding, conscripted Army, it was the Inspectors, directly responsible to the Commander-in-Chief, who in practice shaped and trained all the combat arms and administrative services.

Fellgiebel had thoroughly absorbed the lessons of the previous war which made it plain that, important as radio was, it could not be absolutely secure, not even with employment of the most foolproof ciphers. For the early Enigma machine, wonderful as it seemed in the 1920s, was quickly demonstrated as simplistically vulnerable. Indeed, had Fellgiebel but known it, GC and CS would be breaking by hand those primitive models in 1937. Yet it mattered not that he was unaware of that event. Fellgiebel, who was extremely security conscious, well understood the great truth that the more a code is used the greater the chances of its defeat. From the moment of his appointment as Chief of Staff to the Inspector of Signals he set in motion, in consultation with the Navy, progressive improvements to the Enigma machine which by 1937 seemed not only to have made it impregnable to decryption after intercept but similarly proof even if captured.

Before the outbreak of war in September 1939 he had seen to it that the Wehrmacht's listening and DF intercept sets had been perfected and the Cryptographic Office in Ministry of National Defence staffed and equipped to ensure solution of enemy codes and ciphers as well as keeping secure its own cryptographic systems. More important still was the opportunity offered in 1936 by a National Defence Decree to enlarge nation-wide by thousands of kilometres the existing Reichspost telephone, telegraph and teleprinter cable circuits for use by the Supreme High Command (OKW), the Army, the Navy and the Air Force. Furthermore, the Army, while embracing enciphered radio for mobile operations by the fast troops of the Armoured Corps, was encouraged to make only essential use of these facilities and to use cable or couriers as often as possible instead. For this it was equipped with laying machines which could dispense cable at a rate of 100 miles per day.

Prior to the outbreak of war, Fellgiebel had been granted sweeping powers over the communications of the Reich; but while there was tight control over civilian organisations and structure, the relationships with the Navy and Air Force were very loose. From long association and the evolution of complementary procedures, the Army and Navy got on well. In any case they had only occasionally to work operationally in close collaboration with each other and the Navy was very much the junior service within a land power. With Field Marshal Hermann Göring's new-born Luftwaffe, however, there was constant friction, made worse by Göring's use of Hitler's favour to win priority grants of signals equipment to the detriment of the other services.

In practice, each service tended to go its own way. Only rarely did their networks collaborate mutually; frequently they did not share technical information and habitually each employed their own contractors and manufacturers without consultation. In so far as the Navy was concerned, this raised few matters of concern for Fellgiebel. He was satisfied that the sailors had developed excellent communications arrangements geared for surface and submarine warfare. The B Dienst operated to far greater effect than in World War One both for security and the penetration of enemy communication systems and ciphers. Moreover it was developing a four-wheel Enigma machine (Typhoon) that was even less vulnerable than the standard, three-wheel type (with their two additional spares) that was in service with the Air Force, the Abwehr, the SS, the police, the railways and the diplomatic service.

It was the Air Force which posed the greatest potential for trouble through insecurity. For not only were its relations with the other services fractious, its dependence upon radio for strategic, tactical and navigation signals communications made it highly vulnerable to intercept. This weakness was multiplied by excessive use of Enigma encoded messages on radio when cable would have sufficed, and by undisciplined RT chatter between pilots when airborne.

Nevertheless, well before the start of hostilities, Fellgiebel (who by then was legendary in the Wehrmacht) had created the best communication and information system in the world to give Germany an immense superiority over her opponents in nearly all respects. From the intelligence point of view, this was already apparent to the British.

With the growth of German, Italian and Russian belligerence in the mid-1930s, the quantity of military radio traffic multiplied during training exercises (especially those of the Luftwaffe). Germany's transmissions in the VHF wave band was found by British Y Service to be more and more difficult to intercept from 1937 onward and, after the introduction of the latest Enigma machine, indecipherable on HF. Italy's, on the other hand (including very valuable diplomatic messages), was far easier to intercept from Malta and the Middle East and beginning to yield to a significantly reinforced GC and CS. Russia's, although interceptable, was thoroughly secure.

Nevertheless, now with ample practice, Y was able to make useful progress against Germany, although only marginally against her Navy and the Army which were sparing in the use of radio. The key to success was to be found in the attack on the Luftwaffe, which was prolific in its use of radio and therefore wide open to TA and DF. Not only were locations of over sixty airfields revealed (in due course to be confirmed by clandestine observation from the air and on the ground by attachés) but so too were the identity of aircraft units in flight. At the same time, experience in the breaking of low-grade book codes was obtained. Such was the success of these relatively limited achievements that complaints from a high level were being shot at the SIS, which had been allowed to run down dangerously and was producing little information of real substance – except for what the French supplied. Not that TA's discoveries provided anything better than rough guide lines as to German strengths and order of battle. Indeed, come September 1939 and the invasion of Poland, the former was grossly exaggerated and the latter virtually non-existent – a criticism that equally could be applied to tank strengths and Army order of battle at that time.

The state of the overworked Y Service on the eve of the Munich crisis in 1938 may be compared in microcosm to Britain's shocking unreadiness for war and slow rate of production and rearmament at the hands of a government which was singularly ill-informed by an arrogant Foreign Office with its scanty interest in military intelligence. There was a desperate shortage of suitable receivers and DF equipments as well as trained people to work them. Much the same could be said of GC and CS, even though steps were being taken to recruit past members of Room 40 and MI as well as newcomers found by the Foreign Office from the universities. These came together for the first time in September 1938 at the architecturally uninspiring manor of Bletchley Park, that stood with its cottages and out-buildings in 581 acres near the A5 road, forty-seven miles to the north of London. What at the time was thought likely to be a move for the duration of the coming war served then as a short and most useful practice mobilisation exercise. Socially it seems to have gone fairly smoothly, but it indicated too that extensive building and communications work would be required should the real thing occur in the almost predictable future.

This would be the home of C where he controlled the SIS, GC and CS and the Y Service throughout World War Two. The latter pair of organisations referred to by GC and CS's Head (Commander Alistair Denniston who sat on the Y Sub-Committee) as '... an adopted child of the Foreign Office with no family rights, and the poor relation of the SIS, whose peacetime activities left little cash to spare'. There emerges, in fact, a distinct impression that the Foreign Office, in its smug detachment from the military scene, treated military intelligence and, indeed, the rest of the world, as participants in a vulgar brawl.

The situation really was menacing as Germany's corrupt intentions progressively revealed her expansionist intentions after the absorption of Austria, the take-over of the Sudetenland, the occupation of the remainder of Czechoslovakia and the mounting threat to Poland. Not to be brushed aside, too, was evidence that the Enigma decryption problem, which was stubbornly proving so intractable, might soon be exacerbated by yet another encoding machine of formidable capability.

In 1932 the Metropolitan Police intercept station at Denmark Hill and the GPO station at St Albans working for the Y Service had picked up a new kind of high-speed, non-morse transmission coming from Germany. It was transmitting at 25 characters (four words) per second in the International Teleprinter Code but was not enciphered. These transmissions continued intermittently and were judged as experimental. GC and CS was alerted to what the Germans called Geheimschreiber (secret writer), sometimes by the German signals officers as G supplement and, occasionally in intercepted Enigma messages, as Sägefisch. This led eventually to GC and CS naming its variants generically as Fish.

Fish was kept in mind. But it was Enigma in its progressively improved versions which demanded the highest, almost desperate priority for cracking. The story of how this was done is best described in its complexity in Professor Sir Harry Hinsley's monumental *British Intelligence in the Second World War*, Vol. 3, Appx 2. Here it must suffice to record that the struggle to break Enigma continuously was the result of an epic piece of Polish, French and British collaboration.

This team work began in 1931 after Captain Gustav Bertrand, of the French Service de Renseignement, acquired from Hans-Thilo Schmidt, of the German cipher branch, manuals and operating instructions for Enigma 1. In December he offered them to the British, who for technical reasons were initially lukewarm, and to the Poles, who were extremely interested. They were given more documents in 1932, including sufficient settings for Enigma to enable the Poles, until late in 1938, to decrypt, first the Army, then the Navy and the Air Force version and also that of the Sicherheitsdienst (SD). By then, moreover, the Poles had solved the complex wiring system of the wheels, had built replicas of the Enigma machine and designed and built six models of an electro-mechanical decoding machine, programmed by perforated paper sheets, called Bombe. By this time, in fact, GC and CS had worked out a hand method (called Netz) which could cope with Enigma 1.

At that point, however, the radical improvements incorporated by the Germans into Enigma 1 had worked their spell. Enigma 2 was made impenetrable and crisis among the Allies reigned supreme. In January 1939 Bertrand called a meeting with the British and Poles which led to

Bertrand delivering in person to C at Victoria Station, London, on 16 August, an Enigma replica along with drawings of the Bombe which enabled GC and CS not only to build but also vastly improve the Polish version. This enabled a team, led by a brilliant young mathematician named Dr Alan Turing, to exploit the Netz method and focus his genius on making the improved, renamed Bombe which, seven months later, was capable of solving the Enigma 2 keys with consistency and speed.

CHAPTER SIX

FOUNDATIONS

After World War Two Nigel de Grey, of Zimmermann telegram fame and, throughout most of the war, Deputy Director of GC and CS, held the view that Bletchley Park, with its false mellowness, would gradually become an historical factor that was impossible to ignore. Without doubt on its mobilisation in September 1939, this looked a distinctly remote possibility as an odd collection of academics, civil servants, sailors, soldiers and airmen rubbed shoulders in surroundings which were anything but well organised or cosy. The manor house, surrounded by huts, accommodated the Naval Section, the Military Section, the Air Section, the telephone exchange and the teleprinter room. Among the huts No. 6 would house the Army and RAF Cryptanalytical Section; No. 3 the Army and RAF Intelligence people; No. 8, in due course, the Naval Cryptanalytical Section; and No. 4 the Naval Intelligence people who dealt direct with the Admiralty. Eventually these four expanding, key sections would move into newly built, enlarged accommodation. But like Room 40 after it moved to better accommodation in World War One, they retained their original names.

At Bletchley Park, the war was fought against the Axis Powers at the same time as sectional combat was joined between GC and CS's denizens to resolve numerous problems which had been overlooked or never could have been foreseen. Into this mélange the Y Service, groping with the unimaginable, began to feed in the raw material without which the war would be lost.

By grace of Adolf Hitler's improvised grand strategy, Bletchley Park and its satellite Y searchers were granted the month-long Polish campaign, plus six months' Phoney War, to improve or activate a few important operational systems and administrative arrangements before the war hotted up in April 1940. The crushing air attacks on the civilian population which had been expected did not materialise. Instead Air Intelligence (AI) in the Air Ministry, which was tasked with responsibility for Meteorology, found itself working with the Meteorological Office in the hunt for new sources of weather data for essential forecasting. This was because on 3 September the Germans had started using low-grade encoding of their broadcast weather bulletins in the International Meteorological Code; and soon they were copied by the Russians, thus depriving the French and British of vital data from most of eastern Europe and northern Asia.

This had been anticipated. The task of deciphering was passed to the Air Section at BP, where it became the baby of Professor Josh Cooper, a scruffy, slightly deaf, brilliant mathematician. He depended upon the Meteorological Office's radio intercept station at Dunstable for material from German and Russian weather broadcasts (of which those from Russia were the most important). After two months of frustration, Dunstable admitted it was not making progress. So the business was moved to BP where Dr G. C. McVittie took charge. He was an applied mathematician who had been studying weather reporting, but who lacked experience, with cryptanalysis. So to begin with he attended a three months course in codebreaking and two forecasters from Dunstable began working at BP. The longer-term aim was to send intercepted material by teleprinter to BP for rapid decryption (for it was pointless, due to the ephemeral quality of the data, to waste a moment of time) and then return the decoded data by teleprinter to Dunstable.

Because this did not work at all well it was decided that McVittie should stay at BP until the codes were broken and then go to Dunstable. In the event he remained at BP for the duration of the war since it was found (as later will be described) much more productive for him to work alongside the other cryptanalysts in Hut 3 rather than with specialist weather men.

Meanwhile the French had enjoyed some success reading the less important German data and Cooper and McVittie had agreed with them that BP should concentrate on the Russian code and there should be a mutual exchange of results. This too broke down when France collapsed in June and the cross Channel teleprinter cable was cut. Happily, at the last moment however, the French did bring to England their results on the German code.

Here for the time being we will leave the Met situation since, from

1 July 1940 onward, it was much more a code problem than one of inter-cept. But its importance and the value of processing without delay via radio intercept and teleprinter had to be judged a model for others to copy. It must never be underrated.

The Allies went to war in 1939 in a strategic position not unlike that which had existed just before peace broke out in 1918. Their navies imposed a blockade and concentrated on dealing with a few surface raiders and U-boats. The armies lined up along the French frontier with Germany but prepared themselves to deal with an enemy invasion of Holland and Belgium. The air forces stood by to support the armies and navies and also to bomb industrial targets in Germany. From the SIGINT angle, an increasing number of listening stations, naval, military or air, were set up near the coasts and in depth behind the frontiers. On the other side of the Siegfried Line the Germans followed suit – except that their intentions were offensive and their security measures, above all SIGINT, bent on concealment.

How successful the Germans were in their measures can be judged from how little the Allies uncovered through SIGINT during the Phoney War. The Allied navies, which had most to do, were least well served by Intelligence. The German Navy's radio silence was outstanding. The few U-boats available made sparing use of radio and their messages were unreadable since all were enciphered by Enigma. Battle-cruisers and cruis-ers tasked to raid convoys came and went unnoticed as, under strict radio silence, they stole along the Norwegian coast under cloak of the long win-ter's night. The German Army, returning to the Western Front from the conquest of Poland, relied on Fellgiebel's cable system for its signals com-munications and carefully broke radio silence only occasionally during training on exercises.

Only the Luftwaffe gave much away. Bombers returning from Poland were detected and located by field units in France when they used radio on approach to their airfields. The few shot down over France yielded priceless information from low-grade code books. RAF Y began rather amateurishly assembling an order of battle from the intercept and TA of bombers and flying boats raiding British naval bases and coastal shipping and, more harmfully, laying magnetic mines in the seaways. Modest though it may have been, it was better then nothing when little was known about the procedure, organisation and deployment of a much publicised and dreaded air force, the strength of which Intelligence seriously exaggerated.

Indeed, that autumn RAF Y found itself in a persuasive position to insist upon large-scale expansion. The ranks of the Navy and Army Y units had been reinforced by recalled reservists. So too had the RAF, but they were very much under strength, although making good use of volunteer, 'ham' operators. Realising that Bomber Command's initial operations had been handicapped by lack of intelligence, Group Captain L. F. Blandy (who in 1924 had served on the original Y Committee), helped by Squadron Leader W. Swanborough, produced a definitive paper for Josh Cooper and the Air Ministry.

Swanborough, who was OC of the Central Intereception Station at Cheadle, summarised the commitments of the RAF Y Service in its wartime task of studying the activity of a powerful modern air force through knowledge of its strategic locations, tactics, radio signalling, codes and ciphers, radio beacons and new secret technical developments brought into use in wartime. He stated that co-operation between Air Section at GC and CS and Cheadle was out of date, insisting that the latter's establishment of listening stations urgently needed increment and enlargement, along with a considerable increase in receivers, DF equipment and teleprinter/morse combined line systems to connect them to Cheadle. To work them he demanded a significant addition of good quality trained people 'at once'.

On Christmas Day 1939, Cooper, acting with all the authority of a principal civil servant, teleprinted his concurrence and continued to press on with what he had started already, the filling of a new War Establishment – which already in places was getting by through the misemployment of Foreign Office emergency staff, including women. The highest priority was given to the recruitment of German linguists as translators and potential cryptographers, the latter incidentally, not recognised on Air Ministry establishments. The ranks of the RAF and university colleges were scoured for suitable employees. So too were those of the WRNS (Womens Royal Navy Service), ATS (Auxiliary Territorial Service) and WAAF (Womens Auxiliary Air Force) – the last, notably at that moment, going to listening stations and Cheadle to join the élite band of ladies who already worked in control rooms of Fighter Command. Some very clever people were discovered and, in due course, were transferred to BP, where staff of their kind were always in short supply.

A tricky problem was how to speed the decoding process to enable vital information to reach RAF Commands in time to be of tactical use. This involved the training of so-called 'computors' (sic) – not machines but human searchers able to produce almost instantly an English translation of a German message, selecting as they went the 'important' ones and ensuring that they were teleprinted without delay to Cheadle and AI (in the Air Ministry). The evolved computor's technique laid down that the German linguist listener wrote in German and inserted the translation between double-spaced lines prior to teleprinting,

In fact, unauthorised as the computors were to attempt any appreciation of the text, they often did so most shrewdly – no mean feat of initiative and insight when it is realised that, in those early days, they were not briefed about Luftwaffe organisation and how it functioned. Indeed, the Air Ministry was very much in the dark about such matters itself!

That Christmas the future handling and value of the material uncovered via Cheadle was in flux. So much depended upon the decryption of Enigma, and doubts actually existed as to the viability of the unproved and very expensive Bombe. This left the far less promising and laborious Netz system as the alternative. (It is on record that there was a convivial celebration at BP that month when the two millionth hole was punched in the large sheets of squared paper employed by the cryptanalysts.) Fortunately Denniston and Commander Edward Travis managed to obtain sufficient money to place a production order with the British Tabulating Machine Company for the first prototype Bombe, thus providing a team of bright young thrusters, headed by the genius Alan Turing and his principal collaborator, Gordon Welchman, with the opportunity on 6 January to solve the Luftwaffe Red key. This momentous event was simply the first of numerous experimental decryptions of three different keys between then and March, all of them leading up to the breaking of a key brought into use for the invasion of Denmark and Norway on 9 April 1940. In the interim, of course, the sight of just a few Enigma decrypts gave Hut 3 sufficient material with which to familiarise its officers with specialised German military terminology and organisation; and then, at relative leisure, to hold post-mortems as part of a training process which proved 'surprisingly accurate' in the desperate days ahead. Also, too, the opportunity was taken to train women to accelerate the deciphering of keys, which had already been solved by using a British Typex machine (derived from Enigma but, significantly, never broken by the Germans).

Close liaison with the French continued that bitterly cold winter of 1939–40. A joint attack was aimed at two roughly defined categories of German radio traffic: Main System (400 messages per day), U System (200 per day) and others (100 per day). The first, initially, were sent untidily and a week late to the principal Army Y unit lodged in an old fort at Chatham, leaving it to the French to deal with the rest because they were intercepting low-powered transmissions on medium frequencies. Come January, blessed by the clear indications of the Bombe potential, Denniston laid it down, in consultation with AI and MI 8 (the Army's equivalent of the RAF's AI), that Air and Army Y stations should concentrate as far as possible on Enigma, while Navy Y stations intercepted their traditional 'clients' and received a mass of their raw material from RAF Chicksands.

MI 8 under Colonel D. A. Butler was engaged, as was AI, in exploiting Y information to gain insight into German Army intentions and order of battle – about which they were largely in ignorance, including knowledge of their call signs and frequencies. Information from France via Chatham contributed; but a small team of volunteers under a Captain Bolitho in London was making little impression, partly because none were trained cryptanalysts. GC and CS seems to have taken little interest, so absorbed was it with naval and air matters. (Not until May would the War Office really obtain a grasp of Germany Army orbat – and then due to the

most fortunate capture in Belgium of a complete copy carried into battle by a wayward German staff officer.) Indeed, at the turn of the year,
GC and CS was virtually unaware of what MI 8 was doing and MI 8 was
baffled by the excellent German Army security measures. Furthermore
the Air Section had not separated TA from cryptanalysis and Hut 3, dealing with the synthesis of intelligence, would steadfastly resist the
introduction of a TA element, even though it was studying the trends of
radio traffic.

In fact it was the Central Interception Station at Cheadle which was
making most headway against the Luftwaffe, its DF network giving such
positive tactical warning of one raid on a convoy that seven out of twelve
enemy aircraft were shot down. Yet even Cheadle at this time was mainly
garnering only peripheral intelligence when detecting such minor organisations as the enemy Observer Corps and the under-privileged Fleet Air
Arm. On the other hand, an important enciphered communication system
called Point-to-Point Networks was discounted by RAF Y and left to Army
Y field stations in France to monitor.

An overriding dread of those in the know about BP and what went on
there – above all the possession of means to read Enigma transmissions
– demanded stringent security measures to preserve the secrecy of the
organisation now called Ultra. Inevitably this affected the Y Service which
was staffed by many hundreds of disparate people, not all of whom were
guaranteed secure. As one of many safeguards it was therefore laid down
by C (Major-General Stewart Menzies) and Denniston that Y's connection with BP must be concealed.

A ban was imposed on contacts between GC and CS and the Air Ministry except through SIS. Among those afflicted by hindrances with simple
internal communications was Josh Cooper (who, of course, was working for RAF Y): he was actually forbidden to appear to be connected with
the material of his own department! Similarly, Hut 3 was ordered not to
include in its reports anything connected with what already had been
reported by Air Section. Anomalies abounded in this jungle that was necessarily fertilised by security. But somehow and suddenly in the first week
of April these things became more bearably important.

DESPITE THE WEHRMACHT'S excellent radio discipline, Y Service's TA had detected sufficient traffic to indicate that something unusual was happening to shipping in the Baltic. This was noticed by Harry Hinsley, a twenty-year-old civilian working at BP who already was the leading expert on German Navy radio organisation. Yet he was only rarely consulted by the OIC (Operational Intelligence Centre) at the Admiralty. His hand-cranked telephoned report to the OIC was dismissed out of hand by the officers responsible – a classic example of the 'Incredulity Factor'. But for this rebuff, it is possible that the Germans might not have achieved the total surprise they managed in their invasions of Denmark and Norway on 9 April.

This German success with the only major amphibious operation ever attempted by her was a masterpiece of planning. The naval and air forces tasked to seize Oslo, Kristiansand, Stavanger, Bergen, Trondheim and Narvik did so in a matter of a few hours with scarcely any resistance. What few contacts and losses occurred at sea came by chance. Indeed, not only did the Germans maintain maximum radio silence until first contact with the Norwegian and British elements, they also benefited from B Dienst's excellent radio intercept and its ability to read some 80 per cent of the Royal Navy's ciphers.

Nevertheless, in this radio war the Germans, unbeknown to themselves, no longer had things absolutely their own way. Within twenty-four hours of the operation's start British Y's searchers had detected a new Enigma code, called Yellow. Hut 6 and the Bombe went to work and on the 15th broke it, to discover that this was a joint Army/Luftwaffe command channel with naval connections. As the messages were decoded, teleprinters in Hut 3 transmitted the urgent ones to London where they were delivered by hand to the ministries. Meanwhile less urgent material was typed and delivered in sequence by motor van. Yellow continued to yield invaluable information until 14 May - by which time Norway was virtually lost, Holland had fallen to the main German offensive and the Allied armies in France and Belgium were in appalling difficulties.

At BP, amid the excitement and tension of a twenty-four-hour day, seven-day week routine, there slowly grew a sense of achievement. But this was a very misleading, academic chimera even to the tiny minority who were permitted full knowledge of what Ultra amounted to and was doing. To begin with, of course, the Allies, who were transfixed by the correct belief that the Germans were on the verge of invading Holland, Belgium and France, had not expected an invasion of Norway which, if suggested, probably would have been rejected by the Incredulity Factor. Thrown off balance into a chaotic situation, the Allied generals in Norway found, that after landing near Trondheim and at Narvik, they were in no position to make good use of intelligence, even if it had reached them – which it did not.

Useful lessons were learned, however, as some reputations were lost – and others made. Few of the latter were more important than those generated by the sinking of the aircraft carrier HMS *Glorious* on 8 June during the evacuation from Narvik. Once more it was Harry Hinsley who interpreted TA correctly and gave early warning of threatening movements in the Baltic by unidentified vessels. On 7 June these were reported as entering the North Sea. But again the OIC, notoriously sceptical about TA and guilty of inadequate liaison with the Admiralty operational staff, chose to take no notice. It did not even issue a warning to the fleet or call for air reconnaissance – despite the fact that it was known that the evacuation from Narvik was in progress. The German ships were the battle-cruisers *Scharnhorst* and *Gneisenau*. *Glorious* and two destroyers were sunk with heavy loss of life.

As a result there was a shake-up of staff duties in the Admiralty and the creation of high respect for Hinsley. In future when the Incredulity Factor appeared in high naval circles, all doubts would be cast aside if it was learnt that Hinsley was the intelligence officer responsible.

TOTAL TACTICAL SURPRISE was also achieved by the Germans when they opened their great offensive aimed at Holland, Belgium and France on 10 May. For two weeks the British Cabinet was kept largely in ignorance of what was going on, so sparse was intelligence on offer. The French (whose extensive and efficient static intercept units had been mostly outflanked) also were largely out of touch with the fast-moving, mechanised corps that were scything westwards from the Ardennes to Abbeville on the Channel coast. Not until 26 May, when GC and CS broke the Luftwaffe Red Enigma code, did a fairly coherent picture begin to emerge. But even this was clouded, partly because Hut 6 was overloaded by a thousand messages a day and was compelled to concentrate only on Red; partly because of ignorance of the enemy orders of battle; and partly due to lack of a proper card index system – which was only founded then when two trained indexers were discovered working on other matters in Hut 3.

There was a dearth of large-scale maps, with Baedekers in demand. Also there was a dire shortage of personnel who were working all hours. The realisation that abject defeat loomed when a Luftwaffe signal indicated that the armoured spearheads, which had reached the Channel on 20 May, were turning north towards Dunkirk. On the 23rd the War Office was forced to conclude that the French forces which had entered Belgium along with BEF on the 10th were doomed to imminent envelopment and surrender.

It was RAF Y, not that of the Army, which made the most useful SIGINT contribution to Intelligence acquisition during the Battle of France.

When the BEF (British Expeditionary Force) deployed to France in September 1939 an RAF field unit belonging to the AASF (Air Advanced Striking Force) went with it and set up a DF base line between Amiens and Bar-sur-Seine. It was regarded as an out-station of Cheadle. Another party was sent to an island known as IDEM off Cannes to intercept Italian radio. The IDEM party had many problems but, despite abysmal administration and poor equipment, managed to make useful interceptions, though without making contact with GC and CS, via very unreliable land lines. Furthermore Squadron Leader Hamilton found it difficult to obtain clear guidance as to what were the intelligence priorities.

On 9 April a field station of the northern party heard, in plain language to the Luftwaffe, orders to attack three towns near Oslo. A month later, when the balloon went up in France, the field units were bombarded with requests for assistance, but failed to provide any bearings of value to the fighters of AASF. On 31 May, when evacuation from Dunkirk was in progress and RAF fighters based in England were doing their best to fend off the Luftwaffe, the unit managed to send weather reports, intercepted enemy reconnaissance reports and also supplied the locations of friendly troops, the last in the hope that they might be given fighter protection – a pious hope in the circumstances. Finally they were evacuated from St Nazaire on 15 June having produced little intelligence of real value.

Likewise the Army Y unit caught up in the retreat to Dunkirk achieved nothing of value and had to be evacuated via Dunkirk to face in Britain an unimaginably disastrous situation which demolished practically every one of the Y Committee's concepts. Already in April a long-brewing storm of discontent concerning resources and priorities had erupted about the state of Y service to GC and CS. The main Y Committee, chaired by Air Marshal Sir Philip Joubert de la Ferté, did not meet. In June the situation was far worse but still nothing seemed to have been done to rectify the dire shortage of receivers and operators – this at a time when invasion was anticipated daily and Chatham actually was taking 85 per cent of Enigma traffic after its number of sets had been reduced!

There were, however, a few bright spots in the performance of Y Service during the grim Dunkirk period. UK-based RAF HDUs (Home Defence Units) not only intercepted and understood Luftwaffe traffic sufficiently to help the Royal Navy control shipping off the beaches, they also identified and effectively jammed dive-bomber communications; and inter-service collaboration still functioned to the benefit of all. In July civilian sets at last were requisitioned, and the Navy and RAF made forty new operators available to reinforce the Navy Y station at Chicksands and the Army one at Chatham. But accommodation was limited and rugged, and many high-quality RAF recruits objected to impressment because they wanted to fly. One young man was slandered by his one-time headmaster for letting the old school down by avoiding active service.

There were of course numerous competing, top priority requirements, very few of which could be fulfilled satisfactorily, and also numerous people in the Y Service who were overworked in action. Take for example a German linguist called Aileen (known as Mike) Morris of the WAAF. In

June she was posted to an RT intercept station at Fairlight near Hastings. Here she would sit during eight-hour shifts, headsets clamped to ears in front of two civilian-type Hallicrafter receivers, twiddling knobs in the search for transmissions on the VHF 40 MHz band from German aircraft. Inside the signals vehicle was the CRT of an oscilloscope to assist with DF and outside the antennae. To hand was the log-book to record for each message time of receipt, radio frequency and call sign plus, on every other line, the original text in German with the translation written on the line below. Searching for signals demanded patience. Staying tuned-in to combat 'drift' was as essentially necessary as was the ability to hear and record accurately faint or corrupted morse at 20 wpm (25 wpm if in Japanese). For an intelligent person it was quite easy to learn, though tiring. For Mike Morris it was extremely difficult because she was never better than 18 wpm – but that soon was of no concern because she was booked for promotion as one of the future stars of RAF Y.

As the Germans drew closer to the Channel in May, the searchers had at last begun to hear VHF RT conversations from marauding fighters and bombers. Morris's colleagues in England (who provided far better material for Intelligence than Y in France) soon became adept at understanding the raw material for TA – breaking down code-words used by the Luftwaffe for air-to-air and air-to-ground communication and registering their use of gridded maps to locate friendly and hostile forces. All of this would find its way to Cheadle for study and, as required, forwarding to AI and GC and CS for filing in the card-index systems as the first steps in assembling an order of battle that included the identity and, sometimes, the location of airfields used by formations and units. Morris arrived at the sharp end when amateurism still prevailed. But the foundations had been laid for the really hard times in the Battle of Britain, which was imminent.

When Morris was learning the ropes, there had arisen in London another sort of vital and unprecedented radio intercept, such as Swanborough had predicted in his paper for Blandy. Early in June, Blandy was alerted to an intriguing Luftwaffe signal referring to Knickebein and Kleve. He called in twenty-eight-year-old Dr R. V. Jones, an Air Ministry scientist since 1936, who was expert in infra-red and electronics and who already was investigating German bombing apparatus associated with pulse radio technology. Jones, who had access to Hut 3 at BP, told Blandy that he thought this signal might refer to a device utilising intersecting beams. He prompted further successful interrogations of Heinkel III bomber crew who had recently crashed in England. That not only revealed that there was such a device but also how it was concealed in a so-called blind landing device. Two days later this was confirmed by another prisoner.

The upshot was a series of meetings at the highest Air Ministry and Y level which convinced the C-in-C Fighter Command, Air Chief Marshal Sir Hugh Dowding, that such a device might exist. His orders were to jam if there was one. Air Commodore 'Daddy' Nutting, the Director of Signals, formed the Wireless Intelligence Development Unit (WIDU) using twin-engine Anson aircraft fitted with Hallicrafter receivers to detect the beams. Winston Churchill was informed. There were more meetings as controversy about feasibility raged among experts, culminating in a famous Cabinet meeting on 21 June which was attended by Dr Jones. At this meeting he held the floor for twenty minutes explaining what nobody else in the room understood. Churchill later wrote that there was incredulity: but he ordered a hunt for the beams in the first-ever attempt at airborne detection. Outside the Cabinet room, however, an attempt was made by a leading sceptic to debunk Jones. He insisted that such a beam could not be detected at 20,000 ft. Promptly the Deputy Director of Signals demanded that the trial should be cancelled forthwith, provoking young Dr Jones to say that the Prime Minister had ordered it – forcing the DDS to give way.

When Nutting asked Jones what they should do if the beam was found, the reply was 'Go out and get tight'. That night an Anson crewed by Flt Lt H. Bufton and Cpl Mackie found two narrow beams with Lorenz characteristics (400 to 500 yards wide) intersecting near Beeston. Nutting skipped round the room with delight. Jones and a friend had a drink or two in St Stephen's Tavern. There would be many more episodes on these lines in the years to come – but that is another story. The point is that what might have been a truly appalling threat to vital targets, such as the Rolls Royce engine factory at Derby, would be largely neutralised by the unique counter-measures that resulted.

So too did the ramifications of security problems raise heart-rending traumas. The complexities of who should speak to whom and about what subjects, as well as when, were stifling of initiative. Later the principle was adopted that, in solving such riddles at the height of an emergency which was centred upon whether or not to divulge a known target, the source of intelligence should never be risked for the sake of a tactical advantage. Nothing like that, however, existed on the eve of the Battle of Britain and the Blitz. Quite often senior officers at GC and CS had to agonise over the need to withhold warning of a known target for fear of disclosing Ultra.

YET EVEN WHEN THESE searing events were stretching the defence of Britain beyond the limit, there were serious distractions in the Mediterranean and Middle East which could not lightly be brushed aside. This already had been the case in connection with the Middle East Intelligence authorities, Whitehall and GC and CS prior to the entry of Italy into the war on the Axis side in June. The bickering which went on from the beginning of 1940 until October was, from the organisational side, pernicious. At root was an unwillingness on the part of the armed services to co-operate sensibly, and how to resolve wrangles over the cryptanalysis of intercepted messages by GC and CS. The internecine 'war' was reprehensible in the light of the quantity and quality of traffic being intercepted by the very experienced Navy, Army and RAF Y units which, as described in Chapters 4 and 5, had been engaged since 1924.

Broadly speaking, London was more interested in intelligence about Russian activities in the region (including India) and any German threat in the Balkans, than it was about Italy in the Mediterranean. But nothing of value from Russia was reaching Cairo and so far only Italy was deeply involved with the Balkans. That summer a vast quantity of excellent, encoded radio intercepts were being acquired by inter-service Y stations, a high proportion of which were being decrypted. In fact, from February onwards these were treated as first priority by Y.

The Middle East authorities (led by the AOC-in-C Air Chief Marshal Sir Arthur Longmore) were anxious to decrypt their 'own' messages. BP insisted that everything should be sent by Typex machine to BP for crypt-analysis and the fully analysed results returned to Cairo in disguised form. A Combined Bureau was mooted, kicked around and dropped. A Y Com-mittee Middle East (called the W Committee) that was locally formed insisted that such material as was locally acquired should be cryptanalysed in Cairo. Furthermore it was felt that each service should retain control of its own staff and share results with the others through liaison officers. It was suggested that the Army and RAF should share a building at Heliopo-lis but that the Navy, true to tradition, should remain in Alexandria. Astonishingly, the Y Committee in London (no doubt fixated by the Battle of Britain being waged overhead) raised no immediate objections. But GC and CS did.

It was pointed out by Commander Travis that what few delays there were to transmission of material could be solved by providing a second Typex machine. That there already were sufficient cryptographers in Cairo to carry out immediate decoding of local messages. That half the material from the Mediterranean area, Libya, the Dodecanese, Metro-politan Italy, Albania (recently occupied by Italy) and Sardinia was intercepted in England. And that the present method was very much the best way to meet Middle East wishes.

Travis concluded that, while GC and CS had sent Cairo everything to hand, Cairo had not reciprocated by sending BP a number of local intercepts, captured documents, cipher keys and items of WT interest which GC and CS did not have.

This did the trick. On 29 September the Directors of Intelligence in London decided that a Combined Bureau Middle East (CBME) under Army administration was required. Tabulating machinery was on the way. Major Jacob was appointed a member of the Middle East Y (ex W) Com-mittee and head of the CBME. For high security communications the number of Typex groups available per day was increased from 7,000 to

12,000. Nigel de Grey wryly commented that, during the six months of 'warfare' needed to reach the new arrangement, a smooth-running machine was steadily producing results and managing to deal with each problem as it arose without undue delay.

It was not a moment too soon. For although the Italians were having a very rough time of it at sea, on the Egyptian frontier, in East Africa and in a misconceived invasion of Greece, there soon would be indications through SIGINT that a strong German presence might be expected in the Mediterranean, North Africa and the Balkans.

CHAPTER SEVEN

ALONE AND UNDER SIEGE

At the end of June 1940 Britain stood alone and, to an alarming extent, weakly armed against the full and exuberant might of Germany. Already the Luftwaffe had executed exploratory night sorties over the country and, due to careless tactics, had suffered quite heavy losses. These, to some measure, reflected significant ignorance on its part about the air defences and, above all, intelligence about radar and the strength, command and sophisticated control system of RAF Fighter Command.

In May 1939 the Director of Luftwaffe Signals, General Wolfgang Martini, had personally flown over England in the airship *Graf Zeppelin* in the hope of detecting radar pulses. He was disappointed, because radar silence was in force for the occasion and the listening RAF Y was tempted to tell him that his signals reporting position were inaccurate! Furthermore the RAF had managed to conceal the flexible system of radio control of fighter formations through sector stations in each Fighter Group. Like their opposite numbers across the Channel, the searchers of the German Horstdienst were busily engaged in trying to fill large gaps in their knowledge.

The balance of air forces at the beginning of July was very much in the German favour both in numbers, doctrine and experience, although, by that time, RAF Y had acquired sufficient information through TA and DF to construct an order of battle which indicated that the disparity was not as overwhelming as recently had been calculated by AI (Air Intelligence).

Assistant Section Officer Mike Morris (now commissioned on 23 July) was busy directing the searchers of an HDU at Dover. She therefore worked in a small building and had under command two or three RT receivers. Each set needed five people (RAF or WAAF) to work a three-shift day, seven-day week. At Dover she was a close participant in the battle as the Germans raised the tempo of operations over what became known as Hellfire Corner. To the sound of artillery (from both sides) and the thunder and whine of aerial combat and bombing, she and her German-speaking girls would listen to enemy pilots chatting as they fought for their lives overhead, sharing with them the humour of a reconnaissance pilot, call sign Amsel Eins, speaking: 'I know you, English listening station, can you hear me? Would you like a bomb on you? Listen – whee – boomp!'; and briefly mourning when this ebullient character was shot down in flames as a result of their reporting his activities. She would listen to German fighter pilots manoeuvring to drop on an unsuspecting fighter flight, hearing one of her girls crying helplessly, ' Oh God ... oh God ... please look up!'; yet cheering when they heard somebody reporting a comrade as shot down.

The part played by that HDU (linked by telephones to RAF Kingsdown on Wrotham hill) was not restricted to monitoring enemy aircraft. It also assisted the Royal Navy by reporting enemy E-boats coming out to attack convoys. It was the Luftwaffe, nevertheless, on which Mike Morris's searchers concentrated. They noticed the rigidity of command and methods of its fighter pilots and sensed how, as the Battle of Britain progressed through August into September, their chatter would indicate waning self-confidence and morale. Bomber pilots, whose morale was no stronger, were far less talkative because they could speak to their crew and flew to a prearranged plan. They tended to give most information when requesting a homing course to base. Most important were the occasions when HDUs, in plain language, heard formations assembling for a raid. This gave valuable strategic and, ever more frequently, tactical warning in advance of radar detection reports. Moreover, it helped fighter controllers to be more economical in the scrambling of fighters during the first phase of the battle when machines and, above all, pilots were seriously in short supply. To this day, radar, unjustifiably, still gets a lion's share of the credit for winning the battle; but radar was more than simply complemented by the work of the Y Service which undoubtedly provided the highest proportion of useful intelligence about imminent events.

Intercepted Enigma messages played little part in giving early warning of daylight attacks. Those emanating from the Luftwaffe High Command could not be relied upon because sometimes they were modified later at a lower level. In any case these ceased to be heard when, towards the end of the battle, land line was laid to HQs of the air fleets involved. At GC and CS, Squadron Leader Robert Humphreys, was positioned in Hut 3 tasked to keep touch by telephone with Cheadle and relay immediate operational and technical intelligence. This was an appointment of crucial importance, for Humphreys was a very forceful character who had served with Intelligence at HQ RAF in France and who had come to appreciate the value of the Hut 3 material he had received. Moreover, he was a good German linguist who realised how vital was the necessity for far wider, secure dissemination and understanding of Hut 3 material at all levels.

Initially, therefore, Humphreys set about forging stronger links between Hut 3 and the Air Ministry's Intelligence Branch – to the benefit of both organisations' understanding of each other's point of view. Rapidly he began to assume a central role in the running and expansion of AI and Hut 3, where his qualifications and experience as a staff officer enabled him to dominate many a contentious empire-building debate. Soon, under his tutelage, the four bright young RAF officers (without wings) whom he recruited began, with mixed blessings for GC and CS, to make far greater use of the vast amount of acquired material awaiting exploitation.

Driven by sheer necessity, there evolved a far stricter organisation of intelligence at GC and CS in the recording of enemy call signs, frequencies and identities. The last emerged more frequently when the experienced computors at Cheadle realised that they could profitably exploit recognisable evidence of call sign changes and procedure variations – a technique first known as 'foot printing' and later as Radio Finger Printing (RFP). This method was formalised in December 1940 when Cheadle computors spent some time working with Hut 3 people – to the mutual benefit in understanding of all concerned.

A major improvement called systematic log reading was introduced by Army Y officers who had served in France. This was a very effective sharing of resources and information which grew up not only between service people but also with the GPO and Scotland Yard (Denmark Hill), who were monitoring diplomatic traffic. On the other hand there were lapses, such as the occasion when the War Office, without letting GC and CS know, changed the tasks of six sets at the key Chatham control unit. Self-indulgent, ill-advised inter-service wrangles were never entirely discarded.

Naturally, pre-invasion anxieties affected performance as intercepted Enigma messages provided accumulating evidence of German preparations for Operation Sealion. These, nearly all contributed by the Luftwaffe, began to appear fragmentarily in July. It was not until early September, however, that the arrival of large numbers of ships and barges at the Channel ports were detected – and then mainly by PRU (Photographic Reconnaissance Unit) missions rather than SIGINT. Before that, however, Navy Y searchers of U-boat transmissions (whose naval Enigma had yet to be decrypted) had twigged through DF that they had been withdrawn from patrol – as they had been prior to the invasion of Norway. Soon after that, from U-boat claims of sinking ships in the western and eastern approaches to the Channel, it became clear that they were being concentrated in support of Sealion – although SIGINT did not record that code word for invasion until 21 September. By that date Hitler had virtually abandoned the operation and relegated it to a diversionary role in his revised grand strategic plan that was based on the intention to invade Russia in 1941.

So far Admiral Dönitz's few U-boats had done relatively little to impose an effective blockade on the British Isles. A fairly successful experiment in October 1939 with radio-controlled Pack Tactics (which had been developed pre-war by Dönitz) had not been repeated. Allied shipping losses, though heavy, were not yet crippling and had mainly been inflicted on ships sailing out of convoy. U-boat losses had hardly been replaced: rarely were there more than ten boats patrolling singly at a time. Co-operation with the Italians, who wanted their submarines to operate in the Atlantic, was never satisfactory, Dönitz seeing them mainly as a reinforcement of his reconnaissance arm. Intercepts of convoys were becoming more difficult, very largely due to insufficient support from the Luftwaffe. On the credit side, however, stood the possession after the fall of France of the Biscay ports, notably Brest, Lorient, St Nazaire and Bordeaux, and the declaration in August of unrestricted submarine warfare.

The resumption of Pack Tactics and the adoption of night attacks on the surface against convoys began tentatively in October. It achieved a significant rise in sinkings to 350,000 tons per month, but also instituted a dangerously mounting increase in the volume of radio messages from shore to boat and boat to shore. For this helped Navy DF to provide a better guide to the locations of U-boats, although nothing about their or Dönitz's intentions. Occasionally, by courtesy of good fortune in the capture of Enigma wheels and documents containing key settings, GC and CS could give more precise intelligence. But not until February 1941 did the real breakthroughs begin when Dr McVittie and his team broke the German naval meteorological cipher. This triumph was boosted when, in May, it was discovered that U-boats employed that same cipher for their weather reporting, messages which divulged boat's daily positions in the Atlantic. That was not all. Resistant as the naval operational Enigma remained until late spring 1941, the cracking by hand of certain naval codes, including that used by the dockyards, helped BP's cryptanalysts to master the operational Enigma as well. Thus almost every scrap of intelligence wrenched by Y from the copious U-boat tactical as well as strategic traffic became invaluable - for the time being.

As the Germans began to play the pack card, Y Service helped to contribute to a partial neutralisation role when KG 40 of the Luftwaffe joined in. This unit of Focke Wulf 200, four-engine bombers trained specially for the anti-shipping role, had first been identified in February. In August they were spotted making weather flights between Stavanger and Bordeaux, supplemented with sporadic attacks on ships sailing alone. RAF Y units kept Cheadle well informed of its expansion to twenty-nine machines and its location at Bordeaux in October. From several sources AI constructed a clear picture of its support for U-boats by reconnaissance and its successful attacks on shipping. By mid-November a detailed dossier on KG 40 had been assembled, resulting in an extremely damaging raid by Bomber Command on its base on 22 November.

Thereafter, with its strength reduced to fifteen aircraft, KG 40 carried on sinking a few ships and working ever more closely with the U-boats, although feebly managing only one mission per day. Yet, notwithstanding

Hermann Göring's antipathy to the use of 'his' Luftwaffe in this role, it was reinforced in February 1941 by KG 27's He 111s, duly identified by Cheadle as based on Brest. Its activities at first inflicted much harm until Y provided sufficient information about its forthcoming raids as to make their interception by the RAF an extremely effective deterrent.

In the meantime, as the U-boats temporarily enjoyed what their crews called 'a happy time' and German surface warships joined strongly in the Battle of the Atlantic (see below), there were tumultuous fluctuations in the skies above Britain, where the Luftwaffe, defeated in daytime, concentrated on the nightly bombing of cities – what the British misnamed as the 'Blitz'. Against these raids the Air Ministry, Dr Jones and the Y Service wracked their brains and talents to win the ceaseless radio war in their endeavours to outwit the German scientists and technologists and thereby prevent accurate German bombing. Time had to be bought until the multi-cannon Beaufighter night fighter, equipped with airborne radar and guided to its prey by ground controllers, became operationally effective in the shooting down of the enemy in telling numbers. And, indeed, to begin with the German bombers were very inaccurate, to some extent due to the jamming of Knickebein.

At the same time, HDUs, which had first intercepted strange, unintelligible Luftwaffe air-to-air communications in the summer, were joined by the BBC's Tatfield monitoring station in making wild guesses as to what they were. In due course it transpired that they were air-to-ground links for the very recently founded German night-fighting organisation under General Josef Kammhuber. In like manner, it was noticed by Hut 3, in consultation with Cheadle, that German intercept stations at Cherbourg and Cap Gris Nez were concentrating on RAF fighter nets; and also that there was a Luftwaffe experimental unit which was engaged in trials of radar and other night-fighting devices. These were the prologues to the future, prolonged air battle of Germany.

Then there was the 'meacon versus beacon' contest. Before the war it was known that the Luftwaffe favoured radio, ground beacons as navigational aids and, by March 1940, forty-six of them, with evidence of increasing numbers, had been located. Dr Jones' No. 80 Wing RAF's intercepting Ansons and Cheadle were tasked to defeat this system. This they did in July by 'meaconing' – that is, re-radiating the beacon signal to give false bearings to the user aircraft. The method caused deep concern among German aircrew who HDUs heard blaming the system. Worse still from the crews' point of view, many got so badly lost that they crashed or landed in Britain. This contest would proceed, phase by phase, for years to come as the Germans introduced counter-measures to counter-measures, thus breeding an increasing and sometimes confusing complexity for either side.

It was X-Gerät transmitters which caused most trouble to Dr Jones, GC and CS, Y Service and the city of Coventry. These were brought to Jones's notice on 4 September by BP whose cryptographers had broken a new line in Luftwaffe Enigma transmissions. Within three weeks it was discovered that it was a combination of beams: a director beam aimed at the target from Cap de la Hague and three intersecting signals sent from Cap Gris Nez. The three crossing signals told the bombers of the specially trained KG 100 their distance from the target and when to drop their bombs. In fact the system had been tried against Birmingham on 23 August, followed by other experiments against various targets as night bombing took over from the daylight offensive.

This led up to Operation Moonlight Sonata, the concentrated attack by 509 bombers on Coventry. SIGINT gave warning on 11 November of an unusual operation in full moonlight to be led by KG 100 and focused either on Wolverhampton, Birmingham or Coventry, as confirmed in a KG 100 Enigma message of the 12th. Yet AI and GC and CS, influenced by the previous misleading, experimental X-Gerät signals, overlooked this and believed the target would be London. On 14 November, Y intercepted a signal indicating that this was the day. At 1500 hrs Ansons of No. 80 Wing reported that the beams intersected over Coventry. Jammers were switched on but were ineffective because they were wrongly set. Under the pressure of war errors, inevitably, are all too common, but this one was fundamental, ensuring as it did that the pathfinder KG 100 simply could not be deflected from hitting the target with outstanding precision.

Of the 449 bombers which devastated Coventry in bright moonlight, only one did not reach home. Even if there had been time to reinforce the city's defence the outcome would not have been much different. For in those days, even in moonlight, the chances of fighters without airborne radar finding and shooting down bombers were poor in the extreme. This was made all too plain until, only towards the end of the Blitz on 10 May 1941, did the much improved air defences begin to take sufficient toll of the bombers to make their disenchanted and weary crews only too pleased to be called eastwards to grapple with the less efficient Russians.

Weariness was common to both sides during the Blitz. Mike Morris does not exaggerate when she describes the intensity of her work at Kingsdown. The checking of translations and codes of the operational traffic from HDUs, the keeping up-to-date of enemy signals, the reading of logs, the reports to write and the scanning of reports from other Y sources all piled on the demanding pressure. Once, completely exhausted while discussing a night's activities with a colleague, she found it impossible to stand up in order to walk to her nearby billet, and recalled how he picked her up and carried her to a car.

The end of the Blitz granted Britain a brief relaxation of the siege at about the time one of the peaks in the Battle of the Atlantic was reached and passed; and as the epicentre of operations shifted to the Mediterranean, North Africa, the Balkans and Russia.

NAVY AND RAF Y Services were forever vigilant in the search for evidence of commerce raiding by German surface vessels. As was usual, Luftwaffe Enigma was most helpful, although in the circumstances that was not saying very much. For the German Navy's signals discipline was generally excellent, with radio silence adhered to until contact with an enemy occurred. When the pocket battleship *Admiral Scheer* broke out in October 1940 the first indication of her presence at sea arrived when she homed on to a convoy to sink the armed merchant cruiser *Jervis Bay*, although she sank only five out of thirty-seven ships. This was the overture to a five-months' voyage in the South Atlantic and Indian Ocean before she returned to Germany with the score of a mere sixteen ships to her credit.

Likewise the cruiser *Admiral Hipper*, which broke out on 7 December 1940, remained undetected until running into a strongly escorted troop convoy on Christmas Day and being forced by minor damage to make for safety in Norway. However, she did rather better in February when she surprised an unescorted convoy (and GC and CS and the Admiralty) on the 12th off Freetown, sank seven out of nineteen ships and then retired to Brest to refuel.

Y did better in January 1940 when TA discovered that the battle-cruisers *Scharnhorst* and *Gneisenau* were preparing to break out. This time the Admiralty accepted uncorroborated TA and sent the Home Fleet to sea, resulting in a contact by a searching cruiser south of Iceland that persuaded the Germans to withdraw and refuel in the Arctic Sea. On 8 February they reappeared but, upon intercepting a battleship-escorted convoy, again retired. Later they sank six merchant ships before heading for Sierra Leone where they picked off sixteen ships belonging to a dispersing convoy. They then made for a delusive safety in Brest, having sunk 115,000 tons of shipping and badly put the wind up the Admiralty. For by 21 May Y and other sources had uncovered sufficient intelligence to suggest that the brand new cruiser *Prinz Eugen* and the great battleship *Bismarck* were poised to enter the Atlantic via Norway, possibly to join forces with the two battle-cruisers at Brest. The oft-told saga of the sinking of the *Bismarck* will only be detailed here in as much as is necessary to relate Y's vital, yet unsung, contribution. The two ships, whose intentions had been anticipated from other sources, sailed from Bergen on the 21st and were not seen or heard of again until the evening of the 23rd in the Denmark Straits, where they were found and shadowed by cruisers. Following that contact, during the fight with HMS *Hood* (until she was sunk) and HMS *Prince of Wales*, and until managing to shake off her shadowers at night on the 25th, *Bismarck* sent twenty-two radio signals. Those by Enigma stated her intentions but their decryption was delayed until far too late on 28 May. Instead it was DF of those signals, amplified by RFP and by TINA (which analysed the touch of morse operators) which helped Y and the OIC to surmise her course with commendable perspicacity. But the really decisive intercepts by Y were those derived from analysis of the three messages which, presumably inadvertently in breach of radio silence, were sent after the break from contact. These positively revealed Brest as *Bismarck*'s destination, and were later confirmed by a quickly decrypted Luftwaffe Enigma signal. Thereupon the Admiralty and the two Royal Navy squadrons from Britain and Gibraltar were able to concur on where to find *Bismarck*. It also narrowed the areas of search for flying boats. Then at last, at 1030 hrs on the 26th, visual contact was made by a Catalina flying boat.

Bismarck's fate was sealed at 0840 hrs on the 27th, bringing to an end Atlantic commerce raiding by big German warships for the rest of the war.

CHAPTER EIGHT

MEDITERRANEAN IMBROGLIO

As the invasion threat to Britain temporarily receded, the opportunity for both sides to reinforce the strategically vital Mediterranean, Balkans, North and East Africa could not be resisted. In this vast area the widespread Italian empire was both a threat to and a tempting target for the British Empire which enjoyed inner strategic lines splitting the Italian empire in twain. Moreover Italy, by its failure in September to overrun Egypt, its brash invasion of Greece on 28 October 1940 and the sinking of capital ships at Taranto by British torpedo aircraft, was so overstretched as to plead for German help.

This the British were made aware of in November from an ample harvest of long-ago decrypted diplomatic and military codes, plus many other sources. The many years of interception by Y Service from Heliopolis, Sarafand, Aden and Malta since the early 1930s had not been wasted. The delayed agreement to set up the CBME had occurred, most fortunately, at precisely the right moment to make good use of profuse intelligence material. As the Italians struggled to regain the initiative in Greece and then, unavailingly, defeat the Greek counter-invasion of Albania, the British held firm and began to receive from the United Kingdom, India, South Africa, Australia and New Zealand, vital army and air reinforcements that included Army Special Wireless Units (SWU) and RAF field intercept units.

Never would British Y be without the means to read most of the flood of useful enemy transmissions which poured in from Greece, East Africa and the Western Desert as the Italians began to withdraw in defeat after defeat: especially from the desert after the Italian Tenth Army was routed during December into February under the hammer of General Richard O'Connor's Western Desert Force. True the British use of it was sometimes faulty. Also it has to be said that the British and Greeks were helped mightily by lax Italian security, which leaked like a sieve, and by the timely arrival of an Intelligence School in Egypt on 1 December 1940, sent by MI 8.

The attachment of an Army intercept station to HQ Western Desert Force in August had given valuable warning with tactical as well as strategic implications to O'Connor when the Italians advanced to Sidi Barrani in September. Reinforced in September by the specialist Italian sections of No. 2 WT Company, it was not only poised to provide good SIGINT when O'Connor struck on 8 December (Operation Compass), but also to build the foundations of radio intercept in mobile operations such as had not existed in France. It was essential, too, to forge easier working links via CBME to GC and CS at a time when signs of German involvement in the Mediterranean and Balkans were becoming very noticeable.

Operation Compass, which overran the forward Italian positions in Egypt within twenty-four hours, was planned largely on SIGINT. Apart from a few minor omissions and faults, it showed in detail where the main enemy forces were deployed and in what strength. This service by Y continued almost unabated due to the outstanding efforts of the small No. 3 Mobile Section of No. 2 WT Coy. It kept O'Connor fully supplied with hundreds of decrypted enemy tactical messages and strength reports as he drove across Cyrenaica. He was fully aware of the Italian withdrawal from Tobruk to Benghazi at the end of January, enabling him confidently to launch relatively small mobile forces across the desert to cut off and annihilate the remnants of Tenth Army at Beda Fomm on 5 February.

The pattern of events in Italian East Africa to some extent was a replica of that in Cyrenaica. Initial Italian offensives into the Sudan and Kenya were checked and British Somaliland evacuated by the tiny British garrison. Neither PR, secret agents nor SIGINT had contributed much intelligence about this phase of operations.

In the New Year, however, that situation changed radically when SIGINT came into its own, virtually filling the intelligence vacuum in East Africa. Indeed, reinforced Y units supplied CBME with such a large volume of material that it became overloaded in the process of decrypting the Italian Army's new high-grade code and numerous low-grade ones. From that moment there was very little that was not known about Italian retrograde intentions, declining strengths and impoverished logistics from the highest level downward. In consequence it was safe to bring forward in time the counter-offensives which, on all fronts in the coming months, would trigger the burgeoning rout of a demoralised enemy that led to the abject capitulation of all Italian forces in East Africa on 18 May.

Thrilling and satisfying as were the debacles in North and East Africa, it was fully recognised in Cairo and in London that the real threat building in the Mediterranean was German. Since October GC and CS and Y had been monitoring the infiltration of German air power and their vanguard of Y units into Romania, Bulgaria and Sicily. The presence of General Wolfram von Richthofen's VIII Air Corps, with its dive bombers, in the Balkans and of General Hans Geisler's X Air Corps in Sicily was worrying; especially when, on 7 January, the latter began a series of deadly attacks on Malta, on warships and convoys which, due to lack of co-ordination between the Admiralty and Air Ministry, caught the British by surprise.

As usual the Luftwaffe supplied the bulk of SIGINT, the increasing volume of which came to hand (despite the relative lull in German operations during the winter of 1940–1) due to the significant growth of intercept receivers and decryption facilities and through cryptanalysts' skills. Attacks upon lesser keys to the operational priority Red and Brown Enigma keys were now feasible, permissible, quicker and highly profitable. Once again there was trivial, factional friction between Cairo and London. This time the telegrams concerned Typex machines in Egypt, which were in short supply, mainly carried RAF traffic but mostly were owned by the Army. To make matters worse, each Ministry in London was independently distributing identical material in three different codes: a great waste of effort and time on air that also threatened serious risks for breaches of security.

Typically there brooded a lack of goodwill between the services which the Y Committee was slow to tackle. Not until 4 March did GC and CS resolve the matter by reaching agreement that the passage of Y material should be from Hut 6 to Hut 3 and thence to the ministries, with simultaneous transmission by Typex to the head of CBME in Cairo for local distribution. Meanwhile CBME would handle and distribute Italian high-grade air material. Paradoxically, this squabble gave impetus to improvements to the security of Typex machines and the setting up of SSUs (Special Signals Units) to carry and keep secure Enigma intelligence traffic between the UK and other countries. It was pure coincidence, no doubt, that on 14 February the Y Committee had been renamed the Y Board. The fact remained that chronic squabbles would persist as the strategic and operational situation was dramatically transformed, although in due course the arrival of an SSU in Egypt in June would relieve the CBME of the laborious deciphering task.

Due to tight security in Italy, which made spying by the SIS extremely difficult and PR from Malta very hazardous, SIGINT was the principal source of impressively accurate intelligence about the increasingly rapid spread of German air and land forces into Italian territory on both sides of the Mediterranean. The arrival in Tripoli of General Erwin Rommel's Africa Corps at the end of February should have been no surprise since the movement of convoys and transport aircraft to Tripoli had been noticed on 9 February and confirmed as German by the 15th. But, although GHQ in Cairo recognised their import on the 17th, the London ministries resolutely declined to do so until the end of the month – even though British armoured cars had already encountered Germans at El Agheila on the 22nd.

In the Cabinet, at GHQ in Cairo and, moreover, in Berlin, the Incredulity Factor intruded. Nobody could envisage a virtually unknown Rommel attacking with his advance guard before his main body had arrived and his logistic base was established. Furthermore, it was known via SIGINT that he had been ordered by Berlin to do no more than defend Tripolitania until mid-May. Yet Y intercepts of Luftwaffe Enigma in March repeatedly were indicating that a real threat was building. Still London and Cairo declined to recognise the danger and reinforce their light forces in Cyrenaica. They all underestimated the ambitious dash of a supreme tactician whose concealment measures, including typically strict Army radio security, deprived the British of any worthwhile tactical SIGINT.

No. 3 Mobile Section's searchers were caught on the hop. The Italians had improved their radio security and rarely mentioned the Germans. The Mobile Section was untrained in German procedures and ciphers.

TA was not attempted. The German Army Enigma was unbroken. Rommel, on the other hand, was replete with SIGINT and fully aware through the reading of British Army field codes of his enemy's weak spots and intention to withdraw. It would be June before the British, stunned by disasters in the desert, in Greece and in Crete, would get round to tackling these deficiencies. Therefore their inexperienced, newly arrived armoured division fought blind of the enemy, and the Western Desert Force was ignominiously pitched out of Cyrenaica, except for a determined garrison left behind in Tobruk. It was a rout which Y Service was no more able to cope with than they had in Belgium and France the previous year; and the weakness was exacerbated by the reluctance of CBME and GHQ, for justifiable fear of compromising Enigma, to send forward vital information.

As the above events were in train, the British were sending troop convoys to Greece; the Germans were on the verge of invading Yugoslavia; and the Italian fleet was putting to sea to play a part in the evolving Axis strategy of Balkans and Middle East conquest by raiding those convoys.

Luftwaffe Enigma on 25 March aroused suspicions in the Admiralty that a major naval operation was impending and this was confirmed by extensive Axis air reconnaissance. Unusual and rare use by the Italians of their Enigma told of special interest in British convoy movements between Alexandria and Greece on the 26th. This, along with a sighting by air at 1230 hrs on the 27th of Italian cruisers at sea on course for Crete, was sufficient to prompt Admiral Sir Andrew Cunningham, C-in-C Mediterranean, to cancel convoys and unobtrusively put to sea on the night 27–28th: a wise move justified by a deciphered Italian signal saying the British Fleet was still in port. What followed on the 28th was Matapan, an important (though not decisive) battle which witnessed the torpedoing of an Italian battleship and the sinking of three cruisers and two destroyers – an encounter which would not have occurred without preliminary British SIGINT. This might have had a different outcome if Axis radio silence had not prevented a further contribution from radio intercepts during the course of the battle, or if Admiral Iachino had not allowed himself to be misled by faulty reports exacerbated by his rejection of a DF report warning of the close proximity position of three British battleships and an aircraft carrier.

British and Australian Army Y field units were among the first of the Allied corps under General Henry Maitland Wilson to arrive in Greece at the beginning of March. By the 11th they were searching successfully for both German and Italian transmissions. They monitored the *coup d'état* against the pro-German government in Belgrade on the 27th and the German advance into Yugoslavia after it began on 6 April. But, in fact, the most prolific, invaluable strategic intelligence received by Wilson came from GC and CS, based on decrypts of Luftwaffe Enigma. Much of this information, along with that from the field units, was wasted because its passage to the right HQs was confused and often either delayed or mislaid. Yet the strategic SIGINT helped Wilson immensely as the Greek Army collapsed before his own troops were seriously involved in combat. Using it shrewdly, he was able to time his retreat to the sea admirably. But the Y field units were caught up in the withdrawal and on the 23rd forced to abandon their equipment, join the rout and escape to Crete.

As with events in Greece, the Allied commander in Crete, General Bernard Freyberg, received far more intelligence from GC and CS than from the meagre field units on the island. Few German operations can have been more anticipated than Operation Mercury, the exclusively Luftwaffe, airborne and amphibious invasion of Crete. Long before this opportunist attack was approved by Hitler on 25 April, SIGINT was finding proof of a forthcoming, special airborne operation. Although its objective remained in some doubt on the British part, that was banished by a flood of Enigma decrypts which, after the 26th, named the island; though without yet specifying the tactical objectives. These followed in great detail after 6 May and, quite logically, named the places already selected by General Freyberg as the best places to defend. Indeed, the only major discrepancies in thinking between the two contestants were the estimated sizes of the forces committed. The British, based on SIGINT and TA, calculated between 25,000 and 30,000 airborne troops, when in fact there would be only 16,000 plus 7,000 in the seaborne contingent. The Germans guessed wildly at a garrison strength of between 8,000 and

12,000 when, in fact, there were 27,000 British and 14,000 Greeks. But whereas the Germans were heavily supported by air power and extremely well trained and armed, their opponents lacked air support and sufficient heavy weapons and were of variable quality.

The outcome of the invasion was a tight run thing. Fighting was fierce and German losses far higher than could be afforded to an elite force, bearing in mind forthcoming, ambitious plans for the invasion of Russia (Operation Barbarossa). A bill of over 4,500 airborne troops and 170 Ju 52 transport aircraft was not readily set aside, especially since it convinced Hitler that there was no future for that kind of operation.

The Y Service did far better in Crete than it had in Greece. Before the actual landings on 20 May, the field units which had escaped from Greece managed, by energetic improvisation, to establish a useful twenty-four hours' watch that provided Freyberg with information about enemy occupation of nearby islands, intense air activity around Athens, arrivals of Ju 52 transport aircraft and also German reports on Royal Navy movements. Lacking vital equipment, the men of the SWUs searched wrecked ships and brought ashore, among many treasures, a working DF set.

Once the invasion had been launched, the Army units continued to monitor flights of aircraft to and from Greece as well as providing tactical intelligence from enbattled sectors. Moreover, they accidentally complemented the work of seaborne Y on the 21st by picking up two approaching convoys of caiques on their way to Crete with the amphibious force. Initially this contact was mysterious to the searchers until a German radio operator was heard calling a shore station 'landlubber'. As a result there occurred notable interceptions at sea by the Navy which forced the convoys, at great loss, to abandon the amphibious part of Operation Mercury.

This is not the place to criticise the defence of Crete, except to say that SIGINT provided a wealth of intelligence which might have been put to better use. On the credit side, however, it could be claimed that the experience gained by the field units' searchers who got back to Egypt added considerably to the store of knowledge for future use in mobile warfare.

With the stalling of Rommel at Tobruk and on the Egyptian frontier, and the pyrrhic victory at Crete, the Germans had temporarily shot their bolt in the Mediterranean. Yet it did not at all look that way to those in Cairo and London who assumed that Crete might be a stepping stone to the capture of Cyprus, followed by a take-over of Vichy French governed Syria and a role in Iraq which had attacked British bases on 2 May.

In fact, the presence in those countries of the Luftwaffe and a group of diplomats and Abwehr agents posing as tourists, backed up by a few Luftwaffe machines importing arms, represented little more than the advance guard of a highly speculative opportunism that did not fit well with basic German Grand Strategy. This was plainly evident from the prolific gatherings of SIGINT which frequently carried contradicted reports from diplomats, spies and the anti-Vichy Free French. That there was an Axis threat to vital British interests was beyond doubt, but the tendency to write down SIGINT was in reality a manifestation of very worried people taking excess counsel of their own fears.

In the event, rational SIGINT persuaded those in London and in Cairo to strike without delay even with forces that were weaker than those of the opposition. Tactical SIGINT played no part in the defeat of the Iraqi forces by 30 May. But when Syria was invaded on 8 June the survivors of the field unit which had escaped from Crete were flung into action. They helped to amplify the plentiful supply of tactical intelligence provided by reconnaissance and POW (prisoners of war), many of whom were anti-Vichy.

Strategic SIGINT, on the other hand, was voluminous, drawing as it did on generous Lufwaffe Enigma offerings which not only disclosed its own activities but also the movements and intentions of the Vichy French forces at sea and on land. Of even greater assistance on the diplomatic front was the fact that the Abwehr was using Luftwaffe Enigma, thus disclosing its dealings with the French High Commissioner, who admitted to such exhaustion among his forces that they could only be kept in the fight by reinforcement of German forces. This most certainly would not be available since, by then, the Wehrmacht was fully stretched at war with Russia.

Meanwhile the fighting in Cyrenaica had waxed and waned mainly to German advantage and very much due to the imbalance of competing Y Services. From the moment of their arrival the Germans had benefited from experienced searchers in their well-organised and equipped radio intercept units. They were aided greatly by captured British codes, call sign lists and slipshod security which simplified TA and DF and continued to be of immense strategic and tactical help for at least the first eighteen months of the German sojourn in North Africa.

It goes without saying that British Y found the Africa Corps security more difficult to overcome that than of the Luftwaffe's African units and the Italians. Yet, although unable, at first, to break the Army Enigma, the Y field units often did read lower-grade codes, mainly those used by reconnaissance units. It was, therefore, freely read Luftwaffe Enigma which kept General Wavell and the Western Desert Force best informed about their enemy's strategic intentions and rising strength, as well as his logistic state. But tactically Y was of but little assistance, usually because the decrypts of Enigma by GC and CS arrived far too late. Furthermore there was poor performance by intelligence officers who were far too slow passing on the results of their synthesis.

A counter-attack launched against the Germans in the direction of Halfaya Pass on the frontier on 15 May (Operation Brevity), despite sound timing against a weakened enemy, failed in its aim because of weak field intelligence as well as superior German tactical insight and use of powerful weapons. Those intercepts in clear which were achieved after the Germans broke radio silence on contact were wasted by inferior handling. The same could be said of the much larger-scale Operation Battleaxe on 15 June, when Rommel benefited from superior SIGINT in launching his decisive counter-stroke against divided armoured columns. Nevertheless Rommel's interpretation of interceptions of British radio traffic, which divulged his enemy's panicky sensitivity to blows against flanks and rears, taught him a false lesson which led him into error in the future.

CHAPTER NINE

TOWARDS ARMAGEDDON

The first concrete evidence that Hitler might have designs on Russia came to British notice from SIGINT. It arrived as no surprise to those with knowledge of the mounting volume of lies, rumours, hints, reports, deceptions and incredulity which had kept the world on tenterhooks since the fall of France. Nor was it astonishing to GC and CS and Y that the leak came from Luftwaffe Enigma when, in a typical fragmentary reference to an Army matter, it mentioned the intended transfer of armoured formations from the Balkans to Cracow on the day after Yugoslavia signed the damning Alliance Pact with Germany. But it was dramatic on 27 March 1941, immediately after the coup in Belgrade had rejected that pact, when it revealed that the transfer in part had been cancelled. From this change of plan both AI and Winston Churchill became convinced that Germany would invade Russia in the near future.

On 3 April Churchill sent Stalin a careful guarded warning of the threatening danger. It was not delivered until the 19th. But Stalin already was in possession of intelligence which grew in conviction by the day from numerous sources. Meanwhile SIGINT, usually of the Luftwaffe Enigma variety, was divulging very positive evidence of the enormous scale of the impending invasion. On 10 June it forecast a likely starting date after the 15th. On the 14th, appeared a warning order for the 17th, updated on the 16th to the 19th. And on the 21st came a clear indication that crossing of the frontier was imminent.

Yet the Incredulity Factor was present and widespread. Official opinion in London clung to the belief that there was no immediate threat. In Moscow Stalin only came to the correct conclusion on the 21st that he was standing on the very eve of invasion. His inexplicable hesitation was to cost his country dear on the 22nd as Germany and her allies struck with complete tactical surprise and success along an enormous frontage from the Arctic to the Black Sea. Rarely in the history of war can there have been such self-delusion by the governments of great nations in the face of such overwhelming evidence.

Here we shall not examine the course of the campaign in Russia that torrid summer and during the ensuing chill autumn and freezing winter. Mainly we will deal with the impact of events on the Y Service and their assistance to Ultra and the wider aspects of the Allied cause.

It might have been hoped that quickly there would have been a far freer exchange of information between Britain and her mighty new ally, such as already was burgeoning with the USA. But this was never achieved. Dr McVittie and his meteorological organisation at Dunstable and Bletchley Park continued to depend on decrypts of enciphered Russian met reports.

This was hardly surprising bearing in mind that when, in July, what was known as No. 30 Mission (led by General Mason Macfarlane) went to Moscow to probe for the nature of a Russian Y Service and to establish collaboration with it, the reception was far from co-operative. The Russian attitude was likened to that of a horsedealer who thoroughly enjoyed cut-and-thrust bargaining. Mutual trust always was lacking. Sqn Ldr Scott-Farnie's requests to visit a Y station was rebuffed and he was left to guess that the Russians, like the British, spread their intercept stations along the front. But this treatment, coming as it did when the German advance was thundering eastwards with undiminished vigour and success, undoubtedly reinforced the initial British decision not to disclose the existence of Ultra to the Russians, whose survival during a series of defeats was very much in doubt. It was decided to bargain with offers to share the keys to low-grade codes in exchange for other intelligence. Yet there was little response of any value.

The Royal Navy did rather better when, by February 1942, it had, through local negotiations, established a Y unit at Polyarnoe to support the movement of convoys to Murmansk. In return for passing intercepted air intelligence to the Russians, the Navy was permitted to listen to enemy transmissions which were inaudible to searchers in Britain. It enabled them (with only one break when the Russians objected to a meacon that was installed at Murmansk to jam Luftwaffe navigation beams) to monitor air and surface threats to Arctic convoys, including that of the principal warships, *Admiral Tirpitz* and *Scharnhorst*, until they were sunk. The station remained in operation until near the end of the war, featuring as the only Y unit directly to achieve any intercepts of importance from Russian soil. Virtually every other attempt to do so was frustrated. Indeed, as the tide turned in Russia's favour in 1943, No. 30 Mission was ignored by people who were 'swollen-headed with success', and who recklessly employed low-grade codes to carry high-grade material.

Meanwhile the march of events made improvements to weather forecasting vital, especially to the RAF as its bombing campaign over Europe (the only means available to strike heavy blows at the German war economy) was stepped up. Since July 1940 revised Axis meteorological ciphers had made decryption extremely difficult. Furthermore the staff at Dunstable tended to concentrate more on the weather than codebreaking. Staff shortages were acute and it was realised that meteorologists were not necessarily competent cryptanalysts. At times it had to be wondered at that so many codes were broken and some sort of effective service rendered.

Early in 1941 moves to bring the whole meteorological business under one head – the Y Service – began. The process dragged on and on until, after much wrangling, the Dunstable intercept station came under Y on 20 November, Dr McVittie's Met-Sub Station at Bletchley Park was incorporated in GC and CS's Air Section and, in December, the Dunstable intercept station, reinforced by RAF personnel (including WAAFs), all of whom had to be trained, came under the control of Cheadle. Yet it was not until March 1942 that improvements were completed when an enlarged cabin was built at Dunstable to house between forty and fifty receivers. The majority of these were used successfully against enemy traffic and the remainder monitored Allied messages, including some from Russia. Furthermore, all these decrypts were supplied to the Middle East Command, at its request.

Dr McVittie had many problems, not least the morale of his people whose excellent services were taken for granted by the customers. They dealt with anything up to 17,000 observations a day and usually teleprinted or sent OTP (One Time Pad) decrypted material within an hour of its receipt. He alone knew how effective they were. Only occasionally did his people fail to deliver. Yet virtually the only times the customers spoke up was by way of complaint on rare occasions when delivery failed. Praise was at a premium for these unsung workers, although it certainly arrived when it was discovered in December 1942 that the decryption of weather reports (in the so-called Willi Willi code) from U-boats not only enhanced weather forecasting but also for a few weeks, by indirect means in Hut 6, provided the first entry into the difficult U-boat Triton Enigma code which had baffled the cryptanalysts since the previous February.

FROM 22 JUNE 1941 onward Germany was battling on four fronts: the enormous Russian front, the vital Atlantic Ocean front, the Western Europe, mainly air, front and the extensive Mediterranean front. Holding these theatres of war together for Germany was the complex and very efficient communications and information system ruled over by that rabidly anti-Nazi General Erich Fellgiebel. Well knowing the inherent vulnerability of extensively used codes, he had, since the fall of France, been energetically extending the cable communications network throughout France (where alone during the four year occupation the existing 3,750 miles of trunk cable were increased to 6,900), Belgium, Holland and Poland. This reduced reliance on radio and, but for Luftwaffe's wanton carelessness, improved signals security. Additionally, when the Wehrmacht advanced into the depths of Russia it constructed a network of simple, poled, bare-wire lines: which, of course, were vulnerable in hostile territory to tapping and cutting by partisans. Later some of these lines were replaced by the latest microwave beam communications to span hostile territory in security.

Fellgiebel's outstanding, yet seriously flawed, organisation was thus potentially a most profitable target for the Allies to attack. Therefore GC and CS with the supporting Y Service, were both the spearhead and shield of Britain as she struggled to fend off Axis thrusts and schemed to seize the initiative with economic, offensive action.

As mentioned, there was no hope of radio intercept collaboration

with Russia. Yet it was from the Russian front in June that Y searchers
first managed to find a German Army Enigma, the one to be known as
Vulture. GC and CS broke it only occasionally at first, but regularly from
December onward. Although this traffic was useful for indirectly keeping track of the secretive Russians' situation, it was regarded as of low
priority and only to be studied at leisure.

Far more important was the Battle of the Atlantic, which hinged
entirely on the success of a rapidly rising number of new U-boats which
were finding their operations much tougher to execute in face of more,
better trained convoy escorts. Since February, Admiral Dönitz had been
forced to send his boats farther and farther west to evade strong coastal
defences. But out there making contact was more difficult due to lack of
adequate air reconnaissance and radio intelligence. Instead of raising
the rate of tonnage sunk per boat per month, it fell from 20,000 tons in
August 1940 to only 3,700 tons in July 1941. The German Naval Staff,
which was well supplied by its excellent B-Dienst with a steady flow of
decrypted messages, began to wonder if the enemy was even better supplied
with that sort of information.

In May an investigation concluded not only that radio intercept might
be helping the British convoys avoid the Wolf-Packs but also that DF might
significantly be making interception of boats by escorts much easier. The
staff concluded that Y stations were located in Iceland, Greenland, New-
foundland, Spain (!) and the Azores: and they assumed that all their radio
messages (including short ones) were being heard and their senders
located by DF. (Strangely they seem to have overlooked or played down
shipborne DF which the Royal Navy was steadily improving with new
technology and techniques.) Not for the last time, orders were issued
insisting on better radio discipline, more changes of frequencies and so-
called 'short signals' procedure, but to no avail. For tactical reasons
captains went on chattering in morse. Nobody suspected that the Enigma
had been penetrated.

Ironically this was a turning-point since only in March had GC and
CS started to make significant headway against Naval Enigma. Partly this
was due to an enlarged staff and more Bombes, one of which, in Hut 8,

concentrated on breaking naval Enigma. But also it was brought about by the virtually inevitable captures of documents and machinery - notably codes from the armed trawler *Krebs* on 4 March, during a commando raid on Norway; the weather ships *Munchen* on 7 May and *Lauenburg* on 28 June with their Enigma machines and papers; and most famously by luck on 9 May, U-110 complete with Enigma and a treasure trove of documents, including Enigma key settings (past and future), 'officer only' signals and the code book used for special 'short signals'.

The fact of the matter was that Y was beginning to win the Battle of the Atlantic when, from June onward, GC and CS was breaking Naval Enigma on a regular basis and Luftwaffe Enigma was making its customary contribution to general intelligence, thus facilitating evasive routing of convoys and reducing losses to a point in the autumn when Dönitz and his staff became paranoid with fear that they were being betrayed: to the extent, for example, that when they lost ten boats in November, they thought messages sent by cable might be tapped and so decided to send them by radio which, indeed, *was* being intercepted and often read within a few hours.

All this took place at a time when the USA had passed the Lend Lease Act and the trickle of supplies across the Atlantic was beginning to rise to what promised to be a flood if the U-boats did not establish a strangling blockade.

The initiative in the war in, or rather, over western Europe had passed to Britain. With the end of the Blitz, the immediate threat of invasion and the need to take as much strain as possible off the hard-pressed Russians, it was essential to take the offensive: meaning, in practice, by amphibious and air raiding. The former could amount to no more than a few pin-pricks and the latter chronically inaccurate strategic bombing of industrial targets, augmented by fighter sweeps intended (not always successfully) to bring an unwilling Luftwaffe to combat. Y Service had to grow in size to cope with huge quantities of naval and air intercepts ranging from E-boats and escorted coastal convoys to the fast-evolving German night-fighter organisation and the latest 'noises' from navigational beams, radar and high-speed morse transmissions. For the time being there was reduced interest in enemy bombers, which rarely put in an appearance, and no important transmissions at all from the highly security conscious Army.

Both sides of course were obsessed with security and benefited considerably from listening to their opponents' errors. Yet each suffered from serious omissions. For their part, the Germans took pains to monitor their air crews' radio transmissions in order to correct recurring breaches of procedures which could be a give-away to enemy tactical analysis. The British, on the other hand, tended to be much more lax. RAF fighter pilots' RT procedures were more insecure than those of their German opponent and often insufficiently checked. And the British Army, especially its tank crews, were notoriously negligent and rarely disciplined. Until mid-1942, out of crass ignorance, they rarely changed frequencies and call signs, continually disclosing unit identities and orders of battle: this was a very harmful fault which could and should have been discovered at a much earlier date.

On the other hand, the Germans, and the Luftwaffe in particular, were completely blind to the accessibility of Enigma. Set against the entire history of code vulnerability, they suffered from an inexcusably arrogant, overconfidence in the self-assumed capability of these state-of-the-art machines to resist penetration, thus providing an outstanding example of the Incredulity Factor which was to cost them extremely dear. Whereas the British, in their breaking of Enigma, simply could not believe their luck would last; they were constantly wary of Typex being penetrated and always fearful of the day when the Germans would twig that Enigma was being broken. In that event, they realised, the Y Service would become even more essentially vital than it already was. Therefore, at the highest level they braced themselves for the worst and soon embarked on a huge expansion programme.

Aileen Morris has whimsically described a December night in 1940 when one of her WAAFs heard a German airman talking about playing with his 'little screw' (to the ribald amusement of fellow aircraftmen) with mentions of 'lantern' and 'closing a parlour'. The traffic was mostly obscure and on a VHF frequency band which could be heard out to five hundred miles by skilled operators – far into Germany on a frontage stretching from Denmark to La Rochelle. This puzzled everybody from the Air Ministry downward, until it gradually dawned that they were listening to a new system of ground-to-air control of night fighters, combined with searchlights and radar, for the interception of bombers. These were the operational trials of General Kammhuber's 'Line', the system of fighter interception 'boxes' designed to shoot down lone night bombers. It was the start of what would become a major undertaking by the Y Service in support of the bomber offensive which eventually would have to run the gauntlet of night fighters in order to devastate Germany.

Naturally this discovery prompted a series of studies, by both sides, of what would grow into a prolonged, major fighter battle. In Britain this drove the three services, GC and CS, the Y Service, CBME in Egypt and the UK operational commands (especially Bomber and Fighter Commands) to work more closely than ever before. From this emerged demands for far better training and systematic handling and dissemination of material gathered by Y and processed by Hut 3. Needless to say, mistakes were made, as for example, by a duty officer at Cheadle who, lacking the very barest knowledge of the Luftwaffe, drew and forwarded a false conclusion which had a trivial consequence, but which triggered an acrimonious departmental row. Computors who had learned their business on the job were bound to make mistakes. Not until December 1941 were courses for them started, with a syllabus that included TA, small code breaking, radio footprinting, German call signs, RT procedure and so on.

The relatively tranquil period which followed the Blitz and preceded forthcoming major campaigns provided the opportunity to consolidate lessons that had been empirically learned in the heat of battle. On 2 July a sub-committee of the Y Board met to address the relationship between SIGINT and cryptanalysis. It was dominated by a long paper, drafted by the very experienced Group Captain L. F. Blandy. He summarised SIGINT in the RAF (including the work of Cheadle, Chicksands, Kingsdown and the Naval Section at GC and CS), and concluded that the two subjects were interrelated and 'formed one indivisible mechanism'. Unfortunately MI 8's impractical contributory paper caused dissent among the cryptanalysts in Hut 6; although, a few days later, this led to an integration of sounder ideas which improved collaboration between the Army and RAF staffs and GC and CS at the moment when the main Army Y station at Chatham was moving to Beaumanor.

The sense of desperation which seems sometimes to have affected the British SIGINT world in those hectic days inspired many important improvisations. For example, GC and CS produced what was called a Fighter RT Diary, based on recorded TA, for its own use, but which proved so useful that it was later most profitably shared with Fighter Command to help improve tactics against the Luftwaffe. There were in-depth studies into Luftwaffe organisation, methods and its call sign system (at Beaumanor) and frequency allocations with their daily changes: these, along with footprinting results, made possible the forecasting of changes.

The work storm of self-examination generated more interception and the need for additional receivers, staff, Bombes and accommodation. For example, Hut 6, which owned six Bombes in July, was soon demanding eighteen by December. This pattern, as will be seen below, was mirrored in the Mediterranean and Middle East at a moment in history when it was becoming plain that Japan might be on the verge of expanding the war to global dimensions. Unfortunately this work storm was accompanied by a dangerous indecision among the small hierarchy at Bletchley Park. Here the head of GC and CS, Lt Cdr Alastair Denniston (who, it will be recalled, worked in Room 40 during World War One) was seen as a block to essential innovations and reform in an organisation which simply had to move with constantly changing events and technology. It was a situation that Sir Stewart Menzies, in his capacity as C, the overall chief of the SIS and GC and CS, should have gripped without untoward delay. Yet, as will be seen in Chapter 11, he failed to do so – with menacing consequences.

Were that not enough for GC and CS to cope with, there was the onset of Fish – the encrypted, very fast, non-morse radio teleprinter which the Germans knew as Geheimschreiber and which the GPO and Y had first detected in 1932. By the end of 1940 there were several versions, called Sägefisch by the Germans and known generically by GC and CS as

Fish, with individual names such as Tunny, Shark, Herring and so on. The first detection of operational use by one of these machines occurred in August 1941 under German Army control. At Bletchley Park the decision at once was taken to concentrate the attack on this experimental version – and with outstanding results in mastering it by the year's end. But at the back of C's mind and those of Denniston and Travis lay the realisation that the day might come when this complex, ten-wheel non-morse machine would supplant the much slower and more vulnerable (in British eyes) Enigma.

Mid-1941 British opinion held that the Mediterranean and Middle East theatres of war were the most needful of reinforcement. As many men and as much material as could reasonably be spared were being sent to Gibraltar, to besieged Malta and round the Cape. Foreseeing the impact of this in May, and in the knowledge that much Enigma traffic was already inaudible from the UK (and would become even more so due to 'summer fading'), the London Y Board and Middle East Y Board agreed that there must be an urgent reallocation of intercept resources in order to impart higher priority to Enigma interception.

Towards the end of April, thirty RAF Y reinforcements had reached Egypt, bringing fourteen sets with them, and more were in transit along with some Army Y. Even so, existing communications facilities were congested, with all high-speed links overloaded. Therefore Cable and Wireless Ltd was pressed into carrying 10,000 groups per day from Malta and 4,000 from Gibraltar. Hut 6 now pointed out that Malta was intercepting more than all the other Mediterranean Y sets combined. It had only three on vital air tasks, whereas Gibraltar had six on less important army tasks, Heliopolis one on air and three on army and Sarafand two on air. To overcome this imbalance it was agreed by the Y Board that an RAF officer should co-ordinate and allocate a common pool of sets dedicated to Enigma traffic. Two of these would be Malta based, eight at Heliopolis and two at Sarafand. At the same time the bottleneck due to too few Typex machines was urgently tackled in order to raise the number to thirty.

The lull in serious fighting on the Egyptian Cyrenaican frontier and at Tobruk persisted until September as both sides reinforced their armies with a view to undertaking major offensives in November. Desert conditions made trunk cable communications almost impossible to maintain. Therefore radio was in constant use and SIGINT from many sources revealed desperate Axis logistic shortages, especially of fuel. Rommel, however, was never one to remain inactive for long, no matter the state of his logistic situation. Acting on reports of a forward British supply dump being built close to the frontier at Bir el Khiregat, he decided to seize it on 14 September with 21st Panzer Division. The raid was to take place in moonlight and would be dependent on well-staged refuelling arrangements. At the last moment it was discovered that there was no dump. But Operation Midsummer Night's Dream went ahead with the revised aim of destroying British light forces infesting the frontier. Rommel led in person.

Everything went wrong. The refuelling broke down. The British, amply warned by patrols (though not, due to enemy radio silence, in advance by Y), contented themselves with long-range shelling and heavy daylight bombing of the stranded Germans. 21st Panzer lost 67 tanks out of 110, thus so seriously reducing the Axis forces strength that they were unready for their planned offensive against Tobruk in November. But Midsummer Night's Dream was more than an operational nightmare; for it marked the first cryptanalytical entry into Panzer Army Africa Army Enigma, known as Chaffinch I. Difficult to read, it dealt with administrative matters and was read only from 14 to 23 November by using keys captured prior to Operation Crusader. The Luftwaffe Enigma and low-grade Army codes, therefore, until well into 1942, remained by far the best sources of intelligence from radio intercepts. By which time the war was on the eve of its most decisive turning-point.

CHAPTER TEN

GLOBAL WAR

Mounting evidence throughout 1941 pointing to the likelihood of war between America and Japan came to a head in July when President Roosevelt, in retaliation for Japanese occupation of French Indochina in September 1940, froze Japanese assets in the USA. Almost at once he was joined in the act by Britain. Provoked by this virtual blockade and a clear warning from Roosevelt, the Japanese opted for war on 5 November. This set in motion their existing plans to strike at the American Pacific Fleet at Pearl Harbor and simultaneously seize the rest of south-east Asia along with its vast natural resources, including vital oil fields.

In Russia, the Germans on 2 October had belatedly opened a massive thrust to take Moscow, an event which British Army Y had foretold through TA of redeploying German formations as well as from Enigma. Stalin was warned, but probably already knew what was coming. Come mid-November what was deemed as the culminating blow to end the campaign began to suffer a series of checks in appalling weather conditions. The German operations stalled at Leningrad and Russian counter-attacks slowed or stopped some advances towards Moscow. And at Rostov in the south a local German withdrawal, surprisingly, was induced on the 28th.

On 18 November, Operation Crusader, the British Eighth Army's major offensive to relieve Tobruk and defeat Panzer Army Africa, was launched. It surprised Rommel who, for two days, refused to believe evidence from his intelligence staff, well-supplied as they were by radio intercepts and other sources, which said that this was no spoiling-attack but a major effort by two corps. Yet Crusader, relatively speaking, was a mere skirmish compared to the awe-inspiring event of 6 December when the Russians, reinforced by numerous fresh divisions from the Far East, tentatively began a counter-offensive which rolled back the Germans from the gates of Moscow and from eastern Ukraine. It came as a complete surprise to their High Command which, until the previous day, had persisted in refusing to taking into account the oft-reported exhaustion of their men and machines at the front.

Hardly had news of the Russian attacks broken than there came news that the Japanese had struck with complete surprise and devastating effect at Pearl Harbor on 7 December; and at British and American possessions in the Far East on the 8th. These surprises were shared, by no means incidentally, by the Germans who had not been told in advance of what was coming from their Axis ally. The shock so unbalanced Hitler that he raced back to Berlin from the front and, without careful consideration as to the consequences, declared war on the USA on 11 December. For there neither existed then nor at any time in the future a properly considered strategic plan of collaboration between two belligerent nations who never entered trustfully into each other's confidence.

The Americans and British, by contrast, had long been allies who had shared ideas and hardware for their common good. By joint agreement the Americans handed Britain the secrets of Japanese codes and in due course they would send officers to work at Bletchley Park. When their Heads of State and Chiefs of Staff met on 22 December to formulate at the Arcadia Conference an agreed grand strategy, first priority was given to the defeat of Germany ahead of Japan. At the same time, it was agreed that the USA should take prime responsibility for intercept and SIGINT in the Pacific theatre of operations and by Britain in the West. These arrangements, as was to be expected, could not and did not always work to perfection. For example, the Americans did not possess the equivalent of Britain's Y Service. Therefore, when GC and CS came to formulate sharing arrangements it found the necessity to forge separate arrangements with the Army and the Navy Departments, which were, in fact, achieved with remarkable goodwill.

Bearing in mind the advanced state of radio intercept by the British, American, Japanese and German intercept services, it may seem strange that at this crucial moment so much strategic surprise was achieved in matters of the highest importance at all levels. In fact, of course, in every case mentioned above, searchers belonging to each side had detected sufficient information for intelligence staffs to draw correct conclusions about what was strategically, and sometimes tactically, in train. The crunch came when forces of different magnitude and experience collided in the uncertainties of confusing circumstances. These were the commonplace realities afflicting all leaders and followers at war.

For example, when Rommel's staff, well supplied by Oberleutnant Harold Seebohm's signals intelligence unit, gave warning about the strength and direction of Crusader on 18 November 1941 once the British broke radio silence on first contacts, Rommel perversely chose to discount it for nearly forty-eight hours, although subsequently he made far better use of what came his way by intercept and reports from air and ground units. Then, having defeated the British armoured formations at Sidi Rezegh and heard signs of panic in the enemy camp, he had launched an intuitive/empirical blow at the enemy rear, only himself to suffer surprise because a similarly well-served enemy chose not to react in the manner he had during Operation Battleaxe. For, unknown to Rommel, the defeated commander of Eighth Army, General Alan Cunningham, had been sacked by the C-in-C Middle East, General Sir Claude Auchinleck, who was made of sterner stuff. Auchinleck, guided by SIGINT, including Chaffinch decrypts, could confidently stand his ground as Rommel led his drive to the frontier where he was soundly rebuffed by a forewarned and prepared enemy. Forced to retreat and discover from his well-informed staff of impending envelopment by a numerically superior and better supplied enemy, this was but the prelude to a general withdrawal to the Tripolitanian frontier whence he had started the previous March.

For the first time British Army Y performed consistently well in this battle, its field units not only keeping HQ Eighth Army, its two corps and various divisions directly and amply informed about enemy deployments and moves, but also capturing an Enigma machine (referred to at the time as a Typex), useful documents, receivers and DF equipment. These were the first significant finds from a local victory, with more to come when a beaten Rommel started to withdraw on Benghazi. Previously, moreover, a Polish Special Duties Section had distinguished itself tactically at Sidi Rezegh by DF fixing of enemy artillery positions accurately enough for counter-battery fire; by locating HQs (including Rommel's) and knocking out transmitters; and on one occasion by giving orders in German to a Luftwaffe flight telling it to return to base on Crete! Regardless of Eighth Army defeats to come, this was a period when the searchers in the field found their feet and established the roots of sound procedures and techniques of the future.

In Russia too the weary but still over-confident Germans seem to have suffered from a sense of disbelief that, after a series of stunning victories in which hundreds of thousands of the enemy and mountains of his equipment and stores had been eliminated, the chances of a Russian recovery was possible. Yet their estimate of eighty-five infantry divisions, fifteen cavalry divisions and twenty-four tank brigades facing Army Group B on the Moscow front had to have some sort of statistical basis, gained largely from SIGINT. But they had no idea what lay in depth behind those formations.

Yet, bearing in mind how shaky Russian signals security then was and the inferior combat worthiness of their worn-down troops, German optimism may well have been the product of the Incredulity Factor; with which the Russians may have concurred since their so-called counter-offensive opened only as a series of half-hearted probing attacks that did not expand until the shaken Germans abruptly gave way on one key front. Thereupon General Zhukov exploited the event with mighty opportunism as a demoralised enemy astonishingly gave way and the front caved in. Inevitably the rapid, though controlled, German withdrawal continued until, in April, the Russians themselves became physically exhausted as their logistic system broke down. SIGINT played its usual part in that process of mutual neutralisation but it was the Germans who made best use of it.

In the vast expanses of the Far East and Pacific Ocean a totally different philosophy ruled, one that was slightly akin (although in different environments) to what had been the case in western Europe in 1940. For here a highly trained, experienced and better equipped Japanese force proved much more than a match for the outclassed Americans, British and Dutch whose crucial sea power, well served by SIGINT, was neutralised within three months.

There is no intention here to analyse in depth the key strategic events of those hectic months – starting with the crippling of the US Pacific Fleet at Pearl Harbor and the sinking of major Allied warships off Malaya and Indonesia. But SIGINT and cryptanalysis played their parts to the full, the Americans much more so than their allies: and the Japanese most diligently of all because, having for so long been at war, they possessed the initiative and understood properly the urgency that it generated.

Ronald Lewin, in his much admired book *The Other Ultra*, emphasises the effects of pre-war 'noise' that saturated the files of American intelligence officers and the mass of conflicting information which prompted distractive considerations that created several plausible options. Inevitably it was extremely difficult to separate the chaff from the wheat. Rationally, however, it was possible, from traditional sources, to discern what actions were pending or on the way. These, amplified by TA and SIGINT at the highest level, were often illuminated by the cryptanalysts, among whom the brilliant Willliam Friedman was king. He it was who had recently penetrated the Japanese Type 97 machine code (known as Purple but not to be likened to Enigma) which carried diplomatic messages telling the American authorities that the Japanese were about to strike. It was not his fault that this information, via Magic, the American equivalent of Ultra, was not exploited in time to avert the Pearl Harbor disaster, or that of Commander Laurence Safford's radio surveillance intercept organisation (which by now had grown to 700 officers and men since its founding in 1924). He missed little of importance during the tense weeks when the Japanese closed on their prey and in October had been instrumental, through TA, in estimating their Navy's exact order of battle.

No, it was the poorly organised, over-security conscious American intelligence system which was to blame for the fundamental reason that it failed to pass vital information in time to the right people – the very same defect that had plagued the defeated British and French in 1940.

Suffice to say that although the initial Japanese movements by sea towards south-east Asia were detected by various sources, including SIGINT, it was spoof SIGINT which most convincingly was employed by the Japanese to delude the American interceptors. For, before sailing piecemeal on 26 November for a rendezvous off the Kuriles, Admiral Nagumo's First Air Fleet of six aircraft carriers, two battleships, three cruisers and nine destroyers not only imposed complete radio silence but also had its radio identity assumed by shore stations. History relates how Nagumo's voyage to within air-striking distance of Pearl Harbor was executed without detection, and how on 7 December he destroyed or seriously damaged all eight battleships present plus eleven other vessels. It also records that all three American aircraft carriers escaped because, fortuitously, they were at sea; and that Nagumo made a serious error by deciding not to send in another strike to wreck the fuel oil tanks and other vital logistic facilities which were at his mercy. Thus he failed totally to neutralise American naval striking power by enabling repairs to be made and mobility restored rapidly.

It was a different matter off Malaya where the battleships HMS *Prince of Wales* and HMS *Repulse* left Singapore, under radio silence with an escort of destroyers on the night of 8–9 December, to tackle Japanese landings said to be taking place at Kuantan. Nothing was heard of them from the Japanese until Y picked up a plain language message from a submarine reporting their position steaming southward. Soon they were attacked by thirty-four high-level and fifty-one torpedo-bombers based on Saigon. Within an hour both battleships, lacking RAF fighter cover, were sunk, thus reducing the naval defences of Malaya, the East Indies, Hong Kong and the Philippines to a few cruisers and destroyers, and exposing to invasion those territories whose armies were neither sufficiently trained nor equipped to cope with the well-armed, experienced Japanese troops.

The survival of Allied Y Services in the Far East was as brief as the short-lived defences they supported. Like those forces, they were too few in numbers and unready for the trials and tribulations of war. In 1935 a Far East Combined Bureau (FECB), mainly Royal Navy-manned, had been set up by Y Service in Hong Kong, tasked to study Japanese Army and Army Air ciphers. Poorly equipped, they heard little army air traffic because its aircraft mostly operated over China more than 600 miles from Hong Kong. However, quite a large amount of naval air traffic was heard and analysed.

In August 1939 FECB was transferred to Singapore, leaving behind an inadequate DF station (paired with its partner at Shanghai) and too few operators to keep a twenty-four-hours' watch. Needless to say, the Shanghai station, along with an American one, was lost the day war broke out on 8 December, and the one at Hong Kong was put out of action before the colony fell on Christmas Day.

Likewise the long-established and ponderously functioning American naval and military surveillance stations were mopped up when the Japanese took Guam on the 10th and progressively worked their way through the Philippines. By mutual arrangement the US Army RI section in the Philippines carried out interceptions and the Navy's unit (called Cast) decrypted a Purple machine, underground on the fortified island of Corregidor. They learned as they went along in the weeks to come. Lacking an interpreter, they did manage to perform a rough and ready TA to forecast air raids and warn anti-aircraft gunners of approaching targets, a few of which were shot down. Better still, on the Bataan peninsula, they later captured Japanese code books which, at last, made feasible the setting up of an effective listening station on Corregidor capable of identifying enemy units. Bataan capitulated on 9 April 1941 and Corregidor on 5 May. It had to be admitted that, as at Hong Kong, little of value had been contributed by SIGINT.

Initially the arrival of FECB in Singapore in August 1939 caused disruption until, like events to come in Egypt, responsibilities and channels of communications were sorted out. There was the usual wrangling over the meaning and relationship of SIGINT and cryptanalysis. And the arrival of No. 52 Wireless Unit shortly before the fighting began seems to have caused as many problems as it solved. None of the operators could read Japanese morse at 25 wpm and had to be trained on the voyage out by Sqn Ldr Garrity. Antennae had to be replaced, receivers modified or borrowed from the Navy. For DF there was no suitable equipment and its implementation was considered almost impossible due to atmospheric conditions which prevented 100 per cent reliable interception of traffic from Indochina.

Garrity discovered that the Singapore Naval Section, in compliance with a strategy which concentrated on defence against attack from the sea and dismissed the possibility of the Japanese fighting their way through the jungle and rubber plantations of Malaya, searched only for naval frequencies. They monitored the movements of warships, including aircraft carriers and land-based naval air units, but missed a great deal of traffic concerning the movements of other address groups.

Eight days before the war began Garrity and Arthur Cooper (a GC and CS expert cryptanalyst on Japanese air ciphers) felt they had grasped the rudiments of Japanese call signs, frequencies and organisations. So when the accurate bombing of airfields began and amphibious forces landed on the north-east coast of Malaya, Garrity, Cooper and their RAF staff were able, with Naval Y help, to manage fairly effectively to intercept and interpret a useful percentage of airborne RT and ground-to-air signals. But they could do nothing to help save the two ill-fated battleships or the outfought land forces as they were thrown back to Singapore.

On 5 January 1942 the FECB, whose senior army cryptanalyst had already departed to Burma to set up a Y organisation there, was evacuated to Java. There it was joined by Navy and RAF Y units and by Arthur Cooper early in February. Their stay was of short duration. Already Japanese warships and aircraft were operating in the approaches to Sumatra, which was invaded on the 14th. Next day Singapore fell and on the 19th Allied cruisers, endeavouring to catch an amphibious force heading for Java, was roughly handled and beaten off. This coincided with a very destructive raid on Darwin by Nagumo's triumphant First Air Fleet – Australia's first taste of modern warfare. It preceded the Battle of the Java Sea on the 27th when the Allied squadron of five cruisers and thirteen destroyers, which for thirty-seven hours had been groping for contact and was short of fuel, found its quarry, only to lose all but two cruisers and five destroyers to its Japanese opponents.

Not only Java but also the whole of the East Indies were at Japan's mercy. It was virtually a matter of every man for himself, a scramble by any means available to escape to Australia, Ceylon or India. A few Y Service men, including Cooper, reached Australia, but Garrity and the RAF Y unit were lost. FECB, in fact, was wiped out.

As a result, the frontiers of practical, land-based radio intercept of the Japanese had been pushed back to locations on the Aleutian Islands, the west coast of Canada and the USA, Hawaii, Midway Island, New Guinea, the Solomon Islands, Australia, East Africa, Ceylon, India and Burma. But the facilities and trained men available to man those far-flung locations were few and far between. Mainly, in fact, they consisted of depleted American units based on Hawaii, survivors from the Philippines and the East Indies in Australia (about to be reinforced by experienced Australian units sent home from Egypt) and in Ceylon where an agglomeration of experienced searchers from India, reinforced by postings from the Middle East and escapees from Singapore and Java, arrived piecemeal.

As later will be described, these were the cadres and foundations of a new organisation which hastily had to be cobbled and welded into an effective Allied Y Service linked to Washington and London.

AT THE HEIGHT OF the titanic struggles engulfing the Russian, the Pacific and south-east Asian theatres of war, two events of some collateral importance were exercising the Allies on the other side of the globe.

On 29 November 1941 Luftwaffe Enigma, routinely heard by Y, announced the appointment of Field Marshal Kesselring to a new task in the Mediterranean. Later it transpired that HQ of his Second Air Fleet with II Air Corps were moving to Sicily to take command of those Luftwaffe units already present, and that he was to be called C-in-C South (OBS). Tasked to stop Malta's nigh-crippling attacks on Axis lines of communication to North Africa, he therefore had direct contacts with Hitler and OKW, as well as with the Italians and Rommel, thus generating additional Luftwaffe radio traffic for Y to intercept.

Despite this, neither Y nor any other Allied intelligence source managed even to discover hints of the limited counter-stroke being prepared by Rommel for 21 January 1942, without consulting OKW (German Supreme Command). Axis Army radio traffic was reduced to the absolute minimum. Neither Chaffinch Enigma nor high-grade Italian traffic could be read and, for once, the Luftwaffe gave virtually nothing away. As German and Italian units moved secretly into carefully concealed and dispersed forming-up places, Army Y detected nothing of significance.

Rommel, on the other hand, was flush with intelligence, the majority of it collected by Oberleutnant Seebohm's extremely skilful interceptors. Through TA, assisted by characteristically sloppy British radio security, he had exposed the temporary, perilous weakness of enemy forces at the front. Further synthesis was confirmed by the breaking of the cipher used by the American Military Attaché in Cairo to report to Washington the state and intentions of Eighth Army. To Rommel's delight, the British folded at Agedabia under the pressure of his initial attack. Opportunistic as ever, he drove fast and hard for Benghazi, chasing an opponent whose shaken elements disclosed to Seebohm's listeners a tale of woe and rout.

British intelligence, having grossly underestimated Rommel's tank strength, now could do little through SIGINT to compute his actual numbers. Army Y, caught permanently on the hop, could only identify a few enemy units but, due to being almost constantly in retreat for over a hundred miles, not their movements. They were not to know that their opposite numbers had heard petulant disagreements among British generals which made it clear that Benghazi was ripe for the taking. Taking advantage of this, Rommel swiftly enveloped the port and, in the process, threw Eighth Army into even greater confusion, compelling it to accelerate its retreat to Gazala, where its remnants stood on 6 February. But there Rommel, who was short of fuel, left them in peace.

If ever there was a tactical victory won by SIGINT, that was it.

Conjoint with Hitler's decision of 2 October to reinforce the Luftwaffe with Kesselring's Second Air Fleet in Sicily, Dönitz had been ordered in September to send U-boats into the Mediterranean, via Gibraltar, in order to support Axis forces in North Africa. Six went at once and another dozen in November at the same time as concentrations of U-boats were ordered to patrol on either side of the Straits. Although they scored some successes (including the sinking of the aircraft carrier *Ark Royal* on 13 November) it had the negative effect of removing all boats from the Atlantic by 8 December. This radical change of strategy was at once detected by Y and by GC and CS's rapid solution of Enigma messages. It led in

November to the sinking of three boats on passage and five forced back to port by damage; and it prompted such misgivings in U-boat Command that an examination of security was carried out - without positive conclusions since, with characteristic hubris, it was assumed that Enigma was invulnerable and TA and DF not all that effective.

Then came Pearl Harbor, which was as much a surprise to Dönitz as everybody else in OKW, but gave him the opportunity to plead for an end to the wasteful deployment to the Mediterranean and the immediate sending of every available boat to the western Atlantic where easy pickings were anticipated. Not until 30 December was his plea accepted. Operation Paukenschlag started on 2 January 1942 when six boats were ordered to the Canadian and American coast. Their arrival went not undetected by Allied Y, but that could not alleviate for the Allies what, for the Germans, was their second 'Happy Time'.

In January 1942 alone 110,000 tons of shipping were sunk off the American coast; and after 1 February, when a new four-wheel Triton Enigma that long-resisted solution, came into operation, the situation worsened as the U-boats extended their activities into the virtually undefended Caribbean. For the American Chief of Naval Staff, Admiral Ernest King, obdurately refused to institute a convoy system until forcefully tackled by the Chief of Army Staff, General George Marshall, with the warning that losses of Army-run shipping were so severe that, this way, the Battle of the Atlantic and the war might well be lost.

In the meantime, with an average number initially of only five boats patrolling singly at any one time in those waters (and only three sunk between March and June) the Germans ran riot each night, picking off ships silhouetted against the bright lights on shore. Moreover, the captains were frequently guided to their targets by intercepting extremely lax American radio traffic which enabled them accurately to plot ships' positions and courses. Also they were much further assisted against convoys in the Atlantic because the excellent B-Dienst intercepts benefited from having broken the Anglo-Canadian-American Naval Cipher No. 3 which related to shipping movements.

Not until June was an effective deterrent to the U-boats off the

Americas in place in the shape of convoys and better directed air patrols. The boats' withdrawal from western waters (except in the Caribbean and off Brazil) may have been premature and, in the opinion of Harry Hinsley, a let-off for GC and CS. For he argued that if Dönitz, in the aftermath of introducing the four-wheel Triton Enigma, had concentrated on attacking convoys in mid-Atlantic, it might have been realised that a likely rise of sinkings was due to the compromise of the obsolescent three-wheel machine.

After all, however, C and his staff at Bletchley Park worked from day to day in the grim expectation that Fellgiebel and his colleagues would rumble the fallibility of Enigma, and either abandon it or further complicate and strengthen its security. Either way, the work of Y Services through TA and DF would then have become far more vital to the function of SIGINT. As will be seen in the next chapter, such an event at the start of what was now a global war would have been even more disastrous in the light of the internal struggle currently then disrupting the hierarchy at Bletchley Park.

CHAPTER ELEVEN

CRISIS AT BLETCHLEY PARK

The growth under extreme pressure of GC and CS, along with its integrated Y Service and diplomatic element, was both rapid, dynamic and huge. Furthermore it comprised a remarkably diverse collection of military and civilian individuals drawn from many walks of life, some of them brilliant, none of them below average intelligence and few who were anything other than patriotic in their zeal to do a vital job really well. Unfortunately it became apparent in 1941 that the sheer diversity and volume of that growth was making demands on labour and machines which were imposing a strain close to breaking point on those engaged. It was not just the stress of long hours worked in trying conditions which were incapacitating. There festered serious clashes of personalities from different backgrounds which were almost irreconcilable.

The fact of the matter was that GC and CS was becoming a victim of Y's output and its own success, along with realisation that so much more needed to be done to ward off defeat and win the war by keeping abreast of the enemy's colossal flood of transmissions. It was also of grave concern that basic administration of Bletchley Park, which still was the responsibility of the Foreign Office, was beginning to crack. Feeding, accommodation, transport for the thousands of workers, medical care, recreation, provision and servicing of simple equipment etc, let alone maintenance of the highly complex Bombes and calculators, were being managed on a shoestring not only for GC and CS but also for the SIS whose chief, Stewart Menzies, spent most of every day working in Olympian detachment on the second floor of the manor. Also, recruitment of adequate staff was falling into arrears of the rapidly growing requirement for high-grade civilians, WRNS, the ATS and the WAAF.

Dissatisfaction with GC and CS's performance from above and below had been steadily mounting throughout the summer of 1941. It is likely this was one reason why Winston Churchill visited Bletchley Park that summer to meet some of the top men – including, of course, Stewart

Menzies, Alastair Denniston, Edward Travis, Malcolm Saunders (Head of Hut 3), Nigel de Grey, Professor John Coleman (the brilliant but easy-going Head of Hut 6), Alan Turing and Gordon Welchman. He toured the premises and asked a number of shrewd questions before standing on a tree stump to harangue selected members of the staff.

Complaints from customers were pressing. MI 8 felt that insufficient use was being made of the impressive TA results that the Y units were sending in and the decrypted material the cryptanalysts in Hut 6 were handing to Hut 3. Y units were very short of intercept receivers and computors, who sometimes were being filched by GC and CS to fill its own ranks. The cryptanalysts were desperate for more Bombes and people to work them. Criticisms from very high levels, as well as from the leading cryptanalysts, began to focus on the Y Board; in particular against its chairman, Denniston, and, by inference, on Menzies.

A complaint in September by the DMI (Director of Military Intelligence) centred on inferior overall control by the Y Board, which met only once a month. He pointed out that, in reality, it was GC and CS which was the real co-ordinator and that its people were out of touch with the Operational and Planning Directorates of the Ministries with '... no knowledge of our future operations'. DMI (briefed by MI 8) went on to propose that direction of SIGINT policy should be removed to the JIC (Joint Intelligence Sub-Committee) which worked for the Chiefs of Staff in London. This proposal was resisted by GC and CS, though with nothing like the conviction that it might have deployed. However, the Navy and RAF did not support the Army. There the matter rested for the time being as pressures on GC and CS gathered from other directions.

Commander Malcolm Saunders, Head of Hut 3, was at loggerheads with his top Army and RAF representatives, who regarded their responsibilities to their ministries as taking precedence over the hut. As an officer on loan from DNI (Director of Naval Intelligence), Saunders delegated his responsibilities to the Admiralty through another naval officer, and took the view that the senior Army and RAF intelligence officers should do the same. A bitter row escalated. Encouraged by their staffs of bright young officers, who were recruited from university dons (and therefore did not take kindly to contradiction), and businessmen (who were of the 'get-on-or-get-out' mentality), the Army and RAF LOs insisted that they should be given authority to deal direct with their own ministries, regardless of the fact that they were neither adequately experienced nor, on the RAF side, qualified pilots.

The dispute was referred to Travis, who discussed it with C's staff, under whom the Army and RAF intelligence officers came. Between them they concocted a complicated set of rules (referred to by de Grey as an ultimatum) for Denniston to approve on 10 October. All it did was create additional irritation and acrimony without solving the problem. De Grey, in his round-by-round commentary on the fight, remarks that it should never have been allowed to happen. He adds that this imbroglio of conflicting jealousies, intrigue and differing opinions was complicated by the clash of two strong and able personalities (the respective MI 8(a) and AI 1(e) in Hut 3) and the constant intervention of a third (unidentified by de Grey but probably Major Curtis). A fundamental cause of the trouble was the determination of the senior RAF officer, Group Captain Robert Humphreys, to take charge of Hut 3 in person. Humphreys, who already had done so much to improve the exploitation and dissemination of Hut 3 material and influence (see Chapter 7), went further than base his claim on his special grasp of the hut's workings: he also demanded the job for himself on the grounds that it mostly dealt with Luftwaffe intelligence. This was a retrograde step to which Saunders was resolutely opposed since it would destroy the vital principal of tri-service co-operation, of distribution, of integration of information and of ideas. As Deputy Director, who was fully in the know and a friend of Denniston from Room 40 days, de Grey levelled outright condemnation of Denniston, who 'was perfectly aware that the intelligence officers were not co-operating with the Head of Hut 3 ... and that the Head of Hut 3 might ... be considered too to blame, though perhaps sometimes acting under provocation'.

The imbroglio sizzled in a tense, unpleasant atmosphere. On 7 November 1941, Menzies issued revised procedural orders which were promptly rejected by the senior officers of Hut 3 as 'unworkable'. They saw that there would be nobody in the hut to act as an arbiter and to supervise the relatively inexperienced and untrained newcomers. In effect, the Head of the Hut would be reduced to an administrator. Travis remarked, 'I do not believe in administrators: I believe in heads!' Which nearly everybody in Hut 3 agreed with. So it was back to the drawing board.

In the meantime another bolt had been thrown into the machine: this time by five senior cryptanalysts in Hut 6, led by Alan Turing and Gordon Welchman. Probably aware of the battle for Hut 3, they were suffering from the same sort of inertia perpetrated by Denniston about which MI 8 was protesting without avail. On 21 October they sent a long letter, by hand of one of their number, to Winston Churchill at 10 Downing Street. It drew the Prime Minister's attention to serious shortcomings which were jeopardising their work in Huts 6 and 8 and their despair at the impossibility of getting anything done through the usual channels.

In summary they referred to overwork and shortages of clerks, typists and those who serviced the bombes in Huts 6 and 8. They emphasised that skilled male staff belonging to the British Tabulating Company, who had been exempt from military service, were now threatened with call-up. Already one section in Hut 8 had been forced to cease night shifts and the 'finding' of Enigma naval keys was being delayed by twelve hours. A similar situation existed in Hut 6 where shortage of typists and the fatigue of decoding staff were deleterious. They also pointed out that in July they had been promised WRNS to perform the testing of 'stories' for the bombes. None had yet arrived, with the result that staff required for other work had to be diverted to this task. To keep matters in proportion it could have been added that ATS and WAAF personnel were also in demand.

They expressed the opinion that the importance of their work was not being impressed with sufficient force on outside authorities. They wrote that they were acting entirely on their own initiative and emphatically made the point that Commander Travis was beyond their criticism. Let it be noted, however, that they did not grant credit to Denniston or Menzies and that the part in this protest played by Coleman (the Head of Hut 6) was obscure.

On the 22nd Churchill wrote one of his most important 'Action This

Day' minutes. 'Make sure they have all they want on extreme priority and report that this has been done.' This landed on Menzies' desk and caused a considerable stir. Four weeks later Menzies reported in person to the Prime Minister that every possible measure actually was being taken, although not yet complete in every detail. No doubt Menzies realised that he personally was under close scrutiny and that a day might come when he might be unable to continue supporting his old friend Denniston, who had been found wanting.

In fairness to Menzies it must be said that he had many more equally important concerns as chief of SIS. Among crucial matters was the nation's security against penetration by enemy agents, the turning of captured agents into double agents to work against their German masters, and the build-up of a network of friendly agents throughout Europe prior to the day when invasion of the Continent became feasible – or even at extremely high risk in 1942 to take pressure off Russia in case she came to the brink of collapse. He knew that GC and CS could not possibly provide all the intelligence required for that event, if only because General Fellgiebel's vast use of cable communications concealed masses of useful information. Yet he could not ignore the fact that the cryptanalysts of Hut 6 and 8 had alerted him to the dangers of the schism infecting GC and CS. So the new orders were imposed, the imbroglio rumbled on – and Hut 3 went on seething.

Intrigue went wild in mid-December when Major Curtis, the Military Intelligence Officer, launched a furiously critical attack on Hut 3 management in two papers to the DDMI (Deputy Director Military Intelligence Officer), one of which he did not copy to Denniston. He summed up by suggesting that all the hut's work should be in Army hands and that he should be in command of military personnel. When Denniston heard of this intrigue he realised that matters were out of hand and that even he was no longer in charge. To that effect he reported to Menzies.

By some miracle, at a time of intense activity in the Atlantic, in the Mediterranean and North Africa (as described in Chapter 10 above) when the number of intercepts multiplied and the cryptanalysts delved, the work of GC and CS, including Huts 3, 4, 6 and 8 actually improved! Despite, that is, the arrival of many new people in need of training and the deplorable atmosphere – as de Grey records. It certainly did not help ease matters when Menzies called in a brigadier (an outsider lacking SIGINT background) to investigate Hut 3. Needless to say the brigadier only distracted hard-pressed officers from their everyday, onerous tasks, although his long report did give Travis the opportunity to comment that he had no time for private armies and looked forward to the day when the SIS was no longer represented in Hut 3.

At last, on 5 February, Menzies, in his capacity of Director GC and CS, called a Y Board Meeting arbitrarily to settle the hierarchical impasse. Having already decided that a new team was needed to replace the old one which had failed, he chose Travis to represent GC and CS at the meeting. He then divided GC and CS into two – a Services Wing and a Diplomatic Wing with Travis in charge of the former and Denniston the latter. In due course a deeply wounded Denniston, along with the Diplomatic Wing, would be transferred to London. Appointed DD(S) (Deputy Director (Services)) Travis not only took command of the Services Wing but gathered within it the administration of the whole of Bletchley Park: thus bringing closer the day when Foreign Office involvement would be terminated.

Four days later Commander Travis was invited to a meeting with C, the DMI and ACAS (I) to settle Hut 3's future. To his astonishment he heard ACAS (I) announce that he no longer wished to be involved, but suggest that Humphreys, the resident Air Intelligence Officer (the AI 1) should be given his heart's desire as Head of the Hut. Under no circumstance was Travis prepared to accept in place the man who had caused so many of the troubles. All he would offer Humphreys was an office outside the hut - a sort of tent for the sulking Achilles (to quote de Grey).

Heads began to roll after yet another new set of rules for Hut 3 was drawn up in March. Like its predecessors it too proved unworkable due, this time, to the introduction of a so-called Triumvirate of three heads (previously seconds in command who were quite incompatible due to disparities in age and experience) chaired by a Foreign Office man who was out of his depth in military matters. Nevertheless, under Travis's leadership and firm hand (he was sometimes referred to as 'die Führer'), GC and

CS's output and reputation began to improve. In three months 19 watch-keeping officers joined Hut 3 of whom twelve were soldiers, four Foreign Office people and only two from the RAF. So it was not entirely surprising when, on 21 June, the incorrigible Humphreys wrote to Travis accusing Hut 3 of working at only 65 per cent efficiency: and once more insisting that Hut 3 should be under a RAF officer – himself.

Travis trenchantly rebutted this conspiratorial move in a definitive letter where he stated: 'I am, and have always been in favour of one man control providing that the right man can be found, that is loyally accepted by all and that he is allowed to work free from petty underground criticism by the Services to whom he does not belong ... I feel strongly that he should be freed from responsibility to any Ministry, that is to say, if he is an airman he should not be regarded as the Senior Air Intelligence Officer at BP but the Head of Hut 3.'

He also pointed out that the decisions of the meeting (of 9 February) had never been implemented by the War Office and Air Ministry, and was heard to say, 'I have not been given the staff officers I asked for.' A week later that wish was granted by the appointment of Sqn Ldr Eric Jones, (a wholesale cloth merchant) who, as an Air Intelligence Officer, had recently been attached to Hut 3 for a short period in which he made such a favourable personal impression that he was approved of by all parties on the Y Board and in the hut. Enough was enough among high-grade people who were fed up with what had gone before and wanted nothing but a firm hand on the tiller held by somebody who really believed in tri-service working. Saunders was moved, as was the turbulent Humphreys. The Foreign Office representative was made redundant, thus eliminating that department's foothold in the GC and CS hierarchy. Jones took over Hut 3 on 1 July with responsibility to Menzies through Travis.

It was not a moment too soon. Since April the war had intensified, crucial battles had been fought and SIGINT was in greater demand than ever as the struggle moved towards major shifts in the balance of initiatives.

CHAPTER TWELVE

POINT OF BALANCE

The ironic significance of Eric Jones's almost fortuitous appointment as Head of Hut 3 in 1942, and therefore as a partner with the absolutely essential tri-service Y organisation, came at a moment when the global war was in a fascinating state of strategic and technical flux. It was also, in the opinion of Nigel de Grey, in the year of most importance in the development of radio interception.

The land campaign in Russia was shaping along classical lines in a contest between armies that were merely supported by air power. But only in indirect support of their Russian allies could the British and Americans do much more than mount a strategic bombing offensive in Europe designed, over a long period in time, to smash Axis industry; and thereby take pressure off her while they built up sufficient strength for amphibious invasions. SIGINT was playing a part on the Russian front but with nothing like the significance of its role in the West where the bomber offensive and tri-service amphibious raiding depended crucially on its contribution.

Similarly, the Battle of the Atlantic, in both its strategic and tactical aspects, was largely ruled, for both sides, by electronic communications. All of these were wide open to intercept by ever better trained searchers and computors along with improvements to techniques that helped the navies and their supporting aircraft to profit from them. But at sea there was virtually no alternative means of communication, like Fellgiebel's network of land lines laid across the undeveloped Russian steppes. In the Atlantic everything hinged on the contest between secure, short, radio transmissions by the U-boats and the ever more deadly intercept technological facilities and the better DF techniques of those hunting them. Significantly indeed, for the following reasons, the SIGINT war at sea was moving in Y's favour, even though the Triton Enigma keys did remain unbroken.

To some extent the same parameters ruled throughout the even vaster sea and land spaces of the Far East and Pacific; except that there sea and air power were considerably more potent than land forces and the Allied Y Services far worse off than those of their compatriots in the West. On the one hand, everybody had to use radio to cover far greater spaces and to span much longer distances across water. This was a mixed blessing for the Japanese since it meant that they were forced to use the more easily interceptable lower frequency bands for their long range, strategic and diplomatic communications. Only when it came to shorter range, RT communications had they a modicum of safety from shore-based listening stations. On the other hand, the Allies had first to acquire sufficient facilities to replace what had been lost in 1942 and then build, almost from scratch, a new, viable organisation. How this task was tackled initially will be described in Chapter 13. Here we will deal with the earlier events of 1942 as they evolved.

FIRST THERE WAS the incursion of Japanese forces to the frontiers and seaboard of India. From a Y Service point of view this can be described quite briefly since they were, to all intents and purposes, inactive. After the Japanese occupied Thailand and bombed Rangoon on 23 and 25 December 1941, the sole warning of their approach came from a single British radar set. This enabled three fighter squadrons belonging to the American Volunteer Group (employed by the Chinese) to intercept and, by superior tactical skill, shoot down twenty-seven enemies for very small losses.

By the time the Japanese Army advanced into Burma from Thailand on 12 January the Y Service officer who had been sent only two weeks previously from Singapore to set up a local intercept organisation from nothing, had made little progress. Yet once more, as the Japanese Army Air Force tried to establish air superiority, it was repeatedly detected by radar and then caught and forced by RAF fighters to abandon day attacks. But after Rangoon fell on 7 March, the British and Chinese armies came under such heavy pressure from a superior enemy that nothing on earth could cancel their retreat. Yet not until 21 March, when radar failed them, were the British fighters caught by surprise on the ground to suffer such severe losses that air parity was forfeit. Come May, the Japanese had reached their strategic objectives by cutting the Burma Road (that carried essential supplies to China) and almost occupying the whole of Burma.

By then the Japanese Navy had made its presence felt most devastatingly in the Indian Ocean where, again, surprise was achieved due to lack of adequate British SIGINT and the fact that GC and CS and Y Service in England were mainly in ignorance of Japanese ciphers, call sign systems and, especially, whether they used RT for their ground to air communications. Furthermore, there was not only a dire shortage of interpreters but also some uncertainty about what sort of people were required in this new theatre of war. Improvisation was the watchword, disasters the pay-off.

When Admiral Sir James Somerville, commanding the British Eastern Fleet, received vague intelligence on 31 March from a Y unit in Ceylon that a major Japanese attack on his main base at Colombo was imminent, it was sufficient to make him put to sea and hope for the best. But it was not until 4 April that a flying boat found Admiral Nagumo's First Air Fleet with six carriers (the veterans of Pearl Harbor and Darwin) within a day's striking distance of Colombo harbour, where he assumed Somerville's fleet would be. But by then Somerville was persuaded that the Y report was a false alarm. So he had dispersed his fleet to refuel, and sent the fast ships to a secret base at Addu Atoll and the slower ones to Ceylon. The rival fleets were approaching each other in radio silence. Only Somerville was aware of his enemy's position, though only because radio silence was broken when the Japanese bombers struck Colombo on the 5th, and began sinking warships from the slow group at sea, including two heavy cruisers and a light aircraft carrier.

Meanwhile a Japanese raiding force of a light carrier and seven cruisers had sailed into the Bay of Bengal where, in three days uncontested mayhem, it sank twenty-three ships with a tonnage of 112,312 tons and bombed coastal targets in India. Nagumo then withdrew unmolested, having failed in his aim of destroying the Eastern Fleet. But he did achieve a strategic victory by starting an invasion scare in India and persuading the Eastern Fleet to retire to Mombasa and Kilindini in East Africa, where it would remain for more than a year.

When Japan decided on war in 1941, her naval C-in-C, Admiral Isoroku Yamamoto, declared he could raise hell for eighteen months, but after that things might be different. Excellent as his own radio communications were and multi-purpose his codes (the vast majority printed in bulky, elaborate code books), he had not taken into account how SIGINT might undermine that forecast – and cost him his life. In April, as Nagumo was venturing into the Indian Ocean, Yamamoto was bent on unfinished business as demanded by the original, pre-war plan – the capture of Port Moresby in Papua (Operation MO), of the Aleutian Islands (Operation AL) and Midway Island (Operation MI) – to establish the perimeter defences of a risky over-extended estate. These plans became known to the Americans early in April through Hypo, the US Navy radio intercept station at Pearl Harbor. There brooded Commander Joseph Rochefort, one of Safford's original colleagues back in 1925, and now a senior cryptanalyst and intelligence officer of high merit.

For a brief, post-Pearl Harbor attack period the Americans had been unable to break the Japanese Navy's JN 25 code, which carried 70 per cent of its operational traffic. Only gradually in April was its improved successor (JN 25b) penetrated sufficiently to make fragmentary sense of messages dealing with MI, AL and MO. Often the cryptanalysts would be helped in the search by the same sort of intercept give-aways as exposed German and Italian ciphers – operators' errors, radio fingerprinting and TA. Indeed, reflecting later about those days, the Americans officially admitted that even without success in decryption of JN 25b messages, sufficient warning of the Japanese intentions would have been given by TA and SIGINT.

Ordered by Admiral King to make an estimate of Japanese intentions, Rochefort produced an almost exact forecast of Yamamoto's plans. King was characteristically sceptical. Admiral Chester Nimitz (C-in-C Pacific Fleet) was not. Each day in Hawaii he was able to read in person and interpret the accumulating evidence from Hypo which fitted Rochefort's forecast like a glove. Then, on 24 April, an intercepted signal actually detailed the force allocated to MO (including three carriers, the key weapon systems), the objective and its almost exact timing. This was followed, day by day, with supplementary intercepts that enabled Nimitz to track the enemy and make the dispositions which, on 7 May, brought on the crucial, four-day Battle of Coral Sea.

Strategically Coral Sea was a victory for the Americans made possible by SIGINT because it enabled Nimitz to place two carriers under the command of Admiral Frank Fletcher exactly where they were required in order to neutralise the effect of three Japanese carriers and thwart Plan MO. During the ensuing battle, in which carriers found each other by air reconnaissance and remained many miles apart, SIGINT could do little to clarify the farrago of errors committed by the contending admirals. Ironically it was the cryptanalysts of Hypo in Hawaii who were among the first and best informed searchers as they roughly translated each Japanese signal on arrival to gauge accurately how went the day. For whereas the Japanese assumed they had sunk both American carriers, when only one had been put down, Hypo from intercept logged one Japanese carrier sunk and another severely damaged, along with heavy losses in élite aircrew. Ironically, however, it was not at that time possible to inform Fletcher in time to be of immediate use.

Absent though the benefits of practical tactical SIGINT were to the Americans, its longer-term strategic uses were invaluable. A week before the Battle of Coral Sea, Nimitz had little reason to doubt the truth of Rochefort's forecasts of Yamamoto's intentions, even though JN 25b was still only about 30 per cent mastered by the cryptanalysts. With the comfortable assurance that the Aleutians were only marginally threatened by Operation AL (as soon transpired when only a few worthless islands were occupied), Nimitz could secretly, under strict radio silence, concentrate his forlorn trio of three fleet carriers and thirteen cruisers (commanded by Admiral Raymond Spruance) to deal with the overwhelmingly imposing MI fleet. To compensate for this imbalance in strength, Nimitz could bank only on the sure knowledge that Midway was the objective, when it would be attacked and where by Nagumo's First Air Fleet, with four fleet carriers, two battleships and three cruisers, which also was the vanguard to the main force, with its three battleships and three medium carriers, and the back-up, amphibious occupation force, with two battleships and four heavy cruisers. Their actual position was uncertain, however, until 4 June.

Plainly it was not enough when, that day prior to the clash of carriers, costly efforts by Midway-based bombers failed to score hits on Nagumo's carriers. Had foiled Japanese SIGINT and incompetent air reconnaissance not then played a decisive hand, the result might have been disastrous for Spruance. But when Japanese radio intercept was thwarted by radio silence, and when one of their delayed, scouting seaplanes sent back two inadequate contact reports before, in a third, mentioning the presence of an American carrier, the odds swung against another triumph for the over-confident Nagumo. As it was, confusing reports, compounding an inherent indecisiveness, tricked him into an order–counter-order sequence of mistakes – errors which exposed his vulnerable, momentarily undefended carriers to devastating attacks by Spruance's bombers which inflicted fatal damage on three carriers and later led to the sinking of the fourth. The disaster persuaded Yamamoto to abandon Operation MI and thus to concede a strategic defeat of catastrophic implications which had been decided by SIGINT factors.

Henceforward for him and his country it was to be downhill all the way as Generals Rommel and Auchinleck stood on the threshold of a strategic decision in North Africa which, like Midway, might easily have swung either way at the almost exact halfway point of the war.

BEFORE THE LINE settled in mutual exhaustion at Gazala on 4 February 1942 it was apparent that the Y Services' main efforts were focusing on the Mediterranean and Middle East theatres of war. Without the remotest possibility of land operations in North-west Europe, General Fellgiebel had managed to divert the major portion of German Army and, to a lesser extent, on-going Luftwaffe signals traffic from radio to cable. Therefore RAF Y was the principal player in air operations based on Britain as well as being heavily involved with support of Y units in North Africa – where the Army was chiefly engaged. It is significant that when young Aileen Morris, now a highly experienced and respected WAAF officer sporting a MBE, went in January to join the joint service staff of HQ Y Service at

Suez Road, Heliopolis, and to help bring RAF Field Units in the Middle East up-to-date with SIGINT techniques, she was sent on a top priority flight among senior VIPs in a Boeing Clipper flying boat.

No doubt her transfer was a result of a recent visit to Heliopolis by the new Inspector of RAF Y, Air Commodore Blandy. For his visit coincided with the influx of units and their equipment and the expansion of RAF Y Service into a wing consisting of ten Field Units (similar to HDUs in the UK) spread from Malta, the Western Desert Front, Alexandria, the Levant, Iraq and Iran. These were tasked to intercept, process and quickly relay, via Heliopolis, to GC and CS the rising flood of unencrypted material for cryptanalysis in Hut 6 and its evaluation in the embattled Hut 3. Unlike the HDUs, however, the RAF Field Units and the many Army Field Units were now mounted in motor vehicles and capable of moving at an hour's notice and setting up close to the battle fronts at headquarters and forward airfields.

The enemy strategic traffic intercepted was usually powerful WT or RT carried on high frequencies, although the VHF RT was mainly monitored by the Field Units. It had been anticipated that co-operation with Army FUs would be very close. But this proved illusory. Airfields and army headquarters tended to occupy different pieces of real estate – the latter liable to move about far more. It turned out that CBME at Heliopolis was the best place to co-ordinate intelligence. Here, far from incidentally, the best source of translators could be found, many of whom were German-speaking Jews recruited in Palestine. Considered by some as a security risk, they proved thoroughly loyal. After all, no race had a greater interest in defeating Germany.

The arrival of Kesselring's Second Air Fleet in January portended an all-out assault on Malta and the convoys from Gibraltar. Needless to say, German and Italian agents in Spain kept ceaseless watch on the assembly and departures of convoys. Their reports usually were sent to Berlin and Rome by radio and therefore were monitored by Y. Each convoy sailing was accompanied by a flurry of Abwehr signals and always came under ferocious attack, usually without tactical warning. Until June 1942, that is, when ships carried so-called Naval Headache and RAF Y computor parties; the former equipped with receivers to monitor enemy airborne RT transmissions, the latter to evaluate their content for instant exploitation.

Similarly, although the air defence of Malta benefited to some extent from sketchy decrypts of Enigma giving notice of selected enemy targets, the best tactical intelligence came from the hard-pressed RAF Y Field Unit and from radar. To train that unit in the latest techniques of VHF RT intercept, Aileen Morris, sponsored by Air Marshal Sir Arthur Tedder, who had to override the trenchant objections of the WAAF Queen Bee in Cairo, was flown into Malta in mid-January. At that time other service women were being evacuated. She spent two months there, repeatedly under fire, and was officially commended for greatly improving the quality of local SIGINT and for shortening the warning times for incoming raids.

These improvements did little to mitigate the aerial bombardment. They simply underlined the old martial lesson that sheer weight of numbers will often neutralise even the highest-quality intelligence. The passing of convoys to Malta became prohibitively expensive at the same time as it became almost impossible to prevent Axis convoys reinforcing their forces in Cyrenaica. Moreover, as SIGINT began to reveal that the Axis were planning an invasion of the island that would be co-ordinated with a major offensive at Gazala, the Luftwaffe on 1 April introduced a radical change in its handling of minor code books that proved so complicated and effective that, for a time, it baffled the Y Service computors – to the extent that it was feared TA would no longer produce enough operational intelligence to justify the existence of the Field Units and, perhaps, the seaborne computors.

Ten days feverish experiment did produce a working arrangement whereby Field Units were concentrated at Sidi Barrani and Alexandria in order to obtain the fullest cover of all enemy frequencies. At the same time CBME at Heliopolis became the collecting centre for the entire Mediterranean, with Cheadle and GC and CS brought in 'at second instance'.

Army Y produced a large quantity of SIGINT material foretelling the thrust line of General Rommel's Gazala offensive which began on 26 May, although Enigma contributed nothing comprehensive in the aftermath of a Chaffinch decrypt on 30 April. Unfortunately for General Ritchie, commanding Eighth Army, his intelligence staff blundered badly by under-rating the accurate evidence of a captured German NCO and failing to connect this with accumulated Y reports of low grade SIGINT that clearly (if controversially) showed that the enemy Panzer Army was going to swing wide to the south to outflank the Army's strongly defended line.

Over a period of four weeks, Y identified and located most of the principal formations and key units of the Panzer Army as they moved into position. But whereas their Field Unit IOs interpreted the intercepts specifically for the operational staffs, they were not in close touch with the intelligence staff. And were therefore in ignorance of what Chaffinch Enigma (usually decrypted a week late by GC and CS) and the German NCO were saying; and unable to contribute to what could, and should, have been a valuable and timely dialogue which might have helped Ritchie to nullify Rommel's chance of surprise.

This is not the place to enter into a blow-by-blow description of the Gazala battle which led, through British defeat, to the surrender of Tobruk on the 20th, which was first notified by an Army Y intercept of Rommel's triumphant claim; nor of the nigh headlong withdrawal to a shortened front at El Alamein, which induced what became known as Ash Wednesday in Cairo and Heliopolis when certain, panicky headquarters filled the air with burnt confidential papers.

Y, of course, played its part to a considerable degree if only because its resources were so much larger, with newly arrived receivers and DF equipment that were vast improvements on the old, and with operators who were better trained than ever before. It had contributed through listening to the usual sources, chiefly the Luftwaffe Enigma, including that of Kesselring's Second Air Fleet. The start time was affirmed by an Army Y intercept and its correct interpretation of the code word Venezia. There can be little criticism of the volume of intercepts registered and their potential for dealing commanders a winning hand. The major criticisms, that were made long before Ultra became public knowledge, largely stand in their castigations of the most senior British commanders, from divisional level upward to General Auchinleck at the top. The soldiers fought well enough given the chance – but all too often were let down by incompetence at the higher levels of command.

Tactical SIGINT from Field Units provided a running commentary on German strengths, logistic weaknesses and setbacks; these might have been exploited – but rarely were. After 31 May, decrypted Chaffinch and other Army Enigma keys were rarely available more than twenty-four hours behind interception and sometimes half that time. This intelligence announced Rommel's defensive/offensive attritional intention when the battle swung against him on 31 May. But he was receiving Seebohm's first-rate interpretation of his searchers – and making superior use of them. Luftwaffe SIGINT was, as usual, its prolific, revealing self and, along with Chaffinch, becoming ever more generous. In fact the Y Service units were providing insight into every Enigma key used in North Africa, all of which were being decrypted to some extent. This was quite apart from low-grade material computed by the Field Units, unless, of course, they were unable to receive when on the run with the rest of Eighth Army, or after they were killed or captured, as quite a number were.

Sad as was the debacle, it had a cheering aspect, illuminated by the steady, empirically, improved use by headquarters staff of Y material – strategic and tactical, low and medium grade. Even if, at times, the sheer pace of events left decrypts in arrears, Y was in process of finding its feet during mobile operations; and the headquarters they served were beginning at last to integrate them fully in response to lessons learned the hard way.

Step by step SIGINT revealed that Rommel, now logistically abundant with vast quantities of supplies captured in Tobruk, was hell-bent on a drive to Alexandria and Cairo, having persuaded Hitler and Mussolini to abandon the invasion of Malta. From the moment Rommel headed for Mersa Matruh, he was being tracked by Army Y besides air and ground reconnaissance. Warned by a flood of intelligence from GC and CS, besides his own resources, and aware of a collapse of morale and the chaotic state of Eighth Army's communications, General Auchinleck (who had taken personal command of that army in addition to his role as C-in-C Middle East) withdrew to the as yet unprepared Alamein line. This was a

Admiral Sir Henry Jackson, the first man to transmit and receive a radio impulse. (*Imperial War Museum* Q80194)

ABOVE A British radio transmitter of 1917. Note the large thermionic valves. (*Author's collection*)

OPPOSITE German signallers transmitting by key in 1914. (*Author's collection*)

LEFT British Command and Control tank T236 accompanied by light tanks for liaison tasks, 1931. Security of transmissions from radio intercept was rudimentary for many years to come. (*Broad*)

BELOW LEFT Brigadier Charles Broad in command of T236. (*The Tank Museum* 1586/A4)

BELOW German radio searchers listening in. (*Imperial War Museum* HU3807)

BOMBE

ABOVE Generals Fellgiebel and Guderian with Colonel Praun, 1941. (*Nachrichtentruppe*)

OPPOSITE, ABOVE A German telephonist in the field. Telephony was secure against intercept, unless the enemy was able to tap or cut the cable. (*Imperial War Museum* STT848)

OPPOSITE, BELOW An American-designed Bombe. (*Imperial War Museum* HU56940)

RIGHT Nigel de Grey, Deputy Director of the Government Code and Cipher School at Bletchley Park. (*Bletchley Park*)

OPPOSITE, ABOVE A WAAF searching at Kingsdown. (*C. Jones*)

OPPOSITE, BELOW A Geheim-schreiber, the German 'secret writing' machine. (*Imperial War Museum* HU54699)

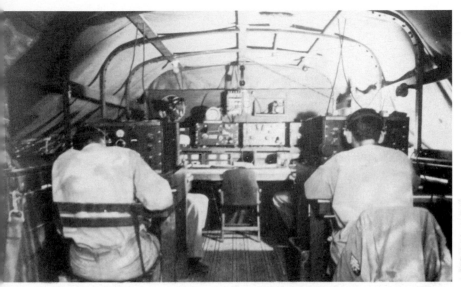

ABOVE Interior of a British radio intercept truck. (*Hugh Skillen*)
BELOW Interior of US 'I' vehicle of 128 RI Company. (*Hugh Skillen*)
OPPOSITE The four-wheel Enigma machine. (*Bletchley Park*)

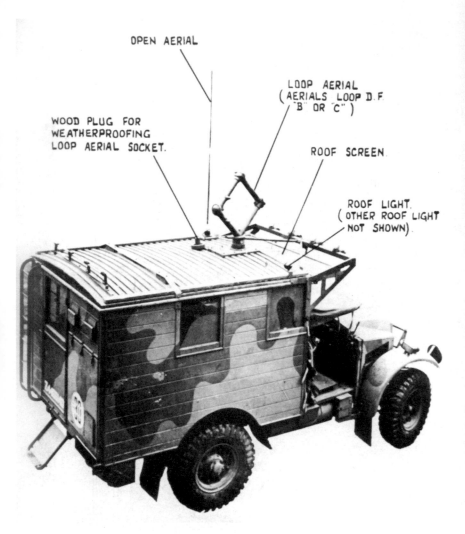

OPEN AERIAL

LOOP AERIAL
(AERIALS LOOP D.F.
"B" OR "C")

WOOD PLUG FOR
WEATHERPROOFING
LOOP AERIAL SOCKET.

ROOF SCREEN.

ROOF LIGHT.
(OTHER ROOF LIGHT
NOT SHOWN).

ABOVE British 15cwt truck DF station. (*Hugh Skillen*)

OPPOSITE An interior view of the same, with the operator's seat removed.
(*Hugh Skillen*)

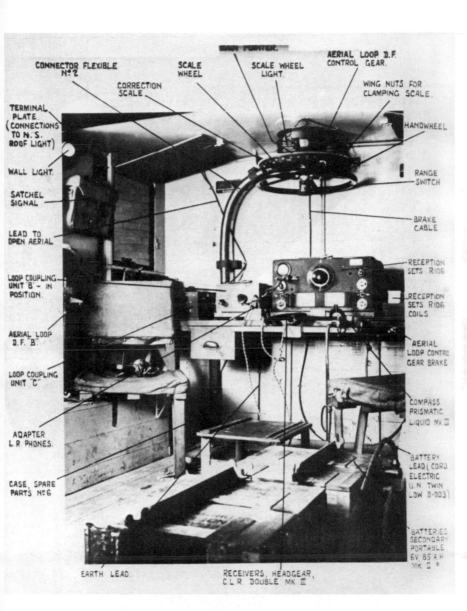

MAIN POWER.

CONNECTOR FLEXIBLE Nº 2

SCALE WHEEL

SCALE WHEEL LIGHT.

AERIAL LOOP D.F. CONTROL GEAR.

CORRECTION SCALE

WING NUTS FOR CLAMPING SCALE.

TERMINAL PLATE (CONNECTIONS TO N.S. ROOF LIGHT)

HANDWHEEL

WALL LIGHT.

RANGE SWITCH

SATCHEL SIGNAL

LEAD TO OPEN AERIAL

BRAKE CABLE

LOOP COUPLING UNIT 'B' - IN POSITION.

RECEPTION SETS R106

RECEPTION SETS R106 COILS

AERIAL LOOP D.F. 'B'.

AERIAL LOOP CONTROL GEAR BRAKE

LOOP COUPLING UNIT 'C'

COMPASS PRISMATIC LIQUID Mk III

ADAPTER L.R PHONES.

BATTERY LEAD (CORD ELECTRIC U.N TWIN LOW 0·003)

CASE, SPARE PARTS Nº 6

BATTERIES SECONDARY PORTABLE 6V. 85 A.H MK II *

EARTH LEAD.

RECEIVERS, HEADGEAR, C.L.R. DOUBLE MK III

ABOVE HMS *Bulolo*, Landing Ship Headquarters (Large). Note the various radio and radar antennae. (*Imperial War Museum* W23598)
OPPOSITE, BELOW Two 'Gin Palace' 5-ton intercept trucks, set up back-to-back with a canopy between them. (*Royal Signals Museum*)

Navy, Army and Royal Air Force operators at work – an example of tri-service cooperation – aboard HMS *Bulolo*. (*Imperial War Museum* A13842)

wise decision taken on the strength of accumulating SIGINT which indicated the failing stamina of the overstretched Panzer Army and the denial
of Luftwaffe support (due to exhaustion) when the RAF was making life
extremely difficult for them.

So promptly were Enigma decrypts now reaching Auchinleck at HQ
Eighth Army that he was occasionally able to make tactical use of them.
For example, the time of Rommel's attack on 1 July was known on 30
June, although the exact plan was obscure and the actual start delayed: not
that it mattered since it gave the defenders more time to prepare and hold
fast against whatever came their way. Moreover, at this critical moment,
Y managed to solve a long-standing disagreement concerning the actual
enemy tank strength, a calculation which was confirmed by escaped
British officers.

Rommel's attempts to break through foundered against an ever-stiff-
ening defence held in place by concentrated artillery fire and bombing of
his troops whose moves were known in advance. Worse still, his own SIG-
INT received a crushing blow early on 10 July when men of the 9th
Australian Division drove back an Italian division at Tel el Aisa and surrounded Seebohm's intercept vehicle. Why it was located a mere 600
yards behind the front is unknown. Seebohm was killed and several of
his men killed and wounded, in addition to junior officers and operators
captured in the fighting and their vehicles seized undamaged.

In that vehicle was found a Pandora's box loaded with everything
to be expected in a very special intercept control room: German orders of
battle, call signs, frequencies and codes in current use or about to be introduced. Far more shattering was the discovery of how well equipped the
German equivalent of a British Field Unit was. Files of cross-referenced
documents revealed the extent to which Seebohm and his people had penetrated British SIGINT security; and the appalling fact that for six months
Kesselring, Rommel and OKW had been privy, through the broken code of
the American Military Attaché in Cairo, whose reports to Washington
revealed very high level intelligence indeed which had been vital
to Axis planning. Moreover, interrogation of Seebohm's second-in-
command, Leutnant Herz, revealed such appalling flaws in British Army

radio procedures that, as a matter of the greatest urgency, the whole system had to be radically changed and all operators instructed in what not to do in the future.

Serious as was the loss to Rommel of Seebohm's expertise and insight into the enemy's mind, organisation and methods, it was not the absolute disaster sometimes suggested. Nevertheless it took two months for the Panzer Army's intercept service to be restored to full strength. But by then the First Battle of Alamein had ended in stalemate and the balance of strengths in the Middle East had changed radically.

Strategically important though the drama of Kesselring's and Rommel's adventures in North Africa were, by comparison with the massive offensive taking place in Russia they were almost incidental. For as the Wehrmacht struck eastward again, heading for Stalingrad and the Caucasus, there now was implanted, for the first time, in Allied minds (if not that of their enemies) a vision of a coherent strategy connecting Rommel's presence at Alamein to the emerging threat from the Caucasus. This made it all the more important for Y Services in Cairo and London to position Field Units in Iraq and Persia, searching for signs of a cogent threat from the north which the ever-secretive Russians might not care to mention.

Indeed it was a matter of Allied concern that the most complete news of the Russian situation and emerging plight came from the Germans, not the Russians. Early in April, Enigma began to give notice of an operational stalemate when the extremely costly Russian winter offensive stopped. Rumour inferred a number of future possible German offensive actions, not all in Russia. But rumour came mainly from dubious SIS sources, whereas SIGINT was usually concrete and, in April, providing evidence of just one renewed offensive against Russia, probably aimed at Caucasian oil. Virtually conclusive were intercepted signals from Oshima, the Japanese Ambassador in Berlin, who fully expected a thrust through the Caucasus to the Persian Gulf. The validity of these signals was reinforced when, on 8 May, the Germans and their Italian, Romanian, Spanish and Hungarian allies resumed limited, preliminary offensive operations in the south between Kursk and Kharkov and in the Crimea. This was followed shortly afterwards by the revelation, when Luftwaffe Enigma confirmed earlier SIS and diplomatic reports, that Stalingrad was an objective.

The main German offensive was launched on 28 June and by its strength and accelerating pace against an apparently crumbling Russian Army gave reason for the Allied Chiefs of Staff to up-date plans designed to take desperate measures in the event of a Russian collapse. SIGINT confirmed Stalingrad and the Caucasus as the main objectives. Stalingrad was reached at the end of August when a German advanced guard was within 60 miles of Grozny in the foothills of the Caucasus mountains. It is against the background of these events that events in the Arctic, Western Europe and over Germany must now be described from Y's point of view.

FOREMOST IN ALLIED strategic considerations was the need to supply the Russians as well as to divert Axis pressure from them. In 1942 the supply route through Persia was not developed and the course through the Arctic Ocean to Archangel and Murmansk at high risk from German naval and air interdiction. Arctic convoys had been started in August 1941 and were not seriously opposed until February 1942 when Hitlerian intuition, convinced of the likelihood of an Allied invasion of Norway, prompted a considerable strengthening of that country's defences. It was a strategy which not only committed troops but a substantial Luftwaffe and naval reinforcement. SIGINT contributed by the Royal Navy's Polyarno intercept station, as well as UK HDUs and Cheadle kept GC and CS up-to-date with the arrival in Norwegian waters of major German Navy units, in addition to some fifteen U-boats by May. The great battleship *Tirpitz* reached Trondheim in mid-January to be followed by the cruisers *Scheer* and *Prinz Eugen* in February, *Hipper* in March and *Lützow* in May, along with escort vessels. All of these movements were notified through TA as well as Enigma.

Convoys PQ 12 and QP 8 which, respectively, sailed from Britain and Russia on 1 March, were the first to be threatened by *Tirpitz*, which put to sea with her escorts on the 6th. The ensuing game of blind-man's-buff was to be typical of more to come when competing SIGINT was either misinterpreted or misapplied in thick weather without contact being made. At one moment *Tirpitz* passed a mere ten miles ahead of the lightly escorted QP 8. At two others, to compound confusion, characteristically long transmissions by a U-boat were attributed to *Tirpitz*. Both convoys got through unscathed and *Tirpitz* also was lucky on her way home not to be hit when attacked by torpedo aircraft.

PQ13 was the first convoy to be attacked from the air on 27 March when the longer summer daylight hours prevailed. It lost two ships out of nineteen from bombs, two from U-boats and one straggler picked off by destroyers. In the spring and summer months to come this ratio of cause of loss shifted in favour of air attack by bomb and torpedo. Between 21 August 1941 and December 1942, out of 533 sailings to and from Russia, thirty-eight were sunk by aircraft, twenty-five by U-boats and only two by destroyers. SIGINT always gave ample warning – of the negative sort through lack of Enigma when the big units chose to stay at anchor. Indeed, at this time, most useful intelligence was being provided by the Swedes who were tapping into the German cable to Norway and passing it on via the British Naval Attaché in Stockholm. It was this source which gave warning that PQ 17 was going to be strongly opposed after it sailed on 27 June.

The PQ 17 story has been told many times and need not be retold here. At the crux of the matter was the decision by the First Sea Lord, Admiral Sir Dudley Pound, to disperse the convoy when it seemed possible to him, on available intelligence, to be directly threatened by *Tirpitz* , *Hipper, Scheer* and *Lützow*. Through radio intercept, submarine and air reconnaissance both sides were sufficiently aware of the other's movements to make sensible plans. The account in Harry Hinsley's *British Intelligence in the Second World War*, Vol. 2, is definitive. Crucially, Commander Norman Denning, the officer responsible for appreciations about the enemy fleet, had assured Pound that he was confident *Tirpitz* was in Altenfjord on 4 July – as soon was confirmed by TA and Enigma and agreed by Hinsley in Hut 8 at GC and CS.

Denning's appreciation was not accepted and Pound, in consultation with the DDIC (Deputy Director Operational Intelligence Centre), concluded that *Tirpitz* had already sailed when, in fact, she did not do so until 1700 hrs 5 July. Therefore, in the knowledge that the enemy were aware through (intercepted) U-boat reports that the Home Fleet (which was positioned to guard against the far greater threat of *Tirpitz* breaking out into the Atlantic) could not reach PQ 17 in time to save it. It mattered not that *Tirpitz* was not sent to sea until the Luftwaffe had located the Home Fleet on the 5th. For already, at 2215 hrs on the 4th, Pound had ordered the convoy to disperse, after an attempt to dissuade him had failed. Hinsley points out that, if Denning had managed to persuade Pound to order the convoy to reverse course, worse might have followed after Enigma disclosed at 1517 hrs that *Tirpitz* was ready to sail, which she did at 1700 hrs. In those circumstance, says Hinsley, ' he would have had no choice but to order it to scatter on 5 July'.

German SIGINT had played a crucial role leading up to the sinking of seventeen merchant ships out of thirty-three by aircraft and U-boats. *Tirpitz* and her surface consorts had been recalled at 2130 hrs, once it was realised that the dispersed convoy was prey to aircraft which, in constant daylight, could at minimum risk hunt their targets over a far greater expanse of water than surface vessels. The PQ 17 disaster amounted to a classic example of the principle that, no matter how complete the intelligence, the uncertainties of war eventually inject the balancing factors of chance, which prey most heavily on the minds of commanders when weighing imponderables.

There would be no more Arctic convoys until September when the nights were longer. Yet, as PQ 17's scattered ships were being massacred, it was Grand Strategy and the vital Battle of the Atlantic which Admirals Raeder and Dönitz had on their minds – factors British SIGINT could read only indirectly.

For his part Raeder, a great strategist, had it in mind that at that moment, when the land war was finely balanced and news from the Pacific most distressing, a German naval reverse was highly undesirable. Meanwhile Dönitz had to report that his U-boats, despite nearly six months of gratuitous successes off the USA coast and in the Caribbean, were no longer having it all their own way. Also he was beginning to worry about being outmatched by enemy defensive measures and technology. He was always very sensitive to conditions which made the U-boats' task so difficult as to be unproductive, let alone costly in boats sunk. As a counter to this he preferred to infest operational areas which were thinly defended; where convoys were meagrely escorted on the surface and not at risk from the air. This meant a return to mid-Central and North Atlantic where air patrols were non-existent.

Most worrying for the U-boats were the increasing number of occasions when hunting craft homed on to them at night. The consensus among captains that radar was responsible received little support from German scientists. Their own proclivity to sending long messages as a welcome aid to Y Service homing by DF was given less credibility. Ignorance of the effect of ship-borne Headache parties and improving DF techniques, erratic as they were known to be, deterred captains and helped contain sinkings per boat at a rate of about 300 tons per boat per day during the 'happy' period prior to June 1942. What made it look progressively worse for the Allies, of course, was the ever-increasing number of boats at sea which rose to about 100 in October – a month when the number of U-boats sunk was eight, but followed the next month by only two.

These benefits seem not to have encouraged the Germans who were much more concerned about the apparently better tactics of those hunting them and the weird 'noises' made by ships equipped with new sonic devices. Only marginally effective as these devices were, they did undermine the submariners' morale, especially when the staff and scientists tended to dismiss their worries. In fact, of course, there were far more hunters now available, although these were still groping for U-boats. Above all, Allied SIGINT was hamstrung by the continuing impregnability of the Triton Enigma. Indeed, as previously mentioned, no headway was made against its keys until December 1942 when the German Meteorological cipher helped show the way shortly before Turing and his colleagues made the big break in January 1943. Until then, therefore, there was acute despondency bordering upon defeatism among Allied leaders, politicians and sailors in the know; such was the importance of SIGINT to those who really had come to appreciate its war-winning potential.

The convoy battles played a part in taking the strain off the Russians. Amphibious raiding of the enemy coastline had little effect. Indeed the summer of 1942 was notable for only one large-scale operation – the notorious landing of a Canadian division supported by tanks and commandos at Dieppe on 19 August.

Correctly the Dieppe raid has been described as an essential reconnaissance in force designed to reveal the problems involved in a major assault on a strongly fortified sector of Germany's so-called Atlantic Wall. It was meant to teach lessons which no amount of study and exercises could do. This it most certainly did in even larger measure than expected due to numerous failures at practically every level by all services involved. The Y Service was no exception to that, although, inevitably, due to routine German radio silence, SIGINT provided nothing of value prior to the landing.

A special, improvised Y plan was made to what was visualised as a very complicated and intense event. An RAF officer from the Air Section in Hut 3, who was a protagonist of centralised reporting of the Luftwaffe Fighter Defence, was attached to the Operations Room of 11 Group to act as a filter for material from HDUs to Cheadle and Kingsdown. The aim was to reduce the time taken to pass decrypted, tactical material from German radar, observer posts and fighter control to one vital point at 11 Group where 'the most expert officer in Y on German Fighter Defence and its ramifications ... was placed ... to act as an interpreter of the material'.

The scheme failed, partly because a quite unprecedented volume of traffic was generated by the massed reaction of the Luftwaffe to the raid, but largely due to the weaknesses of the experimental system which was prepared far too late, lacked proper apparatus and was manned by unbriefed people without knowledge of what was expected of them. For example, Kingsdown (unbriefed about the operational situation) failed to detect the approach of enemy fighter reinforcement of the Dieppe sector from far afield. The special 6IS Fish party (which had only just been set up) had not been given prior warning and therefore was unready and prone to missing important intelligence. The War Room at 11 Group became congested as Luftwaffe reaction multiplied.

The failure of the experiment was not wasted. The lessons learned would be applied not only to the forthcoming amphibious operation in north-west Africa (Torch) but also in support of daylight bombing by the Eighth US Army Air Force, which had made its first strategic bombing attack on a target in France two days before Dieppe, and which also supported the raid.

DIEPPE COST THE RAF 106 aircraft, plus eight American fighters. The Germans lost forty-eight plus twenty-four damaged – well below the ninety-two kills, thirty-nine probably destroyed and 140 damaged claimed by the RAF. Discrepancies of this magnitude were common – the record probably was held by the Eighth Army Air Force which, in a raid on Lille in October, claimed 102 when, in fact, only one German machine was shot down.

The need to help the Russians by every means possible placed a heavy load on the RAF. In 1941 it had suffered badly in fighter sweeps (known as Rhubarbs). These recommenced in March 1942 and losses were heavier still – 259 by mid-June with only fifty-eight German fighters shot down – far less than the 197 claimed. Nevertheless, SIGINT discovered that the strategic aim had, to some extent, been achieved in that Luftwaffe reinforcements were being attracted to France and Belgium (among them the new, powerful FW 190) at a time when it was made plain (again by SIGINT) that the Luftwaffe was overstretched and short of machines.

Meanwhile RAF Bomber Command had suffered heavy losses against the Kammhuber Line in 1941 for poor results against what few targets it found and hit. But in February 1942, under Air Marshal Arthur Harris, it was on the eve of its major strategic offensive. Harris was convinced he could best help Russia and win the war by destroying industrial cities with area bombing, which he also believed would break national morale. To achieve the aim he was dependent on new tactics made feasible by bigger and better bombers, new technology and new techniques. He would be heavily dependent on SIGINT to help overcome the enemy fighter force, anti-aircraft artillery, early warning systems and distractions.

To meet these demands the Chiefs of Staff in January 1942 had authorised at high priority a huge expansion of the Y Service, with sufficient personnel to work the 993 additional receivers on a twenty-four-hour, seven-day-week basis – requiring five people per static HDU set and three per mobile Field Unit set. Administratively this demanded an extensive building programme to house receiver and communications equipment, accommodation, training schools and hard standing for many more vehicles. Cheadle, Chicksands, Dunstable and Beaumanor were enlarged and reinforced by a new station at Shaftsbury in Dorset. Essentially, therefore, many more Bombes were needed in Huts 6 and 8 at GC and CS along with much enlarged buildings to hold them and the teams of RAF men, who were trained by the British Tabulating Machine Company, to keep them working efficiently in compliance with an elaborate checking system. Furthermore, there loomed ahead a totally new requirement, the provision of buildings to accommodate the equipment which would be needed to cope with Fish (Geheimschreiber). For, by mid-1941, Geheimschreiber machines were transmitting high-speed, non-morse encrypted messages over a slowly increasing number of links.

(It is worth noting that, by 1945, there were 212 British Bombes in Hut 6, of which just over fifty were shared with Hut 8. There also were six British Bombes held in America for use by Hut 6, which also had recourse to 112 US Navy Department Bombes).

The complexity of these constantly growing, integrated organisations surely needs no exaggeration. Equally it must not be overlooked that a proper sense of responsibility now spread through GC and CS as Travis and Jones made their exemplary leadership felt. A significant factor in this was the end of Royal Navy separation when, in May, some sailors from Hut 8 joined Hut 3. Also a much more professional relationship with the RAF officers in Hut 3 grew. At last genuine, tri-service collaboration was inducing a more confident mood which raised standards of accuracy by individuals in teams that were handling masses of diverse, yet interrelated, material from numerous sources. Concerning those individuals, de Grey wrote about the qualities needed by anybody tackling controversial material: 'Of him was demanded an awareness of a delicate kind, the hardiest horse sense and a quick power to detect any aroma of suspicion and that he should decide with promptitude.'

These talents, however, had to be succinctly and currently presented to the customers; and it was Messrs Bonsall, Moyes and Prior of GC and CS who, in June 1942, achieved this with what became known as daily BMP reports. These consolidated all the products of SIGINT from sub-sections in a comprehensive picture of the German (Air) Defensive System in action. They were in tabular, column form under the headings of Area of Offensive, RAF Plan of Operation, German opposition reported, German radar plots, Observer Corps reports and Fighter Action. In the months to come they would be elaborated as RAF Y discovered new and subtle changes of value.

BMPs served all RAF operational Commands, but none more so than Bomber Command (when at last it chose to make use of them) as it sought intelligence about ever-reacting Luftwaffe defensive measures. Hut 3's Research Section (3G) was diligently examining all kinds of intelligence which, to a very large extent, came from Y. The list was long but included new and changing codes, code words within Enigma texts, official returns, radar, observer corps traffic, night fighters, Ground-Controlled-Interception (GCI) – all of which were of immense interest to ADI (Sci), Dr R. V. Jones, in the on-going radio war of 'noises' and new, electronic weapon systems. Then there was the search for information about enemy topography, map-grids, thrust lines (Stosslinie), map reference points, anti-submarine patrol areas, Luftwaffe target numbers, Orders of Battle, terminology and technical terms - anything which gave the slightest insight into the scope and workings of the Kammhuber Line. Vital was the study of the Horchdienst's penetration of Allied (including Russian) enciphered signals, plus urgent searching for evolving Fish traffic.

Without this kind of intelligence, Harris and his staff would have been working blind. Largely due to Y, it nearly always could discern fundamental, as well as minor, weaknesses in Kammhuber's defences. The idea for the first 1,000 bomber raid on Cologne on 30 May was based on the realisation that his Little Screw system was vulnerable to the saturation effect on night fighters and their controllers of a concentrated stream of bombers approaching an area target; thus effectively reducing casualties.

Every day a controlling element in decisions concerning if and where attacks should be launched depended upon timely meteorological reports via Dunstable. Such information, of course, was also essential to Fighter and Coastal Commands as well as the Navy, and was often amplified by Cheadle from its listening to low-grade, encoded airfield weather reports.

Needless to say radar was of paramount importance to both sides in the air battles. Germany lagged behind Britain from the outset in this technology and the latter, through intercept of 'noises' and other sources, such as interrogation of POW, was usually well informed about the Freya sets for early warning and the Giant Würzburg sets after they came into service in 1940. Vital equipment from the latter was seized in the famous Bruneval commando raid in February 1942 and its role in the Kammhuber Line for vectoring fighters to close range of bombers was then understood. In due course RT intercepts of night fighter successes in a non-searchlight area around Flushing suggested the existence of airborne radar - such as Britain already had in service late in 1940. This was Lichtenstein with its 200 to 3000 metres range of acquisition. Initially most unpopular with the majority of pilots because its cumbersome antenna reduced speed by 25 mph, it clearly posed a serious threat even to the concentrated bomber stream.

Yet Bomber Command showed little interest at first and it required Air Section's insistence at GC and CS, in a cogent June report, to demonstrate the nature of the threat, though without discovering the frequencies employed. Backed by ADI (Sc), a Wellington bomber from 80 Wing equipped for intercept and manned by an expert operator (Pilot Officer Harold Jordan) was flown over the Flushing area where it was duly attacked by a fighter. Jordan was among those wounded, but he stuck to his post and the vital data from the experiment (including 61 cm frequency) was repeatedly transmitted to base to ensure they were received. Pilot Officer Paulton then managed to fly his badly damaged Wellington home to ditch it 200 yards off shore, where the crew was picked up within ten minutes! From this gallant effort stemmed the progressive policy of jamming German radar in the interests of bomber survival, and the never-ending evolution of Radio Counter Measures (RCM), allied to tactical changes by both sides, which, time and again, were prompted and guided by Y's massive contribution to SIGINT.

The struggle in the skies of western Europe will not be pursued in this chapter, except to say that, although 1942 was the most important year for radio intercept, it had yet to demonstrate its full potential in relation to its size. Nevertheless, without the counter-measures and new tactics, which held bomber losses within acceptable bounds, it might not have been possible in January 1943 for the Combined American and British Chiefs of Staff whole-heartedly to adopt the round-the-clock heavy bomber offensive which, in the months to come, proceeded expensively with controversial results. That story, as it involved SIGINT, will be continued in Chapter 15.

In the meantime, air power in support of sea and land forces was playing a decisive role as the Allies rebounded globally on the offensive.

CHAPTER THIRTEEN

REBOUND IN 1942

To the man in the street, in mid-July 1942, the war situation from the Allied point of view looked pretty desperate. One defeat after another had befallen since the USA had been dragged into the conflict. Only at some scrap of an island in mid-Pacific had the enemy been positively thwarted, although the full meaning of that cataclysmic event had yet to be understood by anybody – including the Japanese.

Immediately after Midway, however, aggressive Allied ideas at the highest level surfaced. They grew rapidly under the urge of Admiral Ernest King (with strong support from the British) and the Combined Chiefs of Staff into Operation Watchtower – a risky invasion of the Solomon Islands of Tulagi and Guadalcanal in the face of assured, extremely fierce Japanese resistance. Admiral Nimitz referred to it as 'shoestring' but the final plan under his command was emblematic of the High Command structure which was being shaped in the south-west Pacific. For within the large amphibious force, under overall American command on the boundary of Nimitz's Pacific Ocean Area with General Douglas MacArthur's South-West Pacific Area, was embodied a truly Allied content, in that it comprised predominantly American forces plus British, Australian and New Zealand units.

Intelligence gathering also was Allied, with emphasis on SIGINT (which depended almost entirely upon TA and air reconnaissance and only marginally on cryptanalysis) and the hundred coast-watching stations which the Australians had established before the war on a 2,500-mile front stretching from New Guinea to the New Hebrides. Needless to say, the radio transmissions from coast-watchers were keenly DFed by the Japanese and many of these brave men were captured. But not only did they uncover priceless information which, in the early days of thinly spread Field Units, filled gaps in Y Services, they always helped to delude the Japanese into blaming them, instead of cryptanalysis, for breaches of code security.

The unopposed landing (except for a few snipers) on Guadalcanal on 7 August and the rapid occupation of its main objective – the airfield under construction by the Japanese – was a triumph for Admiral Kelly Turner, commander of the amphibious force. The six-months' campaign of attrition which ensued, with its heavy naval and air losses for both sides culminating in the crippling of major Japanese forces in hapless defence of their outer perimeter, was a decisive event generally centred on the holding of Henderson airfield. But it was the numerous naval and air battles for that stretch of water generally known as the almost continuous Battle of the Slot which earned Ronald Lewin's true epithet when he wrote that it 'has no parallel in the history of war'. Only in outline will it be described here against the essential background of SIGINT.

Code JN 25b continued to resist timely attack at this moment but minor codes did not. By 30 July the Americans had managed to work out that RX stood for the Solomon Islands, RK for New Britain, RZ for New Guinea and RY for the Gilbert Islands. From this and other evidence they could base deductions about when Guadalcanal was about to be reinforced. For TA provided strategic and tactical intelligence and the coast-watchers filled in with invaluable tactical warnings of air and naval attacks which almost invariably were conducted under radio silence. Yet only once, on the night of 8–9 August, were the Americans taken badly by surprise, and that after TA had given ample (possibly delayed and vague) warning of the approach of seven cruisers bearing down on Turner's anchorage off Guadalcanal. In what became known as the Battle of Savo, four American cruisers and a destroyer and one Australian cruiser were sunk with only minor damage to the Japanese. To make matters more ignominious, the American carriers under Admiral Fletcher were withdrawn, compelling Turner to pull out all his transports and their escorts, thus depriving the US Marines on shore with any vestige of support until, most fortunately, the Japanese withdrew for fear of daylight air attacks.

Essentially SIGINT continued to give a steady flow of information about Japanese commitment to recapturing Guadalcanal and the approach of massive forces under the strategic command of Yamamoto, embarked on the mighty battleship *Yamato*. At once Nimitz, realising the opportunities on offer, threw in everything to hand. He remained at a numerical disadvantage to his foe, yet not in terms of SIGINT. Indeed Nimitz had the advantage from an intercept informing him that the Japanese were convinced their codes were secure. TA to them, it seems, had not been developed into a fine art. Never again would the Japanese achieve surprise. In the Battle of the Eastern Solomons, Yamamoto failed, due to a combination of inferior intelligence and lack of resolve, to press his local advantage to a decisive victory. Thereafter, with every day that passed, he persisted in blindly permitting his warships and transports to be used as a bait that was consumed in ineffectual endeavours to recapture an airfield of diminishing strategic importance. This was a battle of attrition neither he nor Japan could afford. Far too late, Guadalcanal would be left in peace by the defeated Japanese on 7 February 1943 – five days after the German Sixth Army had surrendered to the Russians at Stalingrad and a week before that the Americans suffered a minor, humiliating defeat at Kasserine Pass in Tunisia. But before turning to those events it is desirable to be aware of the reconstruction taking place in the vast Far East quadrilateral that was bounded in the north by India and in the south by General MacArthur's South-West Pacific Area, based in Australia.

In India the DMI (Director of Military Intelligence) had it in mind, as the Japanese drove through Burma, to command the Y Service from Delhi. After all, he was responsible for both internal and external security and so his attention was fixed not only on Burma and Ceylon, but also on Iraq, the North-West Frontier and the activities of anti-British elements in parts of the sprawling Dominion.

Needless to say, the tyranny of distance and the paucity of land and signal communication systems prevailed. Delhi was 5,000 miles from Melbourne; and Colombo was 1,200 miles from Calcutta, which was 1,200 miles from Rangoon and 800 miles from Delhi, which was 400 miles from Rawalpindi. Two-way, macadam roads were few and far between; railway journeys long and tedious, and long-hop flights over undeveloped terrain, with few airfields, hazardous to say the least. Land-line cable routes were meagre and unreliable. Radio communications were hampered by shortage of equipment, atmospheric conditions and the necessity to encrypt nearly everything, when few cipher machines were available.

Trained Y personnel also were at a premium and Japanese linguists virtually non-existent, with schools to train hastily recruited interpreters in Calcutta and London in their infancy. Rapid progress was impossible because Japanese cannot be learned quickly. Moreover, knowledge of their ciphers and codes was almost non-existent. It was not even known if they used RT!

Against this discouraging background, the Inspector of Y Service, (Air Cdr Blandy) arrived in India in February to write what became notorious as the Blandy Scheme. To a large extent it was similar to that of the DMI. Main HQ would be at Delhi, with sub-centres at Rawalpindi in the west and Calcutta in the east. Specifically, to quote from his signal to London outlining the scheme: 'Main and sub-centres to be combined Army and RAF. Control of policy and organisation to be vested in local and or main committee consisting of DMI and SIO to C-in-C and DAOC respectively. Centres will not (repeat not) attempt to break German Enigma but will intercept as required similarly to Middle East. Cryptographers for high-grade Japanese required.'

Blandy's Scheme won the support of the C-in-C (Field Marshal Sir Archibald Wavell) and was accepted by the CIGS (General Sir Alan Brooke) and the Y Board in Britain. But it was received with much consternation by the Air Ministry's staff when it awoke to the fact that they alone would have to find 152 officers (including a Group Captain and ten Wing Commanders) plus 1,367 other ranks to fill such high-grade jobs as computors, cryptanalysts, traffic analysts and RT interpreters. These simply did not exist. So although the Blandy Scheme survived under the Y India Board (in consultation with the London Y Board), its growth was stunted by lack of resources of all kinds.

In fact the first RAF Y unit (355 WU) to reach India did not arrive until July 1942 when it began to train and develop in collaboration with existing Army units. DF was tackled, some Japanese air-to-ground traffic studied and, with the help of a Chinese intercept unit, call-signs and frequencies found and recorded. In due course interpreters trained at the

London School of Oriental Studies would arrive. There were the usual growing pains and complaints about misemployment by officers who felt that their units' talents were being wasted.

A report commissioned by the London Y Committee was accidentally drafted in two versions by Army and RAF officers; although, amazingly, they did manage to concur on many aspects. Lt Col Vernham's paper dealt chiefly with policy and mainly agreed with Wing Commander H. H. Laurie's contention that the RAF units would produce better results than those belonging to the Army. This unanimity persuaded the India Y Board to set up a Y Committee on London lines. At the same time Laurie, who was a very experienced Y officer from Heliopolis, spent considerable time with 355 WU formulating a basic intercept organisation founded upon the EWSC (East Wireless Sub Centre) sitting alongside the IWIS (Interservice Wireless Intelligence Staff) at Barrackpore. RAF WUs, when at last they arrived with equipment, would be formed and attached either to groups or squadrons in much the same way as in the Middle East.

Unfortunately the Y Committee in London continued to be dissatisfied with the standard of raw material coming from India, notably with that sent by Indian civilian intercept operators. Cryptanalysis was improved marginally in June 1942 by a small Japanese section, which mainly dealt with Japanese Military Attaché traffic and only slightly with radio intercepts. Yet there were encouraging signs of closer co-operation with the Americans in Washington when, at the invitation of the Australian Central Bureau in Brisbane, a tripartite conference was held at which the British urged the far more knowledgeable and better equipped Americans to concentrate on the Japanese problem and to head an Intercept Task Control Centre in America, while Britain remained a cryptanalytical centre and India exploited the results. By chance, and most beneficially, a visit by DD(S) of GC and CS to Washington, subsequent to a Y Conference in London in the summer of 1942, drew many threads together in a conference which, among other things, made Britain and India jointly responsible for tackling the main Japanese Army Air cipher (3366) and its allied systems.

The Grand Alliance was working with good intent although the London Y Board was not always in accord with the India Board over cryptanalytical policy and division of labour; this despite a ruling by the British Chiefs of Staff, that 'The whole of the Japanese cryptographic work should be done in India. Long-term research will continue to be handled by BP. It is essential that all raw material be transmitted to BP (GC and CS).'

These problems would gradually be ironed out in 1943 and will be described in Chapter 18. In the meantime great events were taking place in the Middle East and in Russia, all of which would have a bearing on developments in India and the Pacific theatres of war.

WHEN BOTH SIDES ceased major hostilities on the Alamein Front at the end of July it was realised by each of them that the Axis forces had but a few weeks in which to resume their offensive if they were to have any chance of reaching Cairo and seizing the Suez Canal. If they failed to do so, the British flood of men and material pouring into Egypt could never be matched by Field Marshal Rommel and his men, a reinforcement race which certainly should be won by Britain if she managed to cut the Axis supply lines to North Africa. For that reason Field Marshal Kesselring renewed air attacks on Malta in an endeavour to save his convoys from air and sea attacks. And the British did all they could not only to rein- force and replenish Malta but also to furnish themselves with precise information via SIGINT of convoy sailings and courses.

That the British did achieve their aims to a notable extent was due to the twin accomplishments of making extensive use of greatly expanded and more efficient Y Service as well as to advances in the deciphering and exploitation of German and Italian codes. Essentially these things improved admirably after Travis had taken over the direction of GC and CS and Jones was placed in charge of Hut 3. With their tasks clearly defined from above, they enjoyed free hands to guide everybody in the right directions.

Since the Chiefs of Staff's approval on 1 January 1942 for the mak- ing of 993 receivers (later increased to 1,038), the number delivered by June was 700 – although it seems there was considerable uncertainty about the number actually in service. Of more practical importance was the number in use; by November it appears that, to cover all tasks against Germany, Italy and Japan, the Army was providing 179 at home and 191 abroad for use in static and mobile stations; the RAF had 374 at home and 353 abroad; with the balance going to the Admiralty, Foreign Office and GPO. Staffing had barely kept company with demand, although many operators were either still undergoing training or far from efficient. Vitally, there also was a keener sense of necessity in the allocation of priorities to tasks, bringing about crucial reductions in time-lag of distribution of material between GC and CS and the theatres of war.

Thus SIGINT in general was not only beginning to meet all demands, except in India, but also creating a reserve capability to provide adequate intelligence by TA and DF against the event of the Germans perceiving that Enigma was being broken – as always threatened and therefore perpetually dreaded by C, GC and CS, Churchill and the Chiefs of Staff. Indeed, at this very time, it was found, through intercepts of diplomatic messages, that security worries were surfacing among the Germans, most of all in the Navy Command but also within the Luftwaffe. As an indication of this concern, several special Luftwaffe keys were coming into use across the Mediterranean. Difficulties in breaking these at first hampered general intelligence gathering, especially whenever the Army Chaffinch Enigma became intransigent. But the cryptanalysts were up to the challenge and quite soon discovered ways of breaking Chaffinch settings via so-called 'cribs' (textual or other evidence which suggested clues for breaking a signal) from Luftwaffe Enigma keys, by name Red, Primrose, Gadfly, Scorpion and Locust. These valuable breaks were supplemented by extensive penetration of Italian codes of all grades. Come November, some 50 per cent of Hut 6's time was being spent on Mediterranean keys, to the neglect of Enigma traffic from Russia where the struggle was deadlocked. But as de Grey states: 'Hut 6 suddenly found themselves able to turn out a volume of decrypts covering the whole of the Mediterranean operations with a continuity hitherto unexampled ...'

With SIGINT of this quantity and quality stacked against him, it is hardly surprising that Rommel had no chance of defeating a strongly reinforced Eighth Army, under the inspiring leadership of General Bernard Montgomery, at the Battle of Alam Halfa. Accumulating evidence progressively notified postponements of the Axis offensive from 15 August to the 26th, and then to the 31st. Indeed the decrypt of a Panzer Army signal on the 15th laid bare his plan, along with details of its strengths and serious logistic deficiencies. On the 29th it became certain that the 31st was the day, but along with that came an admission that the supply situation (always weak) had deteriorated, partly due to very extended lines of communication but largely because of the sinkings of numerous supply vessels (including tankers and ammunition ships) by submarines and aircraft, whose passages invariably were revealed in detail by SIGINT.

To all intents and purposes the offensive was over within twenty-four hours; stopped dead by a well forewarned Eighth Army, crippled by dire logistic shortages but fundamentally defeated by British Y Service and well-applied SIGINT. This, for the first time, outsmarted Rommel's own SIGINT organisation, although without depriving him of clear intelligence to the effect that he was in for a hiding for nothing, a realisation on his part that the British were encouragingly kept well-aware of by Enigma, just as they were kept informed of Rommel's spell of sick leave in Germany on grounds of ill-health.

The Third Battle of Alamein would inexorably follow on 23 October, a grinding, attritional struggle which was relatively easy for Montgomery to calculate on the detailed knowledge of the enemy vital statistics made available to him by SIGINT and the assurance that the Axis Army would be kept in short supply by the naval blockade. Yet Enigma, which helped expose the complete enemy order of battle on 18 September, played only a minor role in telling Montgomery the details of his opponent's locations because, in the static, entrenched situation, radio silence was strictly observed. Thus Hut 3 at GC and CS depended upon Y inference and reconnaissance patrol reports (by both sides and often in low-grade code or in clear), amplified by intensive study of complicated Panzer Army Quartermaster returns (sent by Enigma) which gave ration strengths. This information disclosed what became known as 'corseting' – the intermingling of German and Italian troops down to battalion level to stiffen the latter's unreliable resolve.

To put it in a nutshell, long before 23 October the Axis situation was hopeless. The fact that the battle lasted for over a week simply was a testimony to the skill and resolve of the nigh exhausted and out-numbered Axis land and air forces and their commanders; and Montgomery's desire to minimise his own losses as far as possible. Naturally, once the offensive started, strategic and tactical SIGINT was supplied in abundance by Y units and handled with dexterity. Nevertheless there were lapses which on 2 November, due to several hours' delay in distributing decrypted tactical messages from Heliopolis to HQ Eighth Army, permitted heavier losses than might have been the case. This was an unlucky incident, typical of war, from which lessons could be learned.

By and large, however, as the Axis front began to disintegrate that day, both Army and RAF Y units were able to give an accurate and timely running commentary which provided Montgomery with clear insight into his enemy's mind. It proved an invaluable advantage that continued with enormous benefit as Eighth Army went on the move and its mobile Y Field Units joined their parent formations in the pursuit to Tunisia.

CHAPTER FOURTEEN

THE FLICKERING TORCH

Uppermost in the minds of the Allied leaders during the Arcadia Conference in Washington in January 1942 was the need to keep Russia in the war on their side. As much as any other factor it was this essential consideration that formulated the Grand Strategic aim of giving priority of effort to knocking Germany out of the war ahead of Japan. This decision automatically instigated the ensuing, prolonged debate, stimulated by urgent populist demands for a 'Second Front Now', about where and when to strike. The American Chiefs of Staff strongly favoured a cross-Channel amphibious operation in the summer. Their British opposite numbers were vehemently opposed to this on practical objections based on an adverse balance of strengths along with insufficient landing craft and logistic shortages. Only in the event of an impending Russian collapse would they approve a major landing in France. Instead they favoured attacking the periphery of Axis territory by invading French North Africa in the hope that the French would raise no more than token resistance before the Germans and Italians reacted in force.

In June President Roosevelt and the Prime Minister opted for North Africa in what became known as Operation Torch. The American Chiefs of Staff persisted in their opposition until 24 July when Roosevelt and Churchill insisted that Torch should be launched 'at the earliest possible moment'. The plan, as eventually evolved by General Dwight Eisenhower in order to gain control of Morocco and Algiers, was to land simultaneously at Casablanca, Oran and Algiers, followed a few days later by a landing at Bône, which was a doorway into Tunisia. The date was finally fixed for 8 November, which was calculated as the earliest possible arrival when troops from the USA could arrive at Casablanca. By this time, it was hoped, Rommel would be in full retreat to Tunisia having been defeated at El Alamein.

Torch was destined to establish the principles of Anglo-American military collaboration which carried them to final victory. Under Supreme

Commander Eisenhower, senior commanders would have equal status at most levels of high command where their staffs would be integrated American and British officers. Naturally, therefore, British Y and American Radio Intercept staffs and units (henceforward for convenience referred to as US Y) were intended to work alongside each other. In fact, joint arrangements had been established in 1940, although Americans were excluded from access to Enigma, until the necessity arose. Now it had.

Fortunately, a mission led by Commander Sandwith RN had visited Washington in June to discuss technical matters. A month later it was learned that a US Y unit was scheduled to come to Britain. It was preceded by a US Army Y officer who visited intercept stations and GC and CS. His stay was badly handled by MI 8, which failed to consult its opposite numbers at the Air Ministry. It resulted in an inaccurate US report which underrated TA and gave offence. It did, however, recommend that a US Army/Air Y unit should be trained in England (where German transmissions could be heard easily) since it was impossible to do so on live traffic at home. Regrettably this was not done prior to Torch.

Affairs were put straight when Colonel Bicher arrived in September as the US Army and Air Y representative responsible for the training of operators, He was invited to join the Y Committee and allocated a site for a future intercept station. A few days later Colonel Hayes, US Y commander in North Africa designate, arrived. Communications with the Americans seem to have been plagued at first by security formalities. De Grey (who, like C, was reputed by some as being not over pro-American) facetiously refers to a 'penumbra of "off the record" information as to what was "cooking"'. But these trivial attitudes soon evaporated as mutual appreciation developed.

Gibraltar, where HQ Allied Forces was to be located, was the obvious forward communications and radio intercept centre for Torch. But there were worries about the capacity of the Rock's cable links to carry messages to and from GC and CS: and also speculation as to whether the French Algiers cable could be utilised for that purpose when it fell into Allied hands. This was fundamental at a time when Typex machines already were too few for existing traffic to and from the UK, Malta and the Middle East. At one period an average of 2,500 groups per day were being processed at Gibraltar by Typex, making it necessary, for a while, to encipher all outgoing signals by cumbersome code books and by OTP.

To make matters worse, the delays in finalising the Torch plan prevented detailed Y planning and essential, combined training until the end of September. For example, the training of the US Army's 128 RI Company (which came direct from America) was so lacking that, in January 1943, Colonel Hayes decided to merge them with British Army 55 WI Section. But neither they nor other British Y units had, prior to the landing, worked up sufficiently alongside the HQs they were to support. Furthermore the two RAF Y units, tasked to accompany squadrons ashore, were adversely rated by their Technical Officer. He said of 380 WU that only four operators were 'any good, about 25 were only lacking in experience but the remainder no good at all'. He might also have said that their equipment was poor.

This harsh judgement of RAF Y did not apply to the computors embarked in the huge convoys to give air-raid warnings, as already they had done on Malta and Arctic convoys. Indeed, considering the hasty, pioneering circumstances, overall performance was reasonable, the faults that occurred being largely laid at the door of inexperience, serious undermanning of the SLU party (which controlled secure distribution of Enigma material), overloaded communications at Gibraltar (where 351 WU was located) and on the HQ ship, HMS *Bulolo*, which embarked an RAF party to handle, with the assistance of Cheadle, low-grade Luftwaffe traffic. In the event staff shortages were sometimes overcome by borrowing Navy Y operators, but Cheadle's signals were not received due to a combination of inexperienced RAF signallers and seasickness. This, wrote the OC Cheadle, was 'typical of the present operating efficiency in the RAF Y Service'.

Reports by two experienced RAF computor officers, one on shore with an HQ staff, the other in HMS *Bulolo*, are explicit and justified. The officer ashore in Algiers wrote that communications were 'the bugbear', with poor interception conditions, and that the presence of Middle East experienced officers would have been useful. The one afloat also complained about 'lousy' congested communications partly caused by

Admiralty intelligence signals which were 'not well selected ... largely redundant and late': and that he did not receive vital codes until the day after they were in force. He goes on to reveal that he only found out by chance that there was a radar 'filter room' on board, which proved really useful in helping him perform his task of air-raid warning. Also that his discovery of Enigma signals on board (to which he had no right of access) was of assistance! In essence this enterprising RAF officer implied the need for HMS *Bulolo*, which had been plagued by acute disorganisation during the Dieppe raid, to assemble all SIGINT facilities in one place and to get its act together for the future.

Improvisation was often the order of the day at all levels. It is difficult to escape the conclusion that it was fortunate that French resistance was short-lived before they joined the Allied cause; and that the completely surprised Axis were slow in mounting air and submarine attacks on shipping. Like Operation Watchtower in the Solomons, Torch initially hung by a shoestring. There was no air defence radar ashore until the end of November. Not until four days after the landing did 380 WU arrive in Algiers, but it was the 20th before it became operational for air defence, and the 27th before communications were established with Cheadle: and even then it had to borrow two sets and four operators from Gibraltar. Fortunately, Flt Lt Waters, an aggressive, so-called Y-U Fusion Officer was flown into Algiers. His task was to merge high-grade Enigma with lower-grade Y intelligence from Field Units and from Cheadle for the tactical defence of RAF airfields in Algiers, and also for subsequent offensive operations, including those by Twelfth USAAF with which there was close Air Intelligence integration. At first he found 'cleavage in the organisation' but managed to get things moving on the right lines in due course

The situation at Bône, where British troops landed on 12 November, was even more tenuous from an air defence angle. Situated some 350 miles from Algiers, it was several days before any semblance of fighter defence against fierce Axis air attacks could be in place to prevent severe shipping losses. Meanwhile SIGINT was disclosing that the Axis were occupying Tunisia in strength by sea and air – and that Malta was the only base from which effective physical and radio interception might be mounted. In fact, as the First British Army (General Kenneth Anderson} led the race for Tunis and Bizerta against toughening German resistance, it was largely without early warning from either radar or from Y through the RAF's WU 381 (which, like 380 WU, lacked Italian interpreters). Indeed, Army Y (like its RAF counterpart) was 'in disorder and confusion': and it remained that way until February 1943 when joined by a unit from Eighth Army. Meanwhile both TA, DF and technical competence, admittedly in difficult mountainous terrain over long distances, remained poor and sometimes made it necessary to position listening stations on hill tops some thirty miles from the waterlogged airfields they served. Furthermore, early in 1943, the Luftwaffe started using VHF RT transmissions which demanded more receivers and special VHF DF sets.

First Army lost the race for Tunis and Bizerta before it had begun and the campaign became bogged down as the Germans allowed Eighth Army to race almost unopposed to the Tunisian frontier, where it was confronted by the Mareth Line. Neither British nor American Y were to blame for the failure to reach ambitious objectives. Chief among the many weaknesses were logistic difficulties and poor signal communications with AFHQ. But at the time there was no doubt that Y had failed utterly to provide the service expected of it. Its problems would be tackled on the spot when a North African Y Committee (chaired by Colonel Hayes USA) was formed to act as the only source for all to deal with prior to the formation of the Allied 18th Army Group in February.

Meanwhile Malta, which at last had been relieved from its long siege, could now make use of its highly experienced Y organisation, along with the GC and CS and Middle East services, to play an offensive role. At once it contributed to the interdiction of Axis transport to Tunisia from both Italy and France, soon after the Germans had occupied the Vichy zone. As the noose slowly tightened around the Axis forces in Tunisia, the expertise of Malta's 10 Field Unit's computors in reading German RT and WT kept well-informed the gradually increasing number of aircraft, submarines, cruisers and destroyers available for strikes against shipping at sea and in ports. But the fact remained that, in those crucial, early months of Torch, the Germans enjoyed air superiority. If only the Allies had got their whole act together in November and December (when vital Axis shipments got through with small loss), the campaign in North Africa might have been ended far sooner than it was.

ON 19 NOVEMBER, when General Anderson set forth for the front in Tunisia and Eighth Army arrived at the outskirts of Benghazi, the Germans in the huge Stalingrad salient were hit on both weakly held flanks by a totally underestimated (though not wholly surprising) Russian counter-stroke which, within eight days, had encircled the Sixth Army within the ruined city. In the days to come, when official information from the Russians to their Allies in the West was, as usual, far from generous, the most reliable commentary on the progress of the fighting in the Caucasus and around besieged Stalingrad came mainly from the searchers of 3 Field Unit in Persia and Iraq who listened to the Germans. Almost in a flash the Grand Strategic meaning of the calamity brought about by Hitler's foolhardy intention to supply the encircled Sixth Army by air, pending its relief by Field Marshal von Manstein's Army Group Don, were made plain to the Allied High Command by British Army Y sections monitoring the German Vulture Enigma messages.

Manstein's counter-stroke was heard to wither and then die on Christmas Day. On New Year's eve, it became apparent from Y that a belated German withdrawal from the Caucasus was under way in order to escape envelopment by Russian forces which were advancing rapidly against the lines of communication passing through Rostov. There no longer existed a threat to Middle East oil. Russia would survive belligerently in the struggle. The Luftwaffe, especially its transport aircraft, would be detected by Y as a wasting asset fruitlessly failing in its attempts to supply Stalingrad. The result was the airlift into Tunisia was noticeably, drastically curtailed.

It was time for the British and Americans, with the initiative unexpectedly thrust into their hands, to plan ahead in the most expansive manner towards the day of Italian and German surrender. On 14 January 1943 at Casablanca, Roosevelt, Churchill, their Combined Chiefs of Staff and North Africa commanders met under the code name Symbol to establish policies and decide strategy and forthcoming operations.

CHAPTER FIFTEEN

THE SYMBOL EFFECT

Pre-eminent in Winston Churchill's mind when he met Franklin Roosevelt at Casablanca was the urgent need to win the Battle of the Atlantic which, in mid-January, seemed to be swinging Germany's way. Win that contest soon and it was only a matter of time before Allied might, backed by the USA's vast resources, would win the war. Therefore the Symbol conference took place under the fairly confident assumption that the Allies held the initiative in all other theatres of war, with the exception of the Atlantic and, marginally, the Pacific Ocean where the Japanese, at exorbitant cost, still clung to Guadalcanal. This assurance was founded on excellent intelligence founded on the Y Service and SIGINT which, overall, were delivering information of a quality and quantity unprecedented in the history of war. Symbol therefore mainly concentrated on measures to win the Battle of the Atlantic; how to wreck the Axis war economy by a Combined Bombing Offensive; how to help the Russians maintain offensive operations by massive logistic support as well as the development of military operations in North Africa and Europe; and also how to begin the process of breaking through the Japanese perimeter defences in the Pacific and Indian theatres of war as prologues to reinforcing China and striking at the Japanese homeland.

HAD THEY BUT KNOWN it, the Battle of the Atlantic actually was on the verge of an Allied victory based on SIGINT and ever-improving, skilful use of vastly expanded, superior weapon systems.

In December 1942 the initial breakthrough into the Naval Triton Enigma (known as Shark), with the assistance of weather reports codes and German carelessness in December 1942, had been exploited by GC and CS. It would be read with fair consistency and only short delays until 10 March, when the Germans introduced a new code book for weather reports which baffled the cryptanalysts. Despondency on both sides of the Atlantic was terrible at the dread of a three months blackout. Then, against all expectations, the blackout was reduced to only nine days by GC and CS and thereafter Shark was broken nearly every day. But Shark decrypts were just part of the useful contribution made to SIGINT, such as its insight into Dönitz's intentions and his tactical positioning of U-boats which made it so much easier for the Commander Western Approaches to divert convoys from danger.

For, despite reminders from the U-boat Command, its captains persisted with lengthy chatter on HF, thus supplying Y (afloat and on shore) with TA and DF that contained material of immense strategic and tactical value. Meanwhile the U-boat Command, in realisation that if Enigma was broken the foundations of their control system would be undermined and the Battle of the Atlantic would be lost, was compelled to persevere with Enigma in the hope that frequent amendments to its handling would safeguard its integrity. It was a method that demanded additional operating complexities which, inevitably, increased the chances of operator errors that made the codebreakers' task easier.

Moreover, Allied SIGINT was being exploited to far more deadly effect than in the past to counter Dönitz's evasive ploys when he concentrated his boats where the defences were weakest. Assisted by B-Dienst's breaking of the British Naval Cipher No. 3 (known as the convoy cipher), the ploys had worked well for several months after he had withdrawn in July 1942 from the better defended Caribbean and sent his greatly expanded Wolf Packs into the so-called mid-Atlantic gap. Their boat losses were minimised and their kills increased. Yet this was the last wide, happy hunting ground where boats could still attack convoys by night without being detected easily by escorts and aircraft. From 15 December (after SIGINT had discovered the vulnerability of Naval Cipher 3 and made changes to it) B Dienst was temporarily baffled.

The decisive effect of codes in the Atlantic SIGINT contest, nevertheless, was on the wane at the beginning of 1943. Now there were sufficient Allied special hunting groups at large which, guided by their Y searchers' skills, could find, detect and sink their prey with depth charges of far greater potency than of old. Also there was the enhanced threat of air attacks from light aircraft carriers or from long-range Liberator bombers, equipped with 10 cm radar that was aligned with a powerful Leigh searchlight, which could find and hit boats by surprise on the surface. Such a surprise was made all the more deadly because the Germans would no more admit to Enigma being compromised than that SIGINT and 10 cm radar were the causes of their discomfort.

These growing threats were overlooked by Dönitz despite recurring suspicions about the possibility of Enigma decryptions by the enemy – a turning of a blind eye compounded by ignorance of the existence, let alone effect, of the British resonant cavity magnetron valves (invented in 1939 by J. Randall and H. Boot and developed by Marconi Laboratories) which made the key 10 cm radar feasible. For although the Lufwaffe had found one in a shot-down bomber, it had failed to recognise its functional potential and inform the Navy. This pin-pointed a fundamental German departmental deficiency in the co-ordination of scientific intelligence on the highest, tri-service practical level; such as operated, for example, by Dr R. V. Jones, GC and CS and the Y Boards.

The fluctuating convoy battles fought from January to May 1943 were decisive and all the more so because Dönitz was saddled with a weapon system which was obsolete. His U-boats were too slow, too easily detected and sunk, and unable to defend themselves adequately, except by dubious, evasive manoeuvres against hunters whose technology and tactical skills were far superior to that of the Germans. The corrected, post-war figures of their success against losses sustained tell their own story:

Month	Tonnage sunk	U-boats sunk
January	182,000	4
February	301,000	15
March	500,000	12
April	246,000	13
May	212,000	38

Faced with losses of this magnitude, including eight boats in two days against two convoys without a single sinking, Dönitz (who already had been concealing the real truth from his captains) was forced on 23 May to withdraw from mid-Atlantic. This crushing defeat was heard by Y searchers as Dönitz transmitted a flurry of exonerating signals which indicated that, for the time being, he was at a loss to know where best to redeploy his boats. The messages were not decrypted until 31 May, but which were confirmed in all their significance when a signal by Oshima, the Japanese Ambassador, disclosed that Hitler knew 'we have been unable to dominate the seas'.

THE SYMBOL CONFERENCE'S decision to launch a Combined RAF/USAAF Bombing Offensive against Germany gave great uplift to protagonists of strategic bombing, such as Air Marshal Sir Arthur Harris and General Karl Spaatz. At last, with a massive increase in the number available of four-engine bombers equipped with the latest electronic navigation and aiming aids, they could dream of winning the war through a round-the-clock programme of destruction which might obviate the necessity for a prolonged and costly land campaign. Y's part in this campaign was pre-ordained. Over the previous three years it had done little to uncover targets or reveal the extent of damage inflicted on them. On the other hand it had been vitally involved in Radio Counter Measures (RCM) against the enemy early warning systems, as embodied in SIGINT and radar, as well as by its consistently prompt breaking of meteorological codes, without which the confident planning of air raids would have been impossible. In essence the task of Y's searchers was assistance in the discovery and nature of each evolving threat, followed by the monitoring of their own counter-measure's effects.

The search for and identification of the German Lichtenstein air-borne radar set (described in Chapter 12) triggered a prolonged and fierce debate centred not so much on how but whether or not to jam in a whole-sale manner aimed at total disruption of the German fighter defences. The Radio Counter Measures Board, set up under the auspices of the Radio Control Board (which dealt with Research, Development and Operations) faced a very tricky problem. It was generally agreed that the use of 'spurious reflectors' – tiny, aluminium strips which when dropped from an aeroplane would create a sort of smoke screen or false impressions on a radar set's screen. This was called Window.

Dr R. V. Jones was an enthusiastic protagonist of this method, having been in on it since 1937, but he was strongly opposed by those who dreaded a variety of retaliatory measures by the Germans which might not only jam Allied fighter defence radar, but also so reduce the volume of SIGINT as to prevent the acquisition by Y of information about forthcoming hostile, radio measures. So, the first attempt to use Window in a Bomber Command raid in May 1942 was called off after packets of strips already had been loaded. Indeed, not until December, in the face of rising bomber losses, was jamming sanctioned, but only by other means and not Window. Objections to it were sustained, one of them being the quantity of aluminium showered on the enemy in order to guarantee saturation of his radar: calculations ranged between 12 to 84 tons! This compelled Sir Wilfred Freeman, chief executive of the Ministry of Aircraft Production, to point out on 11 April that "By using the foil you save aircraft and crews ... you lose more aircraft off production than you save.'

Meanwhile No. 80 Wing was ordered to study anti-jamming measures and some less controversial devices that had been tried, such as Mandrel, an apparatus to jam the Freya early warning radar and GCI (Ground Control Interception) controls, carried in fighters mixed with the bomber stream. It failed because, as Y soon discovered, the Germans could easily change Freya's frequency much faster than the Mandrel operator could keep tuned to it. Others were Monica, intended to give warning of a fighter's approach, but this was abandoned because it interfered with the new and excellent Oboe blind bombing system; Boozer, which warned crews of transmissions from Würzburg and Lichtenstein radar and helped them take evasive action; and Moonshine, which had the capability of simulating to GCI controllers, via Freya, a large hostile formation. Carried in Defiant fighters on 6 August, it spoofed the controllers into scrambling thirty fighters against an imaginary raid, and on the 17th diverted 150 fighters away from a formation of USAAF heavy bombers. But Moonshine too was dropped due to its complexity and limitations; and also because, by then, Window had been used most effectively on the orders of Churchill – and not a moment too soon.

On the night 5–6 March the first of a series of so-called air battles over Germany began with a heavy area attack by Bomber Command on the Ruhr. Concentration of bombs on target was improved by the use of the latest bomb-aiming device (Oboe), by a navigational aid called H_2S, and by the employment of Pathfinder aircraft to mark aiming points for the approaching bomber stream. Bomber losses were kept within acceptable margins by concentrating that stream within a period of thirty to forty minutes, thus, by saturation, considerably reducing the effectiveness of the inflexible Kammhuber Line.

Gradually, throughout the summer, the new British tactics were countered by variations of enemy fighter operations called Wild Sow and Tame Sow, and by increased use of airborne Lichtenstein radar. Bomber losses rose and Y's searching computors heard the reasons why when listening to fighter pilots' chatter. Naturally pressure to use Window increased until, on 23 June at a top-level meeting, Churchill wound up with the words, 'Very well, let us open the Window.' For fear of disruption to SIGINT during the launching of the invasion of Sicily on 9 July, however, a firm date was temporarily withheld. There was yet another attempt at prevention on 15 July, but Churchill stood his ground and gave permission to use it as of the 23rd. The next night Hamburg was struck a devastating blow, the first of four by night, when the German GCI was completely disrupted by Window: and twice in daylight, without Window, by the Eighth USAAF.

The state of confusion inflicted by Window was clearly audible to Kingsdown. One astonished German controller, totally mystified by the gathering cloud of 'aircraft' on his screen, was heard to exclaim, 'They are reproducing themselves!' Nevertheless, from a total of 3,095 British and 629 American sorties, eighty-six British and forty-three American bombers did not return, indicating that a basis for recovery of German air defences existed – as Y instantly detected, stage by stage, in the weeks to come as their enemies experimented with new methods (see Chapter 17).

THE ADVERSE SITUATION in Tunisia by no means had been rectified during Symbol. Indeed as President, Prime Minister and their Chiefs of Staff were conferring and visiting their troops, there were clear signs (including a decrypted signal from Ambassador Oshima to Tokyo) that the Axis were bent on a counter-stroke. Information about this mainly stemmed from SIGINT, although it must be remembered that only a small quantity of it came from Army and RAF Y units located in Algeria, which remained largely ineffectual. GC and CS, supplied by its long established Mediterranean sources, indicated that although, in January, about 25 per cent of ships heading for Tunisian ports had been sunk, taking with them much needed tanks and motor vehicles, losses of 13 per cent fuel shipped and 11 per cent ammunition were not crippling.

Long before Symbol it was apparent that the convergence of Eighth Army and the Allied forces in north-west Africa demanded their closer co-ordination and joint working. In fact, at the end of November, Wing Commander Rowley Scott-Farnie had put forward a scheme for the creation of a central operational control of the separate Middle East and North Africa Y organisations. Unfortunately he and the newly arrived commander of 276 Wing were involved in an air crash, which killed the latter and consigned the former to a hospital bed whence, with the help of 'Mike' Morris, he kept things running for a month until a suitable replacement, Wing Commander John Davies, arrived. Under the latter's guidance the merger of the separated commands went empirically ahead by leap-frogging Heliopolis units towards Tunis and Algeria and maintaining radio links between them and Cheadle.

Foreseeing the problems that might arise in the event of far tougher resistance to an invasion of Europe than Torch had encountered, GC and CS was pressing hard for a decision as to where the Allies would head once Tunisia had been captured. The answer came from Symbol at the end of January. It would be Sicily. Against this background it was agreed that, henceforward, Army Y units would have to take precedence over RAF, but also that the American presence in command in Algeria could not be overlooked. As already mentioned in Chapter 14, this was settled through the creation of a North African Y Committee under Colonel Hayes. And in due course 380 and 381 WUs in Tunisia would be formed into 329 Wing at Algiers after the arrival of 276 Wing from Heliopolis.

A conference in London at the end of the year had concocted a stop-gap plan which was stillborn because it was overtaken by the rapid advance of Eighth Army to Tunisia and due to poor audibility of radio signals at long range. Instead, the converging armies would function independently until the gap between them was closed. Army Field Units, helped by RAF, would take main responsibility for Enigma intercepts. The bulk of Middle East Y would move to Tunisia and Algeria where 18th Army Group, under General Alexander, would be formed in mid-February. But there was a lot more fighting to do before Tunis and Bizerta were in its hands.

The day Symbol convened it was already known that Fifth German Panzer Army, under General Jurgen von Arnim, had been strongly reinforced, not only from Europe but also by the transfer of a panzer division from Rommel's army. On 18 January the first phase of offensive Axis intent was revealed by surprise with a skilfully executed, three-pronged attack that was undetected by SIGINT. It was repelled by the British at Bou Arada, but succeeded against the French who were overrun by a strong German battle group in the mountainous Eastern Dorsal to the south of Pont du Fahs. Thus encouraged, von Arnim and Rommel, spurred on by Kesselring, prepared three successive operations regarded as spoiling attacks to maintain the initiative.

The first hint to the Allies of what might be in train was obtained from Kesselring by SIGINT on 24 January. But the three plans emerged in such a jumble of negotiations between Kesselring, von Arnim and Rommel that Allied Intelligence branches fell into confusion under a welter of intercepts. Not until late on 14 February, the day of the first attack, was it realised that there were only two, not three, operations. Nevertheless, DF had fixed the assembly area of 10th Panzer Division on the 10th and there was sufficient SIGINT available on the 13th for General Anderson to give timely warning to exposed American units at Gafsa to withdraw. By the 14th, indeed, all the necessary pieces on the board had been notified by SIGINT for Intelligence to say where and when the attack would fall and in what strength. But this they failed to do with conviction. In consequence 1st US Armored Division's Combat Command A at Sidi Bou Zid was caught unprepared on the 14th and overwhelmed, having underestimated the powerful strength of 10th Panzer. And on the following day a brave but foolhardy counter-attack by 1st Armored Division was caught in a trap and virtually annihilated.

From this serious setback stemmed the debacle of what is notoriously known as the Battle of the Kasserine Pass. It evolved from a sequence of headlong Allied retreats to Tebessa, Sbeitla, Kasserine and Feriana, as Rommel's Africa Corps advanced from the south and von Arnim's divided forces which headed for Sbiba and Fondouk as the Allies took action in accordance with what SIGINT, PR and ground patrols contributed to their intelligence branches. Now that the battle was mobile the air was filled by radio transmissions, some in clear and of tactical value if only the field units had heard them when forced back in retreat. Mainly it was strategic intelligence via Enigma, relayed by GC and CS of course, which provided the vital information, and usually within twenty-four hours.

Essentially SIGINT gave clear notice of the direction and, to some extent, strength of the thrusts aimed at Sbiba, via Sbeitla, and Thala, via Kasserine. They also detected uncertainty on the Axis part. As a result Anderson was able, with confidence, to leave Tebessa almost unguarded and to concentrate on Anglo-American blocking positions at Sbiba and Thala, and by the US CCB in the Bahiret Foussana; all of which held firm. Only then did Army Y begin to supply useful tactical information, including Rommel's order to withdraw from Thala on the 22nd – a decisive event which rapidly was confirmed by GC and CS and air reconnaissance.

The German counter-stroke was over, brought to an end by its own weaknesses and by the belatedly improved Allied intelligence work based on the Y Service. But it was not the end of the spoiling attacks. Already Enigma was hinting at a new attack in the north and another in the south, where Eighth Army held a line at Medenine.

Von Arnim's Operation Ochsenkopf in the mountainous north on 26 February achieved total surprise but then was reported by a certain amount of SIGINT before it was checked in heavy fighting on ground ideal for defence. It was called off on 4 March after suffering heavy casualties in men and tanks.

A worse fate awaited Rommel's attack at Medenine when he threw a strong Axis punch against an entrenched British position which, but for three days' warning by Enigma, might not have been nearly strong enough to hold on. For General Montgomery had positioned only one division at Medenine when, on 28 February, he was informed that an attack by two or three panzer divisions could be expected on 4 March at the latest. Frantic reinforcement and hard work quadrupled the strength of the defences. But although nothing happened until the morning of the 6th and GC and CS was unable to send a decrypted message giving the thrust line and time of the attack until after it had started, ample confirmation of what was coming had been received. Air reconnaissance had played its part. TA by Army Y had contributed and the intelligence staffs had worked out both the time and direction of the thrust. Leaving fifty wrecked tanks behind, Rommel withdrew into the Mareth Line and handed over command to General Giovanni Messe, his unannounced departure to Germany being revealed to the Allies by Enigma.

It was Montgomery's intention to storm the strong ex-French Mareth Line by an Alamein-style set-piece assault, although at the same time hedging his bet with an outflanking move to the left by a strong armoured force. Furthermore, he was aware that II US Corps was operating strongly against his enemy's rear from the direction of Gafsa. SIGINT, including Army Y, had acquired useful information about the positions of the panzer divisions after their rebuff at Medenine. 10th Panzer was positioned to deal with the Americans; 15th Panzer was known to be in close support of the Axis infantry in the Mareth Line; and 21st Panzer was poised in central reserve.

The frontal assault on the Mareth Line was soon stalled by a staunch Axis defence on the 21st when 15th Panzer's thirty-two tanks counterattacked. But already SIGINT had disclosed that 21st Panzer had been committed to the defence of Mareth and that the outflanking force (1st New Zealand Division) had been spotted on its way to the Tebaga Gap in the mountain chain. Excellent SIGINT now ruled Montgomery's conduct of the battle. He reinforced the New Zealanders with 1st British Armoured Division and ordered 4th Indian Division to clamber through the Matmata mountains which bisected Eighth Army's extended front. Now, safe in the knowledge that 10th Panzer was committed to the opposition of II US Corps, Montgomery urged the left flank to break through the Tebaga Gap which, he knew, was about to be reinforced by a battery of 88mm guns. He was not to know that German Horchdienst had already discovered what was in train and that this was the real danger spot which they had to reinforce with everything to hand pending withdrawal from the Mareth Line.

The Y Service now gave splendid support. When 10th Panzer Division attacked II US Corps at El Guttar on the 23rd, Army Y gave all the warning necessary for a lethal reception. When the left-flank column delayed its breakthrough at the now strongly held Tebaga Gap, it was RAF Y and PR which, at very short notice, provided much of the intelligence that led to the massive, set-piece air/armoured assault which roared though on the morning of the 26th to force the enemy to withdraw in haste to the Wadi Akarit Line.

With a general retreat to the north of Tunisia now in progress, SIGINT in all its forms provided intelligence of unparalleled importance up to that moment. Very little of what was thought at Axis high level or moved behind their front was not soon known by the Allies. Quite apart from reading minds, revealing current and rapidly diminishing strengths and being fully aware of a deteriorating logistic state as shipments by sea and air to Tunisia were being sunk, there was too the hour-by-hour reporting by Army and RAF Y of the enemy's tactical withdrawals from one delaying position to another. This is not to suggest that SIGINT alone was responsible for shaping the Allied High Command's plans. Many other sources besides SIGINT were tapped and fused with Enigma and Y which, nevertheless, were unique in their revelations of longer-term enemy strategic plans.

Yet the disappointing failure of the Allies to cut off General Messe's retreat from Mareth to Cape Bon must be recorded, even though his fleeing forces, bereft of most of their equipment, found temporary safety on 10 April behind the north Tunisia bridgehead. The fact of the matter was that the Axis troops had run with such speed that they were uncatchable. Y could do nothing about that. Nor could it play a major role in the overrunning of the last-ditch Axis stand in defence of Bizerta, Tunis and Cap Bon. Simply put, the moves of a few run-down, fuel-starved, elite enemy units from one threatened place to another had forfeited military validity. In those conditions it was decrypted Enigma signals, relating to dire fuel and ammunition shortages as shipments fell to nothing, which announced that the fighting would be over within a few days and that no kind of Dunkirk evacuation was contemplated. In fact only 632 officers and men had been evacuated after Hitler and Mussolini, to AFHQ's knowledge through a Japanese decrypt, had turned their backs on such an attempt.

Indeed it was SIGINT which played a leading humanitarian role in alleviating the pathetic throes of some 250,000 enemy troops caught in the trap. Given remarkably accurate information from GC and CS about Axis manpower and logistic state, it was revealed that stocks were more than adequate to feed the hordes pouring into the prison camps, even though the AFHQ had underestimated the total by 50,000.

GC and CS had certainly played a notable part in the Allied triumph, and furthermore was winning a derivative bonus in dealing with an old, lurking threat – the fast, non-morse Geheimschreiber, known as Fish. Looking well ahead since the Vienna to Athens link had been detected in July 1942, GC and CS had ordered the building of a much better sited intercept station at Knockholt in Kent, connected to Bletchley Park by teleprinter and despatch riders. Knockholt (which by the war's end would be staffed by sixty Y personnel) was ready when, at the end of April 1943, Y's searchers (recruited from TA experts) began decrypting Fish messages sent on a link (known as Squid) between Amt Anna, near Königsberg, and Army Group South in Ukraine. At the time it was not known that Herring, a link between Fifth Panzer Army and Kesselring's GHQ South in Italy had been secretly in use since December 1942 because it was working via submarine and land cable.

Fortunately a way to break Fish by hand and calculating machine had been devised in June 1942. But this was so slow and clumsy that, in December, Travis (fully supported by C and Churchill) had ordered a prototype, revolutionary, high-speed mechanical computer, designed by Max Newman, in collaboration with Turing. Named Heath Robinson, this lash-up of machinery was proved feasible in May 1943; when, for want of something better, twenty-four copies were ordered at about the same time as Fifth Panzer Army's captured Geheimschreiber was on its way to England.

In fact only two Heath Robinson's, which examined binary data from a loop of 5-level paper, were built. Among its many defects was a nasty habit of shredding the paper and the unreliability of its switching gear. Realising this, Turing spoke to Tom Flowers of the Post Office Research Station at Dollis Hill in February. Flowers had worked on telephone systems and was an expert on thermionic valves. Contrary to common misconception at the time, he knew that valves were thoroughly reliable provided they were not constantly switched on and off, as with domestic radio sets. He said that Heath Robinson would never be reliable and that its switching gear should be replaced by valves – and that it would take a year to build an electronic computer. Without orders he set to work and, driving his team round the clock, demonstrated in December what would become known as Colossus I, with its 1,500 valves, that could process 5,000 characters per second to break Fish settings, on average, in about three days.

Meanwhile, Erich Fellgiebel, true to his belief in the inherent vulnerability of all codes and fearful that Enigma might be broken, was busy delivering Geheimschreibers at the rate of one per month, for carriage of the highest grade material to and from the HQs of Army Groups and Armies. Priority went to the most active fronts in North Africa and Russia, after the Russians had captured Stalingrad at the end of January 1943 and begun thrusting deeply into Ukraine, taking Kharkov and nearing the River Dnieper. As usual Russian reports to their allies of progress were rationed and the Luftwaffe was the most generous provider in helping intelligence branches to calculate the balance of forces and guessing what either side might do next. It was indicative of overall German strength when, in February, Enigma revealed that the Germans were sending bombers to the West in what would develop into a minor (and incompetent) mini-Blitz of England. For that coincided with Field Marshal von Manstein's brilliant counter-stroke in Ukraine which smashed the Russian spearheads, retook Kharkov and rolled them back to what shaped into the Kursk salient before the thaw and spring rains inundated the battlefield.

At this moment the Allied Chiefs of Staff became enthralled by insight, through an Enigma known as Mustard and by a Fish called Squid, into German assessments of evolving situations as both sides lined up for the summer campaigns. Of these, a Squid decrypt, emanating from one of the most distinguished German commanders, was arguably the most important. Written by Field-Marshal von Weichs, C-in-C Army Group South, on 26 April it revealed the code word Zitadelle as referring to a possible major German offensive against the Kursk salient at an unknown date.

At a stroke the logical opinion of General Sir Alan Brooke, that Hitler would not indulge in an offensive in 1943, was turned upside down.

CHAPTER SIXTEEN

GENERAL ADVANCE

On 11 June the Allies took their first step into Europe on their way to Sicily by occupying the tiny island of Pantelleria (Operation Corkscrew) without resistance after several weeks' intensive air and naval bombardment which destroyed Italian morale. Next day the island of Lampedusa surrendered to an RAF pilot when he made a forced landing. SIGINT contributed to knowledge of the defences along with routine information from PR and prisoners of war (PW). From a Y point of view this was a useful rehearsal for the invasion of Sicily (Operation Husky) since it tested the revised procedures introduced on HMS *Bulolo* since Torch and on the other HQ and air defence ships, *Hilary*, *Largs* and the battleship *Nelson*.

Before Husky took place, however, there occurred another far larger event in Russia when, after several postponements caused by technical matters and Hitlerian changes of mind, Operation Citadel at last started on 5 July. This massive German attack, butting against an immensely strong Russian defence in depth, suffered entirely from lack of surprise. Quite apart from what the Allies provided by way of SIGINT (gathered from 6 Field Unit at Aleppo because No. 3 in Persia and Iraq could no longer intercept once the front moved into Ukraine) the Russians themselves were extremely well supplied by every kind of intelligence. This included that of the Lucy spy ring which drew its information from senior, anti-Nazi German officers, one of whom may well have been Fellgiebel using his private code to send messages through Wehrmacht cable to Switzerland.

Kept well informed by Y's monitoring and, to a far lesser extent, the British military mission in Russia, the Allied commanders could launch Husky on 9 July in the comfortable assurance that any sort of effective enemy counter was unlikely. Such an assurance was made absolute by Knockholt's interception of Fish traffic and GC and CS's triumphant use of Heath Robinson (since May) to break Bream, which was Kesselring's

Geheimschreiber link to OKW. As Hinsley relates in *British Intelligence in the Second World War*, '... throughout the Italian campaign the traffic on this link furnished from the outset a more comprehensive guide to the enemy dispositions and intentions than any of the Enigma keys'.

Nevertheless, although AFHQ was sufficiently informed by PR about the Italian Navy's location and state of readiness and the deployment of land forces, there emerges from Hinsley, from de Grey and from Aileen [Clayton] Morris's *The Enemy Is Listening*, a tone of dissatisfaction with Y's performance, quite apart from zero information obtained by SIS agents and from naval beach reconnaissance.

Morris makes no bones about the superiority of the Mediterranean units (above all 10 Field Unit in Malta) over the newcomers and the HQ ships, although she admits it was a mistake not to send an RAF Y party ashore with the leading troops in order to provide more immediate information. She relates how the Chief of Staff in *Largs* rejected an air-raid warning, based on RT intercept of fighter bombers by Flt Lt Rob Clapham, OC the ship's Y team's party, because he 'could not see any hostile aircraft'. A few minutes later *Largs* was hit by fighter bombers and forced to limp back to Malta. Clapham had an arrangement with 10 Field Unit whereby half-hourly signals gave up-to-the-minute information about enemy aircraft movements, reinforcements, sightings of convoys, forecasts of threatened targets, patrolled areas, airfield servicing reports and air-sea rescue tasks. Furthermore, from RT traffic, it was possible for experienced computors reliably to identify bombers, fighter-bombers, Stukas or reconnaissance missions. These were the priceless benefits bestowed by highly experienced individuals who rarely failed to give warning of approaching raids by day or night.

The same could not be said of parties embarked in *Nelson*, *Bulolo* and *Hilary* whose computors lacked experience of Luftwaffe procedure in the Mediterranean. In his post-Husky report, Clapham summed up to AI that, whereas *Largs* had done well, the others had not been particularly successful; and that, while RT was valuable, 'WT intercept on board ship was almost valueless'. Teamwork between ship and shore stations was highly successful and 'interpretation' a far more technical job than was perhaps realised by the Air Ministry and some of the senior officers in either Signals or Intelligence.

Army Y units also fell well short of expectations. The usual Eighth Army drill of attaching Field Units to the HQs of formations was employed and, as a lesson from Torch, a small Y party was allocated to the tactical HQ of XIII Corps to provide earliest possible information to its commander. But this did not happen: instead HQ Eighth Army's section got ashore first. Not that it would have made much difference because, for most of the campaign, Army units contributed very little. Hinsley ascribes this to much improved security measures by the Germans and Italians – such as more frequent changes of codes and keys and more complex call sign systems. To which should be added that, unlike the desert, Sicily possessed a civilian and military cable communications network which the Wehrmacht had augmented to satisfy characteristic Army standards. Moreover, as had been noticed many times before, troops holding static positions had far less need for radio than when they were mobile.

Only once during Husky, towards the end of the campaign, did Army Y provide useful tactical information, mainly used to confirm other sources. In essence, therefore, it was the experienced 10 Field Unit in Malta and Clapham's party in *Largs* which justified the existence of Y during the operation. This conclusion gave rise to questions in some quarters as to the wisdom of allocating, in face of shortages in material and skilled personnel of high calibre, so much effort and expenditure.

Husky was interspersed by two decisive turning points of the war. First, on 16 July, came Hitler's decision to bow to defeat at Kursk and transfer major formations to the Mediterranean theatre of war. The second, on 24 July, was the toppling of Mussolini from power as it became clear that Sicily would fall into Allied hands as the overture to an invasion of mainland Italy.

No. 6 Field Unit at Aleppo provided initial evidence of the German standstill at Kursk and of the unrestrained thrust of the Russian offensive, which already had begun on 12 July. Confirmatory intelligence from other sources would then report its spread from Smolensk to the Black

Sea, as it lunged westward in an advance which carried it to Kiev in November. Now the Allies felt sure that the Wehrmacht was dangerously overstretched and incapable of a major offensive anywhere on land or at sea. Now too, therefore, the Allies could concentrate their efforts, including that of the Y Service, where they chose. For example, 371 WU at Freetown in West Africa could be brought to North Africa at the same time as some Middle East units could either be redeployed or focused more closely on targets in the eastern Mediterranean and Balkans.

The overthrow of Mussolini, long hinted as possible by Enigma and other sources when Sicily was invaded, nevertheless came as a surprise in timing – as was to be expected bearing in mind the essentially secretive nature of the Italian clandestine coup which brought it about. Likewise the intensive, secret diplomatic activity which cloaked the negotiations leading up to the secret Italian Armistice on 3 September was not the kind to be broadcast by radio either by the Allies (whose leaders happened, most fortunately, to be in conference at Quebec), the Italians or the Germans. But where SIGINT contributed most was in its tracking of German reinforcements as they arrived in Italy, Yugoslavia, Greece and the Aegean islands. This indicated, without undeniable disclosure, Kesselring's preparations to disarm Italian forces in the event of their surrender, while he, through backstairs diplomacy, endeavoured to retain his discontented ally within the Axis and, at the same time, did his utmost to hamper the Allied preparations – besides successfully surmising where an invasion would come ashore.

Fish, Enigma and the Italian negotiators kept the Allies extremely well informed about German Order of Battle and dispositions prior to the invasion of Italy. They enabled AFHQ to assess most accurately the meagre nature of resistance which was likely against Eighth Army's landing in the toe of Italy (Operation Baytown) on 8 September, and the stiff defence mounted against US Fifth Army (Operation Avalanche) in the Gulf of Salerno on the 9th. Eighth Army came ashore unopposed that evening, in advance of the public announcement of the Armistice. The American and British troops of Fifth Army also were initially unopposed as they landed - until they advanced into the hills.

But from then on the Germans reacted fiercely and in an eight-day struggle came close to ejecting the invaders.

So far as Y units at Salerno are concerned, there is virtually nothing of importance to report. The Army units (American and British) which were allocated failed to get ashore for several days. The RAF RT detachment which did arrive suffered casualties to men and equipment, and when, after a forty-eight hours' delay it was able to function, it was located in low ground, and therefore awkwardly screened by the surrounding high ground.

Once more it was 10 Field Unit at Malta which, prior to the invasion, played a leading part, along with others in North Africa and by radar, in skilfully reporting heavy raids mounted by the Luftwaffe against ports and shipping. Y Ferrets (airborne searchers) also managed to find and place enemy radar sets; while some 100 sets with static units covered nearly all of the numerous German and Italian transmitters scattered throughout the region. For Operation Avalanche, of course, RAF shipborne parties were embarked in HMS *Hilary* and HMS *Ulster Queen*. And the American HQ ship, USS *Ancon*, embarked an American Y party which had been trained by the redoubtable Flt Lt Clapham.

Needless to say, the Luftwaffe made a maximum effort against targets in the Gulf of Salerno. Fortunately Clapham, unhappy with tardy naval reactions to air raids, had again made arrangements (as during Husky) with Malta for half-hourly broadcasts. Apart from one major variation, history repeated itself. So long as the ships were not close in shore, and therefore screened by high hills, Y searchers did manage to intercept aircraft RT traffic in time for fighters to be on hand. The significant variation was the introduction of Hs 293 radio-controlled bombs which could be guided to their targets from long range. It was Clapham who discerned that Dornier 217s were releasing these from 25,000 ft, and he who went ashore to persuade a fighter squadron to intercept at that altitude; resulting in one Dornier shot down, another damaged and the squadron involved being withdrawn. (Incidentally the Hs 293 menace was not long-lasting since, in 1944, certain ships were equipped with jammers to defeat the missile's control system.)

Clapham's computors also were able, through radio footprinting, to identify a large concentration of enemy aircraft on the Foggia airfield, and to persuade the Americans in *Ancon* to lay on a big attack by US and RAF aircraft, which did immense damage at a critical moment in the battle for the hard-pressed beachhead. But the result of that battle had been decided by soldiers on the ground, heavily supported by colossal naval gunfire. Decrypted Enigma, which revealed on 17 September that Kesselring had sanctioned a withdrawal northward to the Volturno River, was read after Allied patrols had noticed that the enemy was thinning out. Only then did mobile Army Y, at last given a choice of unscreened sites, began to take part effectively in the land battle that would continue, step by step for the rest of the war, up the Italian littoral.

As the Italian front loosened, strategically important operations on the eastern Mediterranean front, which placed limited demands on British forces, were also taking place. Concurrent with the planning of Husky, the Joint Chiefs of Staff had turned down a proposal from Churchill in May to take advantage of the 'favourable situation likely to develop in the Balkans' by capturing the islands of Rhodes and the Dodecanese (Operation Accolade). But there was consensus with the American belief in the close relationship between the European and Far East theatres of war. It was expressed in agreement for major operations in the central Mediterranean, a commitment to the invasion of France in 1944 (Operation Overlord), and the development of operations in the South Pacific Area and the North Pacific. Given the vast scope of these commitments, Accolade would be rendered logistically impossible.

Already SIGINT had taken a hand with a series of decrypts which spoke of Axis reinforcement of the Aegean in reaction to Allied deception schemes designed to deflect attention from Sicily. But although at the Quebec conference Accolade was rejected, it was agreed that the British should send small detachments of SAS to Rhodes and the islands of Kos, Kalymnos, Leros and Samos in the hope of accepting the surrender of Italian troops between 8 and 16 September. At Rhodes they were pre-empted by the enemy, but the smaller islands were taken and put into a state of defence against the German counter-moves which were anticipated after Hitler demanded, in a decrypted signal, that the islands must be held.

The very nature of the fierce and costly amphibious operations which took place in the weeks to come was a guarantee of comprehensive SIGINT gathering by Y, even though no Y sections were sent to the islands. The extensive use of HF radio by the Germans was inevitable. Therefore, the mere involvement of Luftwaffe transmissions was almost sufficient in itself to ensure a running commentary without supplementary naval and army traffic copiously sent in clear or code. This munificence, however, in no way saved the British from defeat. Indeed, as the struggles for various islands reached their climax and the garrisons lost their radio sets, Middle East Command was sometimes better informed of the disasters by the Germans, via Y, than by any other means.

This is not the place to relate in detail the complex pattern of skirmishes which led to the ejection of the British from the islands by 22 November; or the ill-affordable price paid by the Germans to satisfy Hitler's wild desires. Moreover, as Enigma would disclose in the weeks to come, the island garrisons were a wasting asset in urgent need of logistic support by sea which was vulnerable to naval and air interception.

Likewise there is no need here to go into detail about the Balkans imbroglio that was brewing in mainland Greece and Yugoslavia. Internecine, partisan, guerrilla warfare among the hills and valleys of these tortured nations (encouraged and supplied by the Allies) was raging to an increasingly barbaric extent. The officers and signallers of SOE played their part and the Y Service monitored and relayed to them valuable intelligence dealing with a plethora of political and military matters – including warnings of impending German antiguerrilla operations and the revelation of insecure codes in use by the Yugoslavian factions. Vitally this intelligence contributed to and reinforced the opinion of the Allies that they should cease support for the Cetnik forces under General Mihailovic and switch it, in November, to Marshal Tito's partisans – a move of enormous portent for the future of Europe as well as the Balkans.

But, as de Grey was to write, 'The centre of gravity had shifted from

Cairo ... to the middle point of the Mediterranean with all eyes looking northwards. The need for Italian cover, except for monitoring purposes, was gone for ever and operators were needed at home in preparation for another great adventure.'

In fact, rationalisation was to be the order of the day. Towards the end of 1943 major army formations – British and American – would be on their way to Britain for Overlord. Cross-posting of personnel, brought about, for example, by the amalgamation of 276 and 329 Wings, would take place early in 1944, a change which so upset existing systems as to stir GC and CS to complaint. But in the meantime the global war was shifting inexorably into a totally different mode to that just ending.

CHAPTER SEVENTEEN

MISCONCEPTIONS EXPOSED

Optimistically, in midsummer of 1943, the Allied Intelligence Staffs nurtured delusions that the Germans might collapse under the pressure of disasters on almost every front. Hand in hand with these notions and the euphoria of post-Hamburg raids, flourished the apostles of air power who claimed that the Combined Bomber Offensive might actually work the trick without need to implement a full-scale invasion of the continent – Operation Overlord. Conjoint with that grandiose spasm of wishful thinking grew Operation Cockade, an agglomeration of several interwoven deception plans designed to convince OKW that somewhere, between Norway and Brittany, a major invasion would take place sometime in 1943.

Chiefly designed to deter the Germans from transferring forces from western Europe to other fronts, there lurked in the fertile minds of the British planners an intention to utilise Cockade as an overture to what would become known as Operation Fortitude, which was the major deception cover plan behind Overlord. But in addition to that concept abided a supremely optimistic hope that Operation Starkey, an elaborate simulation of an invasion of the Pas de Calais, might actually bamboozle the Germans into withdrawing prematurely and thus allow the small land forces actually associated with Starkey to land almost unopposed.

Starkey comprised a fourteen-day air offensive by the Allied air forces, such as would precede a major landing, and movements of a fleet of landing craft and shipping sufficient to lift fourteen divisions, which really were represented by only two Canadian divisions and five commandos. At the appropriate moment the invasion fleet (less troops) would set sail, but then turn back in mid-Channel. Attending this activity, of course, were actual minor reconnaissance raids by commandos, the implanting of false information by double agents, and extensive spoof radio traffic to keep the German Horstdienst and B-Dienst listeners and intelligence staffs busy.

Eagerly the Y Service searched for enemy reactions to Starkey, only to be disappointed. For a start the Luftwaffe declined to become heavily involved in countering the Allied air attacks. Although Enigma advertised certain precautionary measures, it was soon realised by the Germans that these enemy activities actually were related to events in Italy and a spell of fine weather suitable for amphibious operations. After the war Field Marshal von Rundstedt (C-in-C West) declared that he was not fooled by Starkey or any of its accompanying deceptions. Be that as it may, both he and OKW henceforward indicated through SIGINT their concern that an invasion might come at any moment, confirming this by a continuing reinforcement of the West, showing, therefore, that they were completely convinced the main blow would fall on the Pas de Calais and nowhere else. As will be told, they too would be disappointed by events in 1944!

Y Service also learned valuable lessons from Starkey. RAF Y was judged too slow communicating with operational headquarters. Partly this was due to separation between Cheadle, Kingsdown and the plotting tables in fighter control rooms. This was rectified to some extent by detaching an officer from Cheadle to HQ 11 Fighter Group; by the refining of procedures and communications with RT intercept at Kingsdown; and by the 'cleaning up of the position of the Naval Air Sub-Section and the Operational watch (in Hut 3) at GC and CS ... which regularised the reporting to Coastal Command which had been rather on Black Market lines'. As in the Mediterranean, it was again recognised that it was a mere handful of dynamic people who actually held the key to efficient success, and that only the best experts, with years of experience (naturally), who would make a good showing. In essence, it was only those who, day and night, dealt with this complex work who could be relied upon 'to interlock theory with practice as they advanced from tyros to experts', as de Grey put it.

Conjoint with Cockade the Allied Bomber Offensive against Germany mounted, day by day and night by night. RAF Y was more deeply involved than ever in the months to come, not only in serving the RAF but also whole-heartedly the Eighth USAAF as a whole, including its 8th Fighter

Command and 8th Air Support Command, which became operational in July 1943. Fully aware of their shortage of previous experience in coping with the Luftwaffe and rarely reluctant to learn from others, the Americans unhesitatingly and happily studied alongside the British at a critical moment in the evolution of aerial combat doctrine. For in the modification of Luftwaffe tactics after the introduction of Window, during the incineration of Hamburg, and on the eve of the Americans attempting to fight their way to the heart of Germany in daylight, technically driven techniques were placing huge demands on SIGINT to keep abreast of successive combat changes.

In the aftermath of Hamburg, RAF Y played a leading role in detecting the drastic tactical changes imposed on Kammhuber's rigid defensive box layout that was based on radar and GCI. Soon the computors at Kingsdown were hearing separate RT running commentaries (as many as four at a time with five different call signs) by controllers directing fighter pilots into the bomber stream as it approached the anticipated target area. There each fighter was expected to hunt 'freelance' with the possible help of Lichtenstein; augmented by anticipated assistance obtained by homing on to 'active' H_2S sets (although Y did not realise this at first).

Running commentaries were quite easily heard at Kingsdown and relatively simple to interpret since they were only thinly coded and based on readily comprehensible place names and beacon locations. This made it possible to know when fighters were airborne and where they were concentrating. A mass of unique intelligence was passed via a 'conference telephone system', to intercept stations and RAF Commands, where they were plotted on a large-scale map, and thence to GC and CS where reports in the form of a General Narrative, Analysis of Patrols and Aircraft Reporting were currently prepared. Sometimes it was possible to change bomber routes and to split raids to confuse enemy controllers; and later to guide escorting night fighters against the German night fighters in the hope of an interception.

Occasionally specially equipped aircraft from 192 Sqn flew with the bomber stream to study the signals that were generated by enemy radar and other devices, as well as by the bombers themselves. From this investigation it was discovered that the pulses from the IFF (Identification Friend or Foe) system carried in the bombers could be detected at long range by the Germans. This was soon stopped. But in the main, Bomber Command seemed to profit most from the early morning report from GC and CS, based on SIGINT, containing as it did a short summary of the previous night's raid with a diagrammatic map illustrating enemy fighter movements.

Post-Hamburg, however, it is apparent that Bomber Command was less interested in tactics than RCM. Fighter versus fighter encounters were few. Mainly the bombers depended upon disruption by jamming of the German radar and communication systems and, starting on 22 October, by distractions from Kingsdown in sending contradictory orders to Luftwaffe fighter pilots. The Germans then attempted counter-jamming by the powerful Stuttgart broadcast transmitter, which for two months ineffectively played loud folk songs, opera and brass bands: to which Kingsdown responded with transmissions from Aspidistra, the most powerful sender in England.

Spoofing, which devised diversionary routes and targets and occasionally fooled controllers into withholding their fighters from the actual threatened target area, would not start until the night 20–21 February 1944, although immediately with a gratifying reduction of losses to a mere 1.5 per cent.

Despite the longer winter nights, as Bomber Command losses increased prohibitively, it was realised that RCM was failing. A seat of the trouble could be found among the planning and operational staffs at HQ Bomber Command, which were obsessed with the false theory that bombing could win the war. They made inadequate use of SIGINT when it did not concern technical matters. It was a struggle to persuade these officers, nearly all of whom were pilots, to take a personal interest in what GC and CS could produce. Not until February 1944 did they began to make fuller use of the daily BMPs, by belated requests for clearer presentation and also for frank criticisms from the authors, Bonsall, Moyes and Prior, for whom this was a great stimulus, enabling them to act outside their brief by making such constructive suggestions as to enhance the authority of BMPs well beyond their original aims. This improvement was consolidated in April when an Air Section from GC and CS was attached to HQ Bomber Command to act as a funnel and interpreter of section output.

Fundamentally, however, the Germans already had temporarily won an air superiority over the Fatherland which was based on both technical and tactical factors. By day their fighters, sometimes reinforced by night fighters, could easily find and shoot down the unescorted American B17s. The latter's worst experience came on 14 October 1943 when they lost sixty out of 291 bombers during a raid on Schweinfurt in which only ninety-five returned undamaged. At night, too, the British were increasingly easy to intercept, especially when sent repeatedly to bomb Berlin in the unjustified hope that destruction of this political target would break German morale.

The sixteen major raids on Berlin, between 18 November 1943 and 24 March 1944, would cost 581 Allied bombers. To this had to be added 1,146 RAF bombers sent against nineteen other major targets, the majority falling to fighters of which many were claimed by Lichtenstein Messerschmitt 110s mounting Schräger Musik, upward-firing, twin 20 mm cannon which struck by surprise from a blind spot below.*

The fact of the matter was that the German Horstdienst, playing at home and providing its Fighter Command with excellent intelligence against an opponent who was playing away, was able to use the Luftwaffe's practised flexibility to devastating effect at minimum cost. And never more so than on the night of 30 March when it detected a force of 794 RAF heavy bombers forming up over East Anglia in readiness for a single-stream attack on Nürnberg, yet without the benefit of a major diversionary attack or of spoofing. To meet this dense stream the Germans had ample time to assemble 294 fighters which managed to intercept and shoot down Lancasters and Halifaxes by the score before Nürnberg was reached, The survivors scattered so that but few bombs landed on the city. In all, ninety-four bombers went down (a monstrous 13 per cent against

* Not until July was the existence of this deadly weapon system revealed to AI by a PW. And not until September, for some inexplicably scandalous reason, was it passed on to RAF Commands.

an average of 3 per cent for the month) and eighty-three were damaged, of which twelve were beyond repair. To this the hardened men and women at Kingsdown were horrified and impotent listeners as each victorious German pilot celebrated and as the score mounted.

In effect RAF Bomber Command's basic strategy and its RCM (Radio Counter Measures) defences were defeated. Promptly it was ordered to turn its main effort to support of the forthcoming Operation Overlord – the invasion of France. The task of winning air superiority over Germany was handed to the USAAF Bomber and Fighter Commands in daylight – but from December 1943 into March 1944 with close, long-range fighter protection provided by that outstanding flying machine, the P51B Mustang. In the simplest of military terms, the air battle was to be decided by sheer weight of Allied numbers equipped with technically, superior equipment and fire power, employing appropriate tactics against a Luftwaffe in fatal decline.

RCM was relegated to a minor role but the Y Service would continue to help enormously. For example, when the Americans penetrated deeper and deeper into central Germany, Kingsdown and its Field Units found it extremely difficult to receive German GCI's RT directions to their fighters. To overcome this difficulty the already RAF established practice of sending monitors in bombers was adopted by the Americans. Selected men flew with a few of the B17s to monitor enemy transmissions in order to give early warning of approaching fighters and, sometimes, managing even to work out their direction of approach. It was a difficult job, made all the more so by the electrical interference from the B17s' engines.

The lady responsible for training these Americans was an experienced WAAF section officer called Rusty Goff. When she criticised the state of their logs after an operation they took umbrage and challenged her to do better. So she took part in a raid to Wilhelmshaven and turned in such a polished document that even the experts at Kingsdown (who were unaware it was Rusty's) gave it high praise.

But in the fight against a new type of aerial weapon, neither SIGINT nor Y could play a leading part. Since 1939, in the highly prescient Oslo report, the British had been aware (with some scepticism at the time) of certain crucial technical experiments taking place in Germany. Among them were remotely controlled gliders and rocket propelled projectiles under development at Peenemunde on the Baltic coast.

The successful use in summer 1943 of air-launched gliding bombs (the HS 293) had confirmed these forecasts. But already, towards the end of 1942, the SIS had received credible reports concerning huge, long-range rockets of devastating power, followed over the ensuing months by several confirmatory items of intelligence on the same subject in which Peenemunde featured. Thereafter concrete evidence accumulated rapidly from PW, PR and SIS agents, including air photos of a rocket (A-4) which, in due course, would be known as V2. And then, on 18 June, came the recognition by Dr R. V. Jones of a smaller, winged projectile, which the Germans called FZG 76, and became known to the British as V1, flying bomb or doodlebug. At about the same time, too, intelligence about the construction of many strange sites across the English Channel, in the Pas de Calais and Cherbourg peninsula, came to notice from a variety sources, including the Y Service

On 7 September a Luftwaffe Enigma request for defence of launching sites came to hand. A week later came another Enigma signal regarding site protection, which R. V. Jones deduced referred to a pilotless rocket (V1) that might well come into action before the V2. Far more revealing, however, were earlier Luftwaffe Enigma signals linking the Luftwaffe Signals Experimental Regiment with the test firing of V weapons from Peenemunde. It had opened a new station on the island of Rügen in the Baltic, linked to a number of others along the coastline and tasked to plot V1 flights. Hut 6 soon broke the special Enigma setting. On 12 October Y intercepts began recording vital data from the plots which revealed that V1 certainly was an aircraft, that its speed was between 216 and 300 mph (occasionally 420 mph), its rate of fall from an operational altitude of 2,000 metres just four seconds and its maximum range 120 miles.

This information narrowed the area of search for the so-called ski-launching sites. By 30 November, eight-two had been located in France. Yet the various government committees examining the complex and often contradictory evidence thrown at them could not produce a consensus as to the nature and timing of the various threats. It took superb analysis by Jones, early in December, to convince them about the nature of the V1 threat. In a detailed paper, based chiefly on SIGINT, he quite accurately described V1's performance, rates of fire, the location of the launching sites and supply centres and the likely fall of missiles on London and Bristol. He was even able to relate the progress of the Germans' trials.

Yet it took two bored radio operators from the Luftwaffe Signals Experimental Regiment to reveal when the attack would commence and, therefore, when best Allied counter-measures should begin. This duo enjoyed chatting in plain morse during many an idle hour on duty. One owed money to the other and made arrangements with a third party to settle the debt when on leave. On 5 December, however, this arrangement broke down when it transpired that a number of the operators were being sent to France prior to Christmas. The implications were obvious: the V1 attack was imminent. On 21 December the RAF and Eighth USAAF launched such a prolonged and devastating offensive against all the known ski sites that the start of the operation was put back by more than five months. It was delayed further by the need for a complete change in the missile-launching arrangements that, in fact, prevented a start until after Operation Overlord had commenced on 6 June 1944: thus depriving it, as will be seen, of a few launching sites.

OVERLORD WAS TO BE part of a co-ordinated effort by the Allies in the Mediterranean theatre, in western Europe and in Russia during May and June. Throughout the winter the campaign in Italy would continue at Cassino and after the amphibious landing at Anzio on 22 January (Operation Shingle/Dragoon).

From a Y and SIGINT point of view, Shingle – later renamed Dragoon – was a small-scale but much improved version of Operation Avalanche. When IV US Corps landed by complete surprise its accompanying Army Y party was soon ashore and established on high ground where it enjoyed good reception of local German transmissions, including those of the gathering Luftwaffe. Meanwhile the by-now almost routine air-raid warning system based on land stations and two HQ ships was functioning with satisfactory results. Luftwaffe reaction was by no means instantaneous. It was all of six hours after the troops touched down before an excited reconnaissance pilot was overheard shouting: 'My God! It looks like another Salerno.' But it was late in the evening before bombers that had flown to airfields in northern Italy from France, Greece and Crete were in action – and then only in small numbers and with scant success since forewarned fighters were awaiting them.

The fact that the Germans managed to confine the Allied beachhead was certainly not due to the Luftwaffe's effort, which, as Y noted, rarely exceeded 100 sorties a day to disclose vividly how depleted German air force was and how vulnerable their airfields were to attack by well-informed bombers. No, the real reasons for IV Corps becoming penned lay with the opposing commanders – on the Allied side the failure of General Mark Clark to press the commander of IV US Corps into taking a calculated risk in order to make full use of initial success by pressing on fast and deeply into undefended territory: and Field Marshal Kesselring's bold and rapid reaction, based more on intuition than SIGINT, in sealing off a stalled bridgehead with hastily assembled formations. For in fact all necessary information was being laid bare to Clark by PR and SIGINT, the latter more than adequately served by Y Service which, despite the transfer to Britain of many veterans for employment on Overlord, were still staffed by numerous officers and men who knew their job well.

Indeed, a point in intercept development had been reached when it could be declared that the British and their rapidly learning American allies had promoted themselves from amateur to professional status. Available now stood a large, well-trained body of searchers – members of an experienced force capable of finding and handling the ever expanding volume of traffic that the Germans were generating, be they in clear, in hand codes or transmitted by Enigma and the Fish machines. Needless to say, this intelligence presented by the enemy was by no means localised but gathered widely from the Black Sea, through Romania and Hungary to the Balkans and northern Italy; and it comprised most useful weather reports as well as strategic and tactical material concerning the Mediterranean and Italian sectors.

Moreover, this coverage was handled by fewer Field Units than before at the same time as British units were being replaced by Americans and as seasoned personnel accompanied both British and American Army formations and units to Britain. But unexpected demands were now thrust upon Y as more and more customers (British and American) hunted for information. Such was the popularity of Y that it became necessary, in the interests of full operational, control flexibility, to discourage what Aileen Morris described as 'possessiveness on the part of certain formations to retain the services of their own Field Units'. At the same time, for security reasons, the Chief Signals Officer in the theatre took personal charge of who should and who might not be placed on the distribution list – to the exclusion of those whose wishes were of mere interest or curiosity.

CHAPTER EIGHTEEN

THE ATTRITION OF JAPAN

If the costly battles of El Alamein and Stalingrad mark the turn of the tide against the Germans and Italians in Europe, the defeat of the Japanese in the Solomons, their withdrawal from Guadalcanal and the subsequent attrition of their forces throughout 1943 signify parallel, deadly reverses for the eastern arm of the Axis everywhere from the Aleutian Islands, India/Burma and the central and south-west Pacific theatres of war. The chronology of strategic events speaks for itself as the Japanese High Command struggled to maintain the pre-planned defence of the widespread perimeter of its conquests against the initial probing of forces which, as Admiral Yamamoto had predicted, were likely to grow overwhelming unless the Allies abandoned the war.

Before his death on 18 April, however, as a direct result of radio intercept, Yamamoto most assuredly was dreading that his gloomy prediction was correct. His fatal visit by air to Rabaul that day to inspect the strategic base, and for chats with the sick and wounded, had been intended for more than that. For it came in the aftermath of disastrous defeats (made possible by SIGINT) at the Battle of the Bismarck Sea on 2–4 March (in which, at a negligible price to American bombers, the Japanese had lost twenty-five aircraft, four destroyers and seven ships that were carrying more than 3,000 soldiers): followed by yet another costly rout of his naval air squadrons in their abortive attempts between 7 and 12 April to destroy Allied bases in New Guinea and the Solomons. In a worried state of mind, he wished to assess the very serious situation in consultation with his subordinates.

Unfortunately for him and his country, however, the encoded signal notifying his itinerary was intercepted on the 14th and quickly broken to reveal that his flight path would come within range of long-range P38 Lightning fighters. Referred to the President, with Admiral Nimitz's recommendation for action, it was decided to shoot him down on the 18th. The only reservations was centred on anxiety that Yamamoto's replacement might be a better commander; and, as the more serious risk, the possibility that the Japanese would guess that their naval JN code had been broken. The former reservation may be debatable, bearing in mind Yamamoto's later known pessimism at that moment. After the deed was done on the 18th, the latter was investigated but ascribed to signals from local radio networks. The JN code continued to yield priceless SIGINT by virtually eliminating the factor of surprise from Allied planning against an outnumbered and largely outclassed enemy.

Hard on the Allies as the attritional struggle would be throughout 1943, the balance of losses, in the final analysis, nearly always tipped against the Japanese, both in manpower and equipment expended. Almost everywhere the Japanese looked they were able to see, or hear, massive forces bearing down upon them – and, as often as not, landing or striking with deadly effectiveness where least expected.

True, the Japanese won a few minor victories. A reinforced Indian division which, starting in December 1942, featured in an offensive in Burma against Akyab in the Arakan, had to be called off in mid-May due to a demoralising reverse inflicted by superior Japanese combat prowess. For similar reasons, so too did Chinese American operations on the India–China frontier in February, and again in October, November and December, come to grief. A deep and costly penetration of the jungle in March and April by several small British columns (called Chindits), despite strenuous efforts in most difficult conditions of adversity, also achieved little – except to impart a powerful propaganda, psychological boost to the morale of British and Indian forces as a whole. Both RAF and Army Y units were placed in support of these operations but they gave little help. The experienced Wing Commander H. H. Laurie (from Heliopolis) pointed out that RAF WUs were more likely to produce operational intelligence before those of the Army, but implied that this would be wasted due to inadequate knowledge in its handling at various headquarters in India, often due to lack of initiative and faulty employment of staff.

Far more effective were operations undertaken by South-West Pacific Command in New Guinea and New Britain by the Americans as the prelude to General Douglas MacArthur's drive for a return to the Philippines.

He had set up his GHQ in Brisbane and had under command Allied land forces (under the Australian General Blamey), Fifth AAF (including RAAF units) (General Kenney) and the Seventh US Fleet (including RAN) (Admiral Carpenter). Under GHQ worked the Central Bureau Brisbane (CBB), consisting of integrated American and Australian elements and directed by General Aikin (USA) with Colonel Sandford, Australian Army, as his Assistant Director.

In the autumn CBB's units included five Australian Army sections (one on duty at Darwin) and three RAAF WUs, although only one of the latter was trained and in support of Fifth AAF in New Guinea. Alongside the predominantly Australian contingent at this time were two American Army RI (Radio Intercept) companies although these were not fully under CBB control. CBB itself was a thoroughly integrated tri-service, Australian/American organisation (about 60 per cent Australian manned) with sections tasked to deal with TA (under an Australian Army officer with Middle East experience); and deciphering (under an American). In addition there was the so-called Collateral Intelligence section, serving Australians only in connections with miscellaneous air/ground solutions. It was run by officers from all three services and nations, plus an Australian professor dealing with meteorology.

Towards the end of the year, as will be seen below, the CBB and Australian Y Service were regarded by the head of IWIS (Interservice Wireless Intelligence Staff) as 'producing very valuable intelligence' from the intercepted Japanese high-grade Army JMA Code (see below), from naval codes, various low-grade codes and signals in plain language. The TA and DF section was particularly successful in computing insecure enemy air traffic that, well in advance, gave profuse and accurate warning of enemy operations.

Not surprisingly in such a diverse set-up as CBB, there sometimes were strained relations. The Australians were more experienced than the newly arrived US RI companies, which were not under CBB control and dealt directly with G 2 (Intelligence) Branch at GHQ. Likewise there were problems in communications between CBB and the Naval Intelligence Bureau in Melbourne. The latter saw no need to co-operate with the former: so the former, desperate for direct contact with Seventh Fleet, established a sort of black market in intelligence with that fleet. Reprehensible in principle it might have seemed – but war is war and the means justify the ends.

The system of international intercommunication in Australia and SWPA was nothing like as complicated as that afflicting relationships over SIGINT matters with Washington. To begin with, as has been noted in Chapter 10, there still was no formal contact at the end of 1943 between the Army and Navy Departments.

There were, however, naval links between Washington, Pearl Harbor, Melbourne and Colombo, and therefore 'indirect', cryptanalytical contacts with GC and CS and London's armed forces ministries for the sharing of random snippets of operational interest. Army and air links, however, were different because they were dealt with by G 2 in the Pentagon and, for Japanese codes, by Signals at Arlington Hall. This material therefore found its way to the Navy, to GC and CS, to India and to CBB by circuitous routes, thus generating duplication, no little confusion and considerable danger of security breaches. The physical schism was never resolved, even though, in due course, G 2 did manage to get its clutches on Arlington Hall.

Mainly by chance, in fact, some significant progress was obtained at the end of 1943 when a bold and innovative officer from Special Branch G 2 in the Pentagon visited Bletchley Park. Sent to make arrangements for setting up a dissemination unit in his branch, this American officer strayed from his brief with GC and CS to explore ways and means of improving the handling of material in general. Then, from a study of British dissemination methods, he moved on to develop policy, in close collaboration with his hosts, of better ways and means of breaking Japanese Army/Air SIGINT.

Against the background of these clumsy, slowly evolving organisation and communication systems in January 1943, American troops established a foothold near Salamua as a distraction. They then used this place as an advanced base for a phased leap-frogging of Australian and American forces, between 4 September and 2 October, along the north coast of New Guinea towards Saidor, via Lae and Finshhaffen. The landings were supplemented by an American invasion of New Britain. These began in October and culminated on 26 December when a strong Seventh Amphibious Force came ashore at Cape Gloucester to wipe out over 1,000 Japanese troops. In all these operations the security of the Allies was well assured in the knowledge from coastwatchers and SIGINT that they were safe from major enemy counter-attacks.

Indeed at this time, as Ronald Lewin wrote, 'the Americans had established a comprehensive mastery over the enemy's military communications'. For not only could they and the British and Australians searchers hear nearly everything of importance transmitted by Japanese radio, they also could break Purple and the naval JN codes and gain much intelligence from TA.

Furthermore, they had at last cracked the complicated and recalcitrant, high-level Army JMA code (known as the Army Water Transport Code). This had first been penetrated by a British officer in 1933, but later was thwarted by a modified version until the Wireless Experimental Centre (WEC) in New Delhi overcame it again in March 1943. Thereafter, a progressive train of discoveries, by British, Australians and Americans, would lay bare its entire workings, culminating in February 1944 with the capture of the code book itself along with certain mechanical devices which exposed to examination 'virtually every field of activity in the Japanese Army'. To this, in due course, would be added mastery, at vast gain, of the Japanese Army Air Force Code (6633) by WEC and other centres.

Meanwhile Admiral Nimitz's massive American naval forces were assembling in the Central Pacific. Their advance guard, comprising elements of the Third Fleet (Admiral William Halsey) and the Third Amphibious Force (Admiral Theodore Wilkinson), opened the offensive on 30 June with the capture of Rendova Island. This was a prelude to island-hopping, covering MacArthur's right flank, that included Bougainville in November and, in March 1944, the capture of the St Mathias Islands. In the course of this advance, which wrested domination of the Solomon Sea from the Japanese, SIGINT and the Australian coastwatchers played their now customary and vital roles by keeping tabs on the movements of enemy ships and aircraft, as well as the strength, outline locations and state of each island's defenders. This was a period distinguished by seven major naval engagements, mainly at night when the Japanese were tactically superior despite their lack of radar. Yet, despite this advantage, the disparity of losses was highly significant in that the Japanese lost a cruiser and ten destroyers (along with many more warships and transports severely damaged) and the Americans only one cruiser and three destroyers. This was an attritional exchange the Japanese could not sustain, especially bearing in mind that on 4 December they were to lose an aircraft carrier to a US submarine to the south-east of Tokyo.

The spearhead of Nimitz's central, island-hopping thrust towards the strategically important Gilbert and Marshall Islands consisted of Admiral Spruance's Fifth Fleet (comprising seven battleships, eight carriers, seven heavy and three light cruisers and thirty destroyers), in company with the Fifth Amphibious Force under Admiral Turner with 100,000 troops. They were tasked to seize the islands of Makin and Tarawa on 20 November as the prelude to Central Pacific Command's prime strategic aim of bringing Japan within heavy bomber range prior to the ultimate invasion of Japan itself.

Intelligence about the strength and dispositions of the garrisons was based almost entirely on PR and SIGINT. Makin's 251 defenders briefly fought to the death with characteristic self-sacrifice. But the 4,700 men on Tarawa held out much longer and inflicted heavy casualties upon the US Marines who repeatedly found themselves mown down by an extremely well-concealed enemy. Not only had reconnaissance and the clearing of lanes to the beaches been totally inadequate, resulting in men having to wade ashore from far out, but also it was belatedly relearned that PR could not disclose hidden bunkers. And SIGINT, which provided precise details of enemy unit strengths and defended areas, commanding officers' names and logistic state, was no substitute for clear pointers as to exactly where each weapon slit was located. In the final analysis it was realised, once more, that even the best-sounding intelligence provides no guarantee against surprise – and that it is ever less valid the closer ensuing combat becomes.

A similar grim story of defeat dismayed the Japanese in the North Pacific Area when, in March, the Americans, with Canadian collaboration, commenced sporadic operations to eject the Japanese garrisons from the Aleutian Islands. On the 26th there was an exchange of fire between cruisers and destroyers (brought on by news from SIGINT) off the Komandorski Islands, which resulted in a timorous Japanese withdrawal. Six weeks later, on 11 May, the Americans put 12,000 men ashore on Attu, virtually unopposed in thick fog. Then, for nearly three weeks, they had grappled amid strong fortification with a garrison of 2,500 men in a struggle that gave a foretaste of what was to occur on Tarawa. Losses, too, were alike. The Japanese were all but wiped out and the Americans suffered 1,700 casualties. It was, therefore, something of a relief when a Canadian–American force, which landed on Kiska on 15 August, found, amidst something of a fiasco, that the 4,500 birds had flown, unnoticed even by SIGINT.

It is therefore interesting to take note, in the aftermath of the Italian debacle but prior to the series of autumn setbacks in the Solomons and South-West Pacific theatre, of a US Y intercepted, and Magic decoded, signal from the Japanese Military Attaché in Lisbon. In this he flatly declared: 'It is generally considered here that the eventual outcome of the war is settled, and that it is now only a question of time. This verdict, of course, includes the war in the Pacific.'

PLAINLY THE TACKLING in 1943 of Japanese SIGINT in the Pacific theatres of war by the Americans was far in advance of that by the British in the Indian theatre.

Progress had been made during the conferences of July 1942 (see Chapter 13) but efforts to reduce the number of centres engaged in Japanese cryptanalysis had broken down because of practical difficulties with GC and CS. Furthermore, the dire shortage of experts and machinery remained as a constant stumbling block even after the releasing of some staff after the Italians surrendered in September 1943. And even then conditions in India precluded the employment of aged or unfit people, or women who were considered 'unacceptable'.

Wrangling dragged on into the autumn of 1943, with GC and CS growing increasingly worried by the situation and its international ramifications. For example, India's wish to deal direct with Washington was objected to by London because it would affect Europe and Australia. Petulantly, India, which felt it was not being supported by London, made it plain in the autumn of 1943 that they did not want any one to teach them its business – although, in point of fact, their people really were in need of extensive tuition.

The problem of obtaining better value from Y resources invested in India was reflected by disquiet not only in London (where it was felt that the prosecution of the whole war effort in the Indian Ocean and Burma was being mismanaged) but also in Washington. Matters had come to a head during the Quebec Conference in August 1943 when Churchill and his Chiefs of Staff decided that conduct of the war in that theatre should be removed from Indian control and placed in the hands of a joint Anglo-American, South-East Asia Command (SEAC), structured on the same lines as in the Mediterranean and West European theatres of war; and that its Supreme Commander should be the 'young, enthusiastic and 'triphibious' Admiral Lord Louis Mountbatten', who enjoyed the confidence of both Churchill and Roosevelt and their Chiefs of Staff; plus an American deputy.

Mountbatten was bursting with bright, new ideas – many of which staggered those currently in power. Upon arrival in Delhi on 7 October he found a thoroughly pessimistic atmosphere and this he proceeded to dispel as quickly as possible. The winds of change blew in all directions and the Intelligence world, with its attendant Y Service, was among the first to feel their welcome blast. With the least delay their organisations and methods were to be steered on to less wasteful and better directed lines that were founded on Allied policy and not hostage to the whims of the died-in-the-wool Indian authorities under General Sir Archibald Wavell. In principle London's policy was to be adopted as laid down in the Laurie and Vernham reports (see Chapter 13).

With the agreement of visiting American officers, the new regime was approved on 13 December 1943 – more than two years after the outbreak of war with Japan! At the same time the alleged paucity of personnel and equipment was addressed in accordance with the long-recognised principles that an efficient and highly trained intercept service should be built up, and adequate liaison imposed between cryptanalysts, TA and intelligence staffs. To implement these principles the London SIGINT Board sent out Brigadier Harris, its deputy chairman, vested with executive powers as Director of Signals Intelligence in India with links to SEAC at its future headquarters in the comfortable hill station of Kandy, at a distance from the fleshpots of Colombo.

Harris, as Director, was responsible to both India and SEAC and the JSIB (Joint Signals Intelligence Board) and determined to cut out a lot of 'top-hamper'. By April he had placed himself strategically between Mountbatten at SEAC and General Sir Claude Auchinleck, C-in-C India, with control over operational HQs and Field Units and with the chairman of the London SIGINT Board. This actually did function in a new atmosphere of 'sweet reasonableness'.

The shortage of personnel and equipment remained, however, even though the London SIGINT Board, in its desire to give Delhi and Colombo a capability to decrypt anything decryptable about the Japanese, had denied resources to units in the struggle against Germany. At the end of 1943 there was in the pipe-line, by various ranks and skills (less linguist/cryptanalysts and clerks), 112 Royal Navy, 1,208 Army and 566 RAF. Of clerks there were 156 – barely enough; while linguist/cryptanalyst at twenty-six Navy, thirty-one Army and fifty-one RAF, although improving, would never be sufficient.

Indeed 1943 for anti-Japanese SIGINT was a year notable for the more professional consolidation of the lessons so painfully learnt by improvisation in 1942. The American/British/Indian/ Australian Quadrilateral was taking shape with remarkable amicability at the grass roots. Indexing work, book-building and cryptanalysis were proceeding in company with TA and dissemination as staffs expanded and tried to improve their efficiency and work more in harmony.

As frequently will be remarked, the handling of material in India left much to be desired and Traffic Analysis was notoriously poor. In a reprimand from GC and CS in October the principles of TA were described admirably: 'The tasks of TA are firstly to tell the traffic controllers were to find any wanted traffic and secondly to discover where to discover where the messages have come from and where they are going to; without these there can be no interception and no intelligence cryptanalytical or otherwise.'

It was pointed out that: 'The complaint against India's TA was that they had in their reports mingled together established facts, surmise and speculation and buried them under a mass of verbiage and useless statistics.'

In other words, there were ingrained clerical minds at work! Not those of trained computors who had acquired their insights in other theatres of war.

Only gradually did there grow increasingly centralised specialisation by subjects. For example, Washington dealt with army matters while GC and CS dealt with air. And with this came the realisation that GC and CS appeared to be the only centre where joint-service matters could be studied as a whole. A step towards this, indeed, was the creation on 4 October at Bletchley Park of a very small, select Japanese Air Intelligent Service (JAIS) of Air Section, drawn from the now redundant Italian Section. This was to be an organisation devoted to the study and dissemination of material (practically all of it code-book type) tasked to act as a mouthpiece for Hut 6 to supply material to the top quadrilateral intelligence branches.

There we will, for the moment, leave the Japanese war and turn to the beginning of the end in Europe as Germany was squeezed between the Russian, the Mediterranean and the Western fronts and torn to pieces by the Combined Bomber Offensive.

CHAPTER NINETEEN

OVERTURE TO OVERLORD

The keen anticipation of a major Allied invasion of western Europe over-shadowed every other great expectation for 1944. It largely centred upon it being directed against France, with landings in the Pas de Calais hot favourite for the likely venue in German expectations. In fact, the Allies were intent only on making it appear that the Pas de Calais was the objective whereas Normandy was the selected place.

To live almost anywhere in Britain at that time was to be made dramatically aware of the certainty of the forthcoming, enormous conflict. Immense flotillas of warships and landing craft harboured in the ports, masses of soldiers (many recently brought back from the Mediterranean) with their vehicles and equipment crammed the countryside and towns, and huge groups of bombers, fighters, transports and gliders crowded the airfields or in huge formations thundered overhead on their way to pound targets on the other side of the English Channel. Here the reinforced Germans worked feverishly to strengthen their much vaunted Atlantic Wall and, like their gathering adversaries, awaited the event in tense confidence of winning a decisive victory – or so their leaders and propaganda told them.

But, of course, as related in Chapter 17, decisive campaigns and fierce battles also were being waged on the other fronts, or were in process of preparation for Europe-wide offensives in the spring and summer.

In the Mediterranean, where Allied vessels now sailed in fair safety, those few U-boats which did get through the Straits of Gibraltar led a very perilous existence and sank few ships. In the Atlantic too it was much the same, especially after attacks by U-boats on convoys were abandoned after the last attempt by a pack was defeated decisively between 14 and 19 February, to raise the total number of boats lost since December 1943 to thirty-two. In March Dönitz was forced to admit that his obsolete boats were hopelessly outclassed and fit only to operate singly against commerce in the Arctic and in distant waters, including the Indian Ocean.

In any case, he now was compelled to deploy almost every available U-boat on anti-invasion tasks. Principally this called for reconnaissance of British harbours and preparations to strike, concentrated against the Allied landing when it occurred.

Needless to say, Allied Y Services provided ample intelligence of these activities, to which Enigma by no means contributed the lion's share. The parlous German naval situation was well known to the Allies, although firm intelligence about the schnorkel apparatus, which enabled a boat to run submerged on its diesel engines and thus avoid radar detection when charging batteries on the surface, did not become available until February 1944. This was followed on the eve of Overlord, via decrypted Japanese messages from Berlin to Tokyo, by details about the new, higher speed Walter boats, then undergoing trials and giving indications that they would not be a serious threat to Overlord.

Also well known to SHAEF (Supreme Headquarters Allied Expeditionary Forces, under command General Eisenhower), as it prepared Operation Overlord, was the Luftwaffe's overstretched condition. Not only, as ever, was it unable to give much assistance to the U-boats, it also was grossly outnumbered, technically outclassed on every front and, come April, defeated in daytime over the Fatherland. Although it benefited from priority of reinforcements for the western Europe to support the defenders of the Atlantic Wall, it still only could scrape together 200 anti-shipping bombers armed with a miscellany of torpedoes and remotely controlled missiles: plus an assortment of some 500 obsolescent machines to support the Army. Awaiting the reconstruction and relocation of easier-to-conceal launching ramps were the V1s that were intended to bombard London and Bristol. But these would not be ready until June. So when Hitler demanded that those cities must instantly be attacked in 1944, it was these few machines which had to be used, despite an obvious need to conserve them and their crews in readiness for the ever-expected invasion.

Thus was born what became known in Britain as the Baby Blitz. SIGINT gave full warning of what was brewing in mid-December and the Air Ministry was well aware of the RCM (including Window) being used, none too effectively, by German night bombers. The first raid by 447 machines against London came without warning by Y on 20–21 January 1944. It was a fiasco of inaccurate bombing by inadequately trained crews. No important targets were hit, only thirty tons fell on London and 270 tons were scattered about the countryside and into the sea. Losses to anti-aircraft guns and rockets and fighters were high throughout the Baby Blitz, amounting to 135 (10 per cent of the aircraft engaged) in subsequent attacks, which ended on 18–19 April in what was to be the last raid of the war by piloted aircraft on London. Kingsdown and Cheadle usually gave warning of up to two hours and were provided with excellent practice in the intercept of DF of both RT and WT transmissions, which also gave valuable information about the latest German radio equipment and RCM. At the end of it all the Luftwaffe's strength had been reduced to 200 aircraft.

Not until the end of March did the Luftwaffe turn its attention to PR of ports and to strikes against likely invasion concentrations. Daylight PR, however, was sketchy and confined to ports alone since it was suicidal to penetrate inland. But it was not until 29–30 April that a heavy and, virtually, ineffectual attack was made on shipping at Plymouth. This was to be the tale of nearly every major anti-invasion sortie in the weeks leading up to Overlord's D day on 6 June, as PR fatally diminished.

On land the armies grappled in Russia and in Italy, while Marshal Tito's partisans increased their depredations in Yugoslavia. A winter offensive launched by the Russians in December 1943 wore down the Germans, who were forced back into the Pripet Marshes and to the Dnieper. Then, starting on 19 January, the besiegers of Leningrad were flung back. And on the 29th the offensive was expanded into Ukraine with heavy losses to both sides before a halt was called by the thaw and mutual exhaustion in April.

Meanwhile in Italy trench warfare was waged in the mountains until stalemate set in across the peninsula at the end of March. Large-scale operations by the Allies were not to be resumed there until 11 May when General Sir Harold Alexander broke through on the left flank, linked up with the Anzio bridgehead and headed northward in pursuit of

Kesselring's outnumbered forces. Rome fell to Fifth US Army on 4 June and the advance continued towards what was known as the Gothic Line, covering northern Italy

Y Services performed as well as ever in keeping track of the strategic aspects of these vast operations when they intercepted Enigma and Fish messages. Tactically, however, it was the ever-generous Luftwaffe which was the most prolific benefactor since it still preferred to use radio and, unlike the Army, was neither so security conscious in its use of land line nor thorough in its imposition of radio silence. So it was those Y stations engaged in intercepting radio links carrying high-grade Wehrmacht material, along with RAF Y, which were of most assistance to GC and CS and, thereby, the Chiefs of Staff. Meanwhile Army Y Field Units, working at corps level and below, in conjunction with Naval and RAF Y, contributed useful tactical intelligence once radio silence was broken. This meant that, prior to D Day in France, all they could do with profit was to monitor radio transmissions during German training exercises. Only when battle was joined and went mobile would they positively contribute tactically. Therefore Air Intelligence would be predominant and of most assistance to the Overlord planners.

IN OCTOBER 1943 the Y organisation received a new charter from the Chiefs of Staff. The Y Board was renamed the Signal Intelligence Board (SIGINT Board) with the role of interception, cryptanalysis, TA and 'Special Intelligence'. Henceforward Y would be called SIGINT and the Y Committee would be absorbed by the SIGINT Board which, thereafter, functioned through specialist committees and itself met very infrequently because its world-wide, operational functions were assumed mainly by GC and CS from Bletchley Park. Here Stewart Menzies (still C, as Chief of the SIS) was upgraded to Director General of GC and CS, with Edward Travis as Director GC and CS and Nigel de Grey as his Deputy Director.

Between June 1943 and June 1944, GC and CS broke over fifty new Enigma keys compared with twenty-seven the previous year. This was a measure of its success as its strength (which was to peak at 8,995 people in January 1945) amounted to 4,352 service people and 3,371 civilians at the end of June 1944. Quite apart from the fact that it was dealing with about 10,000 enemy messages a day and its Cipher Office was enciphering more than three million groups a month, GC and CS also was handling and redistributing a vast quantity of material fed in by various Y stations, such as naval traffic into Huts 8 and 4, plus RAF TA commentaries by telephone from Cheadle and Kingsdown to Huts 3 and 6. Additionally there was the enormous quantity of encoded radio traffic (that was never broken by the enemy) flowing to and from the overseas commands that were spread from the Mediterranean, through the Middle East, India, Australia, via the Pacific, to the USA and Canada.

The refining of organisations and procedures stemming from Operation Cockade and support of the Bomber Offensive (see Chapter 17) laid the foundation of an Air SIGINT service for Overlord, which de Grey considered to have reached its zenith at this time.

At its centre stood the Kingsdown Operations Room where all the intercepts from HDUs were gathered through a network of four so-called telephone 'hook-ups'. Its VHF Traffic Control and DF Network had a central Watch Room which recorded, sifted and distributed incoming traffic of that nature. Next door was the HF Traffic Control and DF Network's Watch Room which functioned in parallel. Then there was the Internal Intelligence Network, connected to out-station watch rooms, which recorded intercepts in German: these were recorded and interpreted by the duty officer and his summary writers, who composed and passed on quick appreciations of ongoing operations. Lastly there was the External Intelligence Network whose duty officer translated material into English and had it broadcast to all concerned.

In short, prior to an operation, its outline plan was explained and displayed by plotters on a central map in the Operations Room. Each network was then briefed and made its preparations with regard to frequencies to monitor, call signs to listen for and so on. When intercepts were received they were passed to the internal Watch Room where they were plotted by the DF operator (VHF or HF). Gradually a picture would build showing both German and Allied formations, the latter obtained from intercepts of the enemy. This picture was studied, interpreted and the current situation, evaluated by the duty intelligence officer, transmitted as a running commentary by duty officers through the External Network to interested commands and units. It was very sophisticated and it worked well for the specific offensive operations for which it was designed. But it must not be forgotten that Kingsdown and its HDUs also had to cope with incoming Luftwaffe missions as well as preparing, as a contingency, for the onset of the as yet unevaluated V1s, if and when they took flight.

Moreover, from April onwards, the BMP Section of Air Section at GC and CS in Hut 3 was connected to the Internal Intelligence Network, making it feasible for the BMP duty officer to keep abreast of an operation by reading the WT reports concurrently with listening to the running commentary and knitting them together for distribution in BMP's summaries. The significance of this was a marginal shift upwards of responsibility for attack on Luftwaffe cipher and signals security away from Cheadle and, to a lesser extent, Kingsdown, enabling the better informed Air Section in Hut 3 to enhance its research – in what was known as long-term collation.

These centralisations, which planted their roots in the Dieppe experience of August 1942, impinged upon meticulous preparations for Overlord when COSSAC (Chief of Staff to the Supreme Commander), who had devised the initial Overlord plan, handed over to SHAEF on 1 January 1944. Already, in fact, it had been deemed essential that a very experienced Y officer should be appointed to CSIO AEAF (Chief Signals Intelligence Officer, Allied Expeditionary Force). The choice fell on Wing Commander Scott Farnie (who had been so badly injured in the Middle East). He initially found himself working with COSSAC's Chief Intelligence Officer (General Whitefoord), who headed a typical Anglo-American, joint-service staff. From this would be formed, under Whitefoord, the SHAEF Signal Intelligence Board comprising Commander Johnson RN, Colonel Scott (British Army), Colonel Brown (US Army) and Scott Farnie RAF.

Automatically the advisors, watchkeepers and signals officers of Hut 3 were pitched into intensive planning sessions to settle the procedures and their responsibilities, while the cryptanalysts of Hut 6, anticipating a much larger work-load than ever before, also worried about the prospects of a possible modification to Enigma machines which had been hinted at in decoded messages – perhaps related to an actual change in Luftwaffe call signs, which caused problems. In readiness to compensate for any loss of Enigma, measures already had been taken in October 1943 to improve the study and handling of Luftwaffe and German Army traffic by the introduction of TA advisers into Hut 3. This Section, named SIXTA, soon was being consulted by Hut 6 cryptanalysts. It almost immediately became a focal point because it alone collected the basic TA picture and was able to speak with authority under the direction of an Army TA addict, Lt Col Edward Cranshaw. So successful was SIXTA that Travis established it formally in February 1944.

SIXTA thus was ready to help deal decisively with the dreaded change of Luftwaffe call signs and frequencies which started on 1 April. At once it was realised by the Heads of Hut 6 and SIXTA that the long-prepared plan for dealing with this event, which threatened absolute chaos, was unworkable. Without hesitation, it was bravely abandoned and a simpler method sought by SIXTA in collaboration with Hut 6. Employing their innate knack of recognising enemy habits and relating these to identities, the TA advisors were able to unravel the new system within ten days. It was an exacting test, based on meticulous research of TA evidence which made it possible to present Hut 3 with network diagrams that exposed the new German system.

This brilliant intellectual stroke was made all the more wonderful by the fact that, throughout the storm (which struck at the heart of TA), nobody, except a handful of experts, was aware of a crisis of such terrifying potential. But to the few in the know it generated an enormous boost of confidence in Hut 6's and SIXTA's elite at an extremely critical moment when the pre-Overlord air campaign was opening, and at a time when the influx of very properly, critically minded Americans into GC and CS, which had begun in the autumn, needed to be convinced absolutely of British competence.

SINCE 1940 THERE had been frank exchanges between the British and Americans over intelligence, Ultra and Magic matters. After Pearl Harbor and the Arcadia Conference in 1941 (with its fundamental decision by the Americans to concentrate more against Germany and Italy than Japan) there occurred the practical expansion, already described, which had functioned with remarkable smoothness in the Mediterranean theatre. Early in 1943, a further step forward had been taken when Nigel de Grey visited Washington to settle technicalities which, as he wrote, 'could not be settled by an exchange of amiable generalities'.

Like most of those at the top, the British were sensibly aware that the 'Germany first' policy was by no means popular in all quarters in the USA. Concessions to American wishes to be involved in everything of importance – of which SIGINT was of very high priority – had to be made to help them 'make a thorough job of it'. On the question of the supply of 'British' intelligence to American commanders in the field, de Grey soon discovered that they were adamant in receiving everything that was to be relevant, and to be free to comment and criticise as they chose. It has been said by an American (Telford Taylor) that C had strong reservations about sending GC and CS material to Washington, and that de Grey agreed with his master. Yet, in fact, it was de Grey who negotiated the guide lines – which became policy – that 'American officers should ... be integrated with the British organisation at Bletchley Park and that the US War Department should not set up a separate organisation in the European theatre for dealing with high-grade German Signal Intelligence'.

Simultaneously, a War Department mission was visiting Bletchley Park, and Hut 3 in particular, with a view to exploring the need for a separate organisation in Britain. De Grey wrote that this 'situation had its awkward features ... but owing to ... the broadmindedness of the "missioners" were brought to a successful conclusion'. Indeed there was friction between the two sides which was not finally resolved until May 1943 when Lt Col Telford Taylor (a Pentagon Special Branch officer and top-grade lawyer who would be a prosecutor at the Nürnberg trial of major Nazi war criminals) was admitted to Hut 3. Here he formed a working relationship with Menzies, de Grey and E. M. Jones, and a close friendship with Travis. These relationships ensured that, as the influx of carefully selected American officers arrived for training in Hut 3 work and indoctrination, their integration would take place smoothly in the coming year. The majority would be posted to every American HQ (air as well as army) which received Enigma, where American commanders ensured that British procedures for the secure handling of intelligence were rigidly enforced. But of the elite who remained at BP, at least one formed a permanent relationship with an otherwise bored WAAF officer who worked in Hut 3.

Integration was indeed a watchword in Anglo-American co-operation, which sometimes turned into a stumbling-block. For example, in the run-up to Overlord the Americans attempted to take command of the Field Units which would support and accompany the army formations ashore. This was based on the same principle that, because the British held command of Hut 3, it was a reasonable quid pro quo. But the British still had far more experience in this work than the Americans and had brought back many seasoned Y Field Units from the Mediterranean. Above all they did not want to see their policy of centralisation at GC and CS go by the board. It was agreed to differ. Integration did not take place and the existing system continued to work harmoniously.

At this time, too, the Fish struggle was mounting to a new climax (see Chapter 15). By dint of sheer hard work Tommy Flowers and his team at Dollis Hill had delivered the first Colossus I, semi-electronic deciphering machine to purpose-built buildings at Bletchley Park in December 1943. It was just in time to tackle an ever-increasing volume of Geheimschreiber, high-grade strategic traffic generated by top German HQs in Russia, Italy, Norway and, from Army Group West in France on 6 January 1944, a new arrival called Jellyfish. To make matters more difficult, in December 1943 the Germans began to introduce a new Fish security device which was in general use by February. This caused a large reduction in decrypts which was only gradually countered by the ingenuity of cryptanalysts in GC and CS. Essentially for Overlord, this did include the breaking of Jellyfish in March.

Meanwhile, Tommy Flowers and the Dollis team had set to work on an order by de Grey for Colossus II, with GC and CS demanding delivery by 1 June. It would be a much more powerful machine fitted with 2,500 valves and a limited capacity memory, based on a photo-electrically-read perforated tape. It would read between 5,000 and 25,000 positions per second and was, in fact, the world's first programmable computer. Even so, it normally took between three and seven days to decrypt Fish messages, although this was still of immense value since Geheimschreiber mostly carried intelligence of the highest grade with long-standing strategic implications.

Concurrent with the planning of Overlord and its associated liaison with GC and CS and SIGINT there was launched a systematic destruction of German transport lines of communications to France which, fortuitously, also began to erode General Fellgiebel's elaborate signal communications system.

Always of fundamental concern to COSSAC and, in due course, SHAEF was the fear that the Germans might be capable of concentrating stronger forces against the invasion lodgement areas more quickly than the Allies could bring ashore their own troops and logistic facilities. The obvious remedy was to destroy by bombing and sabotage the French and Belgian land communication system by what became known as the Transportation Plan. The evolution of the plan was long and painful in gestation for fear of its appalling effects upon the populace when railway junctions, workshops and cuttings were attacked over a period of several weeks by day and night. Trial attacks on these targets early in March were disappointing since, as agents, SIGINT and PR indicated, repairs were rarely long delayed. The main programme which began in April was more encouraging but still unconvincing.

Up to this moment attacks on bridges had been discounted and trials against them in April were unimpressive. Not until 7 May were attacks by US fighter bombers sufficiently effective to bring a change of strategy. From then on bridges became prime targets, especially those spanning the rivers Seine and Loire whose destruction isolated Normandy. Increasingly SIGINT gave insight into growing enemy concern about their logistic consequences and the difficulties of moving troops and their equipment by rail. But what these reports did not reveal to any extent was the growing deterioration of land signal routes laid on bridges or converging in exchanges in towns and cities, be they in the occupied countries or in Germany itself, where the problem also had been worsening and was putting a strain on the Reichspost cable links.

The effect of this unforeseen erosion of cables and exchanges not only threw a heavy load on Fellgiebel's repair services, which often suffered from shortages of equipment and spares, but also enforced the increasing use of radio and thereby provided more transmissions for the searchers of Y to intercept and analyse.

Yet another major blow inflicted on the Germans, probably at the instigation of SHAEF and certainly with Dr R. V. Jones's keen involvement, was the jamming and destruction of his early warning radar sets. All of these had been found and monitored by ground intercept stations and PR by April 1944. Nevertheless, a search for stations which might have eluded detection was carried out by special flights by 192 Squadron – without any luck. Then, as D Day drew near, RAF Typhoon fighter bombers undertook the systematic destruction of these sets and five jamming stations until, on the eve of D Day, only five of the latter were working. A few of the radar sets were left alive only temporarily to allow the Germans to detect a spoof operation in which RAF bombers precisely dropped Window to simulate the approach that night of a large convoy to the Pas de Calais.

Throughout the night 192 Squadron and elite RN and RAF searchers stationed at Acton, Ventnor, Beachy Head and Abbotscliff kept watch. They discovered that, out of forty-seven radar stations between Dieppe and Guernsey, all but five were silenced early but that eleven were reactivated, none of them near the beaches. All, with one possible exception, were promptly, effectively jammed.

Remorselessly the Germans were being brought under terrible pressure from a host of foes. On the other side of an English Channel they could no longer adequately guard, their enemy also was under pressure (of a very different kind due to possession of the initiative) as he moved forces into position, amended plans, put final touches to arrangements, struggled to maintain secrecy and security and constantly strove to be on the alert for some event or snippet of intelligence which might throw everything out of gear. Crucial to all of this, although completely unknown to the vast majority of the millions of people awaiting D Day, was the secret SIGINT effort.

Step by step Hut 4 and Hut 3 links were established with selected HQs to provide the weighty fruits of Y and Hut 6 in high-quality, digestible form that their relatively limited intelligence staffs could swallow. Because of the relatively slow pace of naval warfare, Hut 4's system was much less complicated than Hut 3's. Indeed, at times the centralised organisations, that of Air Section in Hut 3 in particular, became unwieldy due to the existence of too many reporting organisations that slowed reactions and delayed distribution of vital information about fast-developing, surprise Luftwaffe operations. Compromise and condensations became watchwords which, as time went by, solved many difficulties without breaching security.

At the same time, of course, there was the SIGINT input from ships and RAF Field Units supporting the landings prior to the arrival of British, Canadian, Polish and American Army Field Units. Each of three naval vessels would embark three Fighter Director listening parties for early warning during the landing only. Another temporary air defence unit, 85 Group Composite Wireless Unit, was tasked for night and day defence of the beachhead. To be put ashore as soon as possible there were to be four British and five American Field Units (all handling RT) subordinated, respectively, to British 2nd Tactical Air Force and Ninth US Army Air Force, and linked to fixed DF stations in Britain. With the least delay these intercept units would send RT reports to Kingsdown and WT reports to Cheadle, as well as to the local commands, whose SIGINT HQ also dealt with WT.

Needless to say, close liaison between Field Units in France was to be maintained with GC and CS, as well as providing up-to-date intelligence to SHAEF's formations and units wherever they were - be they RAF or Army. Meanwhile army mobile sections were to come ashore at the earliest possible moment in order to seek information about enemy reactions, especially the counter-stroke which was expected from 21st Panzer Division, which was the only armoured formation deemed likely to be available to strike immediately after the British landed on the left flank

On the eve of the invasion (fixed for 5 June but at the last moment, famously for meteorological reasons, postponed to the 6th) the intercept and jamming machinery was at a peak of efficiency. Colossus II had come into service to schedule on 1 June to cater for the highest-grade material being intercepted at Knockholt. The entire SIGINT system was in high gear. It had fixed the location of every U-boat at sea and the handful of surface craft that might intervene, and was able, to some extent, to reveal the movements of enemy land formations, despite their excellent radio discipline. Through Cheadle to GC and CS came a stream of technical data and cryptanalytical recoveries concerning weather, enemy reconnaissance activity and anti-aircraft warnings. And from Kingsdown flowed detailed information about enemy aircraft movements, positions of shipping and their escorts, formations approaching the combat zone and active beacons, plus enormous quantities of decrypts with bearing on call signs and frequencies and the movement of transport aircraft – a great deal of this applicable, of course, to the land battle once it was joined.

These were the products of years of blood, sweat, tears, triumphs and setbacks of a kind Winston Churchill cannot have envisaged when he made his famous call to struggle in 1940.

CHAPTER TWENTY

NORMANDY TO ARNHEM

A few days before D Day of Operation Overlord, Brigadier E. T. Williams, the Chief Intelligence Officer of 21st Army Group, visited GC and CS to present General Sir Bernard Montgomery's plan for the invasion of Normandy. During this unprecedented event, for senior staff only, he explained in detail on a large-scale map the intended phases and objectives of the forthcoming operation, and then answered questions. From that moment his audience benefited not only from a sense of Montgomery's confidence in them but also felt better equipped to make fine-tuned adjustments to their own plans which, it was anticipated, would place enormous demands on GC and CS capacity.

They heard that it was the intention to land on a wide, three Army Corps front, flanked by airborne forces, with the aim of seizing Caen at once and the capture of Cherbourg after the sealing off of the Cotentin peninsula. Battleships, cruisers and a fleet of smaller vessels, in collaboration with massive attacks by aircraft, would give direct support to the landings and fend off grossly outnumbered German naval and air forces.

They also learned about the two crucial deception operations called Fortitude and Bodyguard. The former, which was highly complicated (and sometimes referred to as Appendix Y) was intended to persuade the Germans that the main assault would fall on the Pas de Calais: its aims were to make the enemy retain strong forces there instead of transferring them to Caen; to keep him in doubt about the date and time of the assault; and to maintain the deception for fourteen days. The last was intended to delude the enemy into believing that a cross-Channel invasion was not necessarily the main Allied operation in 1944. There is no need here to elaborate on these highly successful operations except to say that the enemy remained deceived for seven weeks. But double agents played a leading role in their implementation and SIGINT steered each ploy and provided vital confirmation of their effectiveness.

In their histories of events during the Battle of Normandy, as seen by GC and CS, both Hinsley and de Grey make it plain that, apart from a few relatively trivial lapses and minor differences of opinion and emphasis, the SIGINT system worked exceptionally well within its designed capacity.

At sea, for example, U-boat Command was overheard giving instructions to all available boats to form patrol lines covering the approaches through the North Sea and Bay of Biscay, as well as ordering an unknown number (in fact seventeen) to move at full speed on the surface into Seine Bay. The majority of the latter were located by Coastal Command on 6 June, two being sunk and eight forced to return to port by serious damage. The survivors were then given permission to submerge but were found on the 7th, with three sunk and the rest repulsed. This put an end to co-ordinated U-boat, anti-invasion measures. Subsequent, piecemeal operations by individual boats were blocked by overwhelming air and surface forces that were guided by SIGINT: they sank only two ships in the first ten days of the battle.

A handful of German destroyers and torpedo boats did no better. Reported at sea by SIGINT and air reconnaissance, they were attacked from the air and by destroyers. By 9 June they either had been sunk, driven ashore or badly damaged having accomplished nothing.

E-boats and torpedo boats in the Seine Bay and Channel were, to begin with, another matter. They sank or damaged twenty Allied ships within the first week. Until then SIGINT had rarely given much warning about them because they received their orders by telephone or teleprinter. But now, due to disruption of land cable communications, those orders were sent by encoded radio which was quickly broken and therefore of some assistance to the Allies. SIGINT, indeed, scored a notable success when it reported a large concentration of these craft at Le Havre, caused by bad weather, on the night 13–14 June. The ensuing, wholesale sinking of these boats by two very accurate RAF Bomber Command attacks (laid on at short notice) was described by the Germans as a catastrophe that had completely changed the naval situation in the Seine Bay.

As for the Luftwaffe, its intervention, to say the least, was desultory. It failed to detect the approaching armadas at night; in daylight it mounted only a few minor sorties; and the following night, out of 175 machines despatched, it managed only forty actual strikes with bombs and torpedoes which sank only one LST and damaged three ships. The price was twelve aircraft. Four days later and until 10 July their night bombers were tasked, much more effectively, to minelaying. But their numbers were in decline and the failure of aircraft to reach the target area noteworthy, SIGINT being significantly responsible for this.

For it was SIGINT which usually gave the earliest warning of raids not only after but also before take-offs. For example, on 14 June Y intercepted a signal, decrypted the following day, demanding an escorted daylight attack with FX guided bombs against battleships from the airfield at Merignac. A confirmatory signal on the 16th advised the best time for it. But that evening Merignac was heavily bombed and the raid prevented. On a more regular basis, founded on SIGINT, Allied aircraft flew close to airfields by night to intercept machines on take-off and landing, or hunted successfully in the known 'safer' corridors used by transports and replacements. These measures, made feasible by Hut 3 at GC and CS (see Chapter 19) ensured throughout the Battle of Normandy and, indeed, almost entirely for the rest of the war, that the Allied forces on land and sea were kept virtually free from effective Luftwaffe attacks by day and not all that often seriously bothered by night.

For these reasons the actual landings by airborne and amphibious forces on 6 June went ahead with remarkable exactitude and far fewer casualties than anticipated by a great many pessimists. Only on the American Omaha beach was there anything threatening disaster and even there sheer guts and determination overcame the defences before nightfall. True, Caen was not captured as soon as desired and the Cotentin peninsula was not immediately isolated. But the dreaded attack by 21st Panzer Division was seen off by 3rd British Division within sight of the beaches, even though SIGINT was not exploited as well as it might have been. In fact, although the approaching tanks of this formation had been monitored by Army Y and watched by air reconnaissance since 1300 hrs, the vital information was slow to be processed by intelligence staff and did not reach the forward troops before the blow materialised at 1630 hrs. Nevertheless, the surprised British tanks and artillery killed fifty out of 127 German tanks and, in short order, snuffed out the only significant enemy counter-attack of the day – and for several days to come.

Army Y's achievements, although of undeniable assistance, were largely complementary when set alongside other SIGINT sources in Normandy, at a time when German Army Enigma was divulging little of vital importance. They were even more important, in mid-June, when the Germans reintroduced the cryptanalytical security device to Geheimschreiber machines which had proved very effective in March and April 1943 – but which gave the Germans much technical trouble. Early in July 1944 Fish was defeating even Colossus II on all channels and would continue to do so until October when, due to renewed technical difficulties, the Germans were compelled to abandon the special security gadget. Fortunately the Japanese Ambassador and his military attachés frequently chipped in with decrypted messages to Tokyo which gave priceless insight into German appreciations, strategy and declining morale. Meanwhile the Luftwaffe's libations were as helpful as ever.

As a rule of thumb, the more mobile the operations, the better were Army Y's successes. For example:

1. The long-delayed German counter-stroke which hit VIII British Corps after its Operation Epsom had penetrated the thinly held German lines around Cheux on 26 June triggered a flurry of tactical as well as strategic radio transmissions by armoured forces. Many of these were heard by Army Y which provided a steady flow of intelligence for Second British Army, its subordinate formations and 2nd TAF. The result was a storm of shelling and bombing which stopped the Germans in their tracks with heavy losses, and put an end to the last German hopes of ejecting the Allies from Europe.

2. Prior to Operation Goodwood (a southward thrust by three armoured divisions from Caen on 18 July) intelligence about the Germans, based on several sources including SIGINT, was nigh immaculate. Moreover, during the battle itself, after the massed British armour of VIII Corps had broken through its enemy's forward gun line, Army Y's searchers were unique in reporting intercepts indicating that German armour was being sent to occupy the vital Bourgebus ridge with a view to counter-

attacking, and also strengthening the flanks of this position. It was not lack of intelligence (as some have suggested) that failed VIII Corps but the inadequacy of a plan which denied timely and effective strikes against enemy positions set in depth.

3. Most important of all, when on 3 August Hitler ordered an armour-heavy counter-offensive to sever the American spearhead driving south into Brittany by cutting through to the sea at Avranches, it was SIGINT, and Army Y in particular, which first got wind of it through TA and 'a spectacular rise' in German low-grade and high-grade encrypted traffic. True, much of it was of a highly ephemeral tactical nature, but it exposed clearly the enemy's intentions and strength. Thereafter all the routine means of intelligence-gathering were mobilised to complement Y and decisively to repulse the Germans at Mortain. Not only, however, did Army Y continue to monitor wilting enemy offensive moves, it also helped detect inherent weaknesses – which were numerous and ripe for exploitation by an infinitely stronger opponent. As an example of rapidity of reaction to an impending enemy counter-attack was Army Y's warning to XII British Corps' concerning its exposed flank on the River Orne on 7 August. To begin with, they gave early warning of its coming and then of its renewal the following day – which came to grief against a well-balanced defence by 59th Infantry Division.

AT GC AND CS on D Day, Huts 6 and 8 had to cope with little more than the customary flow of material. Yet even Hut 3, which sent 16,000 groups per day to SHAEF and 15,000 to 2nd TAF, was about 10 per cent less than expected on D Day. Also, at 1,000 messages per day, the number of messages concerned with raid reporting and fighter defence was low, varying from 1,000 to 1,500 for BMP work and falling from 500 to 200 per day as time went on and the Luftwaffe was crushed. This is not say that Hut 3 was unexpectedly idle. Far from it! Wing Commander Eric Jones's people were hard-pressed until D+30 or thereabouts. But what few hitches there were about the service rendered were minimal. HQ ships complained that reports were 'few and far between and also very late'. This was put down to congestion on teleprinter lines from Kingsdown and, ironically, the time-lag of traffic from the Luftwaffe due to that organisation's current disorganisation. Be that as it may, there were no serious operational repercussions and whatever improvements that could be made were rarely if ever delayed.

Of course the Luftwaffe's terminal decay helped. Its stiffest daytime resistance lasted but a few days in June and then faded away. Come August, Hut 3's Air Section was under-employed and in process of a radical reduction in strength, despite the V1 and V2 campaigns (see below). For the remainder of the war the SHAEF forces' superiority established on 6 June was maintained. And so, in connection with SIGINT and Y, it is not intended to relate the history of the ongoing campaign except when some critical incident demands it. First for attention, therefore, must be the V1s and their impact on SIGINT subsequent to the start of the air attacks on their launching sites in December 1943, related in Chapter 19.

THROUGHOUT THE winter, air attacks on factories, supply depots and the latest type of more easily concealed launching sites continued: they inflicted damage enough critically to delay the planned, massed salvoes of missiles. To make matters worse for the Germans, their campaign, due to communications and logistic difficulties, went off at half-cock on the 12th. Of the ten missiles launched, only four reached England. Three days later the bombardment began in earnest, but only against London since the overrunning of the Cotentin sites saved Bristol an ordeal by drizzle of bombs. Fifty-five sites fired 244 missiles and thereafter sent over between 190 and 120 per day. But that number declined steadily in the days to come due much more to supply and technical difficulties than the destruction of sites, which only occasionally were found and hit with the loss of only 138 men.

In all 8,893 V1s were ramp-launched, plus 1,500 from aircraft after the Pas de Calais sites were captured in August. Barely 25 per cent reached London, but they killed 6,184 people and caused greater anxiety than the V2s which made their début later and did not announce their arrival. One notable casualty, in so far as the Y Service was concerned, was a V1 hit on Kingsdown in August which made it necessary to move that

establishment to a school on the outskirts of Canterbury. (For convenience it will continue to be referred to here as Kingsdown.) Anti-aircraft
weapons destroyed 74 per cent of those shot down, fighters most of the
remainder and balloon cables a mere handful. What little was received
by SIGINT contributed hardly anything to counter-measures since the
Luftwaffe launching regiment did not use radio. But in several decrypted
reports by the Japanese to Tokyo, a picture of deepening gloom emerged.
In summary, they reported that the Germans were disappointed with the
accuracy and effect of V1 which would not affect the invasion. Only
Foreign Minister Joachim von Ribbentrop sounded an optimistic note
when he stated that V2 was more accurate.

Yet this too was an illusion. When at last, on 8 September, V2s began
to fall in the London area (and later, in company with V1s, on Antwerp
after it had been captured on 3 September), it revealed itself as far more
inaccurate and unreliable than V1. Out of 1,600 sent to London in the
ensuing six months, 485 did not arrive and those which did tended to
land anywhere up to eleven miles from the aiming point. Dr R. V. Jones,
aided by SIGINT (notably RAF Y), played a leading part in laying bare
V2's secrets. And RAF Y was greatly helped by the Swedes who permitted SIS, very secretly in August, to establish a radio intercept station at
Malmo, from where it was easier to plot the test flights of rocket across
the Baltic Sea. Furthermore, the Swedes also made available important
bits and pieces of a wayward rocket which had fallen on their country.
As a result, just a few days before the first operational launching, Jones
finalised an incredibly accurate and complete description of V2 and its
likely performance. Apart from that, however, SIGINT was unable to contribute anything of much use. So the rockets continued to fall until
7 April 1945, after the main launching sites in Holland were cut off
in March.

AS USUAL, BOTH BEFORE and after 6 June, SIGINT had been providing
guidance on Russian offensive intentions. For, also as usual, Moscow was
silent about when and where they would strike. So it was Enigma, principally the Mustard key used by the German Horchdienst, which gave the

best intelligence of Russian plans, without revealing exactly when the blow would fall; and which indicated how poor was Russian radio insecurity and how good were the Horstdienst and the German intelligence staffs. Not until 18 June, in fact, did the Russians officially let slip to her western allies that the 22nd was the day: along with an outline forecast of an initial assault on one front before spreading wide with a series of complementary attacks on an enormous scale which, by 3 July, had engulfed Army Group Centre. This disaster opened the gates to Poland, Finland, Romania, Bulgaria and Hungary as the pulverised Germans were flung back in the ensuing months, until the Russians were forced to pause, mainly from exhaustion and for logistic reasons.

As already mentioned in Chapter 19, the Germans were in full retreat after the capture of Rome on 4 June, and would continue to withdraw into Kesselring's Gothic Line by the end of September. During that retreat SIGINT, as of routine, would supply material of all grades and show beyond doubt, from Bream in particular until July, the parlous state of Kesselring's shattered army and its lack of air support. SIGINT's revelations, indeed, would lend fuel to a renewed attempt by General Alexander, by Churchill and his Chiefs of Staff to renew the debate about the necessity to launch an invasion of southern France (Operation Anvil-Dragoon) in mid-August. Backed by persuasive intelligence, they argued that Kesselring could not possibly hold the Gothic Line and that northern Italy was ripe for the taking if the Anvil forces were thrown into that operation. Moreover, they claimed that this would support Overlord with greater effect than a dispersal of forces into southern France which, in any case, would have to be evacuated. In other words, a resounding victory was assuredly certain.

Initially General Marshall and the American Chiefs of Staff agreed. But at the beginning of July it was thought that preparations for the Anvil–Dragoon plan had gone too far to be stopped, and it was hoped Alexander would break through the Gothic Line with what few forces that remained at his disposal. This, as it turned out in the autumn, was asking too much of them. So American and French troops in Seventh US Army landed near Toulon on 15 August against negligible resistance and only token Luftwaffe activity that placed few urgent demands on Y Service, which had established a listening station on the island of Corsica. It was, of course, already realised that the Germans here, as elsewhere, were incapable of mounting counter-actions of any significant dimensions. Indeed, SIGINT revealed within forty-eight hours that Hitler, in view of the collapse of the front in Normandy, had decided to abandon most of his French conquests. His forces in southern France, less those left behind to hold certain ports on the west coast, were to be evacuated northward, post-haste to hold the Siegfried Line guarding the Rhine.

At this moment the air war in the Mediterranean petered out and, such priority as was granted in this theatre were diverted to operations in Italy, Yugoslavia and Greece – which, from a SIGINT point of view, barely needs description here. Until the inevitable end they had only to search for routine interceptions and process messages of minimal strategic and tactical importance as the focus shifted to Holland and the threshold of Germany.

Yet even on that front, the SIGINT events which call for special mention because they threatened to prolong the war are few. Take Operation Market Garden, Field Marshal Montgomery's imaginative, if misguided, attempt to cut off Holland (with its V2 sites) from Germany by spearheading the advance of Second British Army with a massive drop by three airborne divisions to seize bridges at Grave, Nijmegen and Arnhem on 17 September.

Intelligence about German forces in 21st Army Group's operational zone was extensive and, apart from conflicting reports about the understrength 9th and 10th SS Panzer Divisions in II SS Panzer Corps, said to be in the Arnhem area, was by no means entirely discouraging. Much of this came from decrypted Enigma, but PR, the Dutch Resistance, Army Y and PW all contributed – sometimes in a contradictory manner and never positively about those troops alleged to be at Arnhem. So it was Army Y, early on 17 September, which first raised serious alarm when it reported that both 9th and 10th SS Panzer Divisions were on the move in the Arnhem sector as some of their of their units broke radio silence.

As the battle developed and it gradually became plain that the

Arnhem bridge was one too far, SIGINT (frequently delayed in decryption) provided a modicum of useful strategic tactical material, to which Army Y added occasional flashes of tactical light. For example, on the 18th there was nothing of value garnered from the vitally important and threatened Nijmegen and Arnhem areas, but a great deal heard from the less important Best–Zon sector. Second Army continued to be reduced to guesswork about the enemy at Arnhem on 20 September as, day by day, the chances of beleaguered British troops there being relieved diminished. Indeed one Army Y unit, on the orders of General Browning (Deputy Commander First Airborne Army) found itself swapping humanitarian messages with a German general in negotiations to prevent shelling of a hospital train standing in Arnhem, and making arrangements for the exchange of wounded prisoners. Market Garden ended on the 25th. It was the last German victory of major strategic consequence since it undeniably prolonged the war by several months, permitted the V2 bombardment of England and Antwerp and postponed the transfer of resources, including badly needed cryptographers and Y Service experts, to join in the fight against Japan (see Chapters 21 and 22).

CHAPTER TWENTY-ONE

THE LOOMING SILENCE

For signal security reasons the one great asset the Germans possessed when they backed into the Siegfried Line was the opportunity to make full use of the excellent land line system which had been laid by the Reichspost on the directions of General Erich Fellgiebel and which reduced the need to use radio. But Fellgiebel was not to enjoy that unwanted triumph as Germany faced an absolute disaster nothing could prevent. For he was already dead, executed on 4 September for his leading role in the attempt to assassinate Hitler on 20 July and to seize power through the Revolution by Telephone he had devised.

There is no need here to enter into details about the background, the actuation or the failure of the attempt to blow up Hitler during a conference at the Wolfschanze near Rastenburg. Allied intelligence agencies – those of America foremost – were aware that something was brewing but were not involved. Moreover, their governments had profound reservations about the wisdom of such an attempt. SIGINT learnt nothing until it was all over because the army officers running the conspiracy were committed to Fellgiebel's intention to control and implement a revolution by telephone once Hitler was dead.*

In outline, the attempt was to be conducted from the War Ministry in Berlin by disenchanted serving and retired officers. Colonel Claus von Stauffenberg was to plant the bomb, which would kill Hitler and senior members of his staff in the Wolfschanze conference room, and then return to the War Ministry. Here he would help run Operation Walkyrie that was designed to cope with an insurrection against the Nazi government. Meanwhile Fellgiebel and a handful of senior signals officers would shut down the powerful radio transmitters and take control of the Army telephone system's exchanges, telephones and teleprinters for the dissemination of orders and information throughout the Reich: once, that is, it was known that Hitler was dead. It was calculated that full control of government

* See *Without Enigma* by Kenneth Macksey

had to be in place within six hours in order to be effectively unassailable.

Things went wrong from the start. Because Hitler changed his schedule, the bomb had to be detonated thirty minutes ahead of the expected time. This meant that the three chief conspirators in the War Ministry were still having lunch when they should have been at their posts. Then, crucially by a miracle, neither Hitler nor his most senior staff officers were killed by the colossal explosion, although both Stauffenberg and Fellgiebel assumed this must be the case. Stauffenberg at once flew to Berlin, but was delayed through poor staff work in the arrangement of transport to and from the airfields. Fellgiebel initiated the transmission of the 'good news' by telephone to the key signals officers, and tried to warn General Fritz Thiele (the War Ministry Chief Signals Officer in Berlin) after he discovered that Hitler was still alive. Nevertheless Fellgiebel instantly decided to continue with the putsch and ordered that all messages from the Wolfschanze must be blocked before Hitler ordered a news blackout and the blocking of the Wolfschanze switchboard.

The leading conspirators were still at lunch when Thiele heard at 1300 hrs that Hitler was dead but, a few minutes later, that he was alive and that the plan should be continued as intended. However, lacking guidance from his superiors until 1315 hrs, he did not order the shut-down of the big radio transmitters. This delay was extended when the conspirators, unlike Fellgiebel, dithered until 1355 hrs before deciding to go ahead with the radio plan. Then, to make matters even worse, the conspirators delayed until 1530 hrs before agreeing to transmit the prearranged signals announcing Hitler's death and their assumption of power. Whereupon it was discovered that the two signals girls on duty would take three hours to encode all the messages for radio because nobody had thought of doing so ahead of the event. Moreover, nor did anybody think of sending them by telephone.

Stauffenberg arrived at the War Ministry at 1645 hrs and endeavoured to inject a greater sense of urgency. Encoded messages (which were not intercepted by Y) began dribbling out at 1800 hrs but at once were overtaken by a flood of telephone calls from the Wolfschanze that spread the truth that Hitler was very much alive and kicking. Then, at 1900 hrs,

Propaganda Minister Dr Goebbels, who was busy taking firm control in Berlin, broadcast to the world that Hitler was alive (duly intercepted by the BBC in London) and ordered the Army to arrest the conspirators in the War Ministry. The Revolution by Telephone was broken, stopped by a few rifle shots as troops loyal to Hitler moved in. But, as Goebbels later said, 'With a little more skill behind it and the rifle shots would not have done the trick.' Allied SIGINT did not come into the picture until late on the 20th when it intercepted a message from Admiral Dönitz (decrypted the next morning) giving details of the failed plot and the fierce remedial action being taken.

The war went on but Hitler, in his fury and lust for vengeance, nearly crippled the Wehrmacht when he demanded dire retribution on all those signals officers and men who had been involved in the putsch. So large was that number that, to preserve the communication system in working order, Fellgiebel's successor, General Albert Praun, was compelled to risk his own life by, successfully, pleading with Hitler to relent. In the event only Fellgiebel, Thiele and one other senior signals officer were executed. But for the remainder of the war all Army officers and many others did their duty in peril of their lives.

THE ARRIVAL OF THE Allied armies on the German frontier conferred immense advantages on Y Service Field Unit intercept stations which moved into Holland, Belgium and France and communicated results directly to England. Now, too, the air forces operated almost as they chose against a practically defenceless Reich. The Bomber Offensive (in which the RAF had persisted with night area attacks besides its tasks against V weapons and battlefield targets) was intensified with greater accuracy and lesser risk as the German air defences were reduced in depth and deprived of adequate early warning. Y was able to give much improved warning of threats to the bombers. From 27 August onward fighters based in France and Belgium escorted both American and British heavy bombers with increasing safety and far greater effect by day as well as by night. Moreover, the margin of safety was improved by the ability of aircraft to enter German air space by surprise at low levels on a wider frontage, with far less chance of detection by radar.

In addition to transport targets, oil facilities had been concentrated upon since the middle of May. In some quarters, notably in Air Marshal Sir Arthur Harris's RAF Bomber Command, there resided acute scepticism about the potential of the oil offensive. It was SIGINT, as it accumulated mounting evidence from German and Japanese transmissions which, almost alone, proved beyond doubt the extent of the crippling damage being inflicted on the Romanian oilfields and the numerous synthetic oil plants in Hungary, Austria, Germany and Yugoslavia; and also through the complementary interdiction of transport routes. For not only were railways and roads being severed, so too was the River Danube being blocked as a result of aerial mining by 205 Group RAF based in Italy. This began in July with the intention of cutting off vital oil supplies. It did so with such precision that, for the loss of very few aircraft, it had far greater effect than the expensive bombing of the Romanian fields, before they fell into Russian hands at the end of August.

Convincing intelligence of the dire effects of this minelaying operation on the German war economy and logistics grew profusely from Wehrmacht Enigma and the Japanese diplomatic codes. The latter, indeed, deepened the gloom in Tokyo government circles which were all too aware of a similar oil crisis of their own caused by the American submarine blockade. This stranglehold was made more sombre as news from the battlefronts worsened with the reporting of the succession of defeats and setbacks that poured in from the south-west and central Pacific, the Philippines, China and from Burma. Such news coincided with the first of a series of increasingly heavy bombing attacks that struck Japan itself on 15 June 1944 to bring the war home to the populace (see Chapter 22).

The aerial minelaying of the Danube was soon extended, urged on by Winston Churchill who recognised a good thing when he saw it. Between July and October (when at times the river was totally blocked), seventy-four ships were sunk, twenty-eight damaged and a dire shortage of oil tankers caused – all faithfully reported by SIGINT, which, indeed, was almost the only reliable source on the subject since PR was frequently thwarted in its sorties over vital installations by camouflage and the smoke from fires.

The overriding strategic effect of the complementary transport/oil campaign needs no amplification. It alone was bringing Germany to her knees in a way area bombing had never threatened. So it is all the more astonishing that, in September, Hitler became bent on a major counter-offensive in the Ardennes and that his staff prepared it in the full knowledge that oil reserves were hopelessly inadequate.

Military logic certainly conspired to mislead SHAEF into dismissing the likelihood of what the Germans called Operation Watch on the Rhine. Only a lunatic, it might be said on the basis of the oil shortage alone, would contemplate (let alone attempt), such an impracticable venture when Germany was nearing her inevitable defeat. But Hitler was a dangerous maniac served by frightened sycophants who knew not how to curb the mad dictator's fantasies. Nevertheless, although the Wehrmacht's security for Watch on the Rhine was exemplary because its signal communications excluded the use of radio, its camouflage and deception plans were very effective. Nevertheless sufficient information about it reached SHAEF Intelligence to alert the staff about what was about to hit the Americans on 16 December.

As already mentioned, Fellgiebel's cable system, now controlled by General Praun, made possible a SIGINT-proof communications system for planning and deployment of Sixth SS Panzer Army and Fifth Panzer Army. Damaged though the Reichspost trunk cable system was, Praun was able to patch it up by quickly erecting overhead wire links and by the employment of line-of-sight beam radio, such as had been used prolifically and uninterceptably throughout the Russian campaign. Secret planning was done mainly at meetings. Orders were passed by courier or high-grade, encrypted cable. Allied Y heard nothing rated of obvious strategic value that was not regarded by the War Office, SHAEF and 21st Army Group as contradictory and therefore misleading. Most traffic that Y searchers detected was routine, low-grade material, some of it considered compatible with deception schemes.

And yet, Hut 3 at GC and CS acquired sufficient intelligence from SIGINT to sound serious warning about what was in the wind. In *British Intelligence History in the Second World War*, Vol. 3 Part 2, Hinsley goes into the greatest detail to lay bare the whole complex story. In so doing he exposes how difficult it was at the time to arrive at the actual truth about what actually was in train. To put it simplistically, the sheer volume of true, misleading and contradictory evidence made it extremely difficult to see wood for trees.

Nigel de Grey, on the other hand, in PRO HW3/99, presents a more lucid and succinct case in defence of Hut 3 and SIGINT for its contribution in the Ardennes affair. Writing shortly after the war with a minimum of hindsight, he was fully appreciative, as Deputy Director of GC and CS, of the political implications of the Anglo-American aspects of what he rated as 'the most serious lapse in Intelligence work that had occurred during the war'.

Immediately after the event Hut 3 carried out a post-mortem to discover if it had rendered all reasonable service in the way of interpretation or had commented misleadingly. The findings showed that there was no firm indication that the Luftwaffe or Army had put the matter 'beyond peradventure'; that all had been reported fairly and accurately and that Hut 3's hands were clean. But he underlines that there was the perennial problem of the reliability of the intelligence available which always had to be addressed by Intelligence experts. As an example, de Grey laid special emphasis on the quantity and value of intercepted and decrypted messages sent by the Japanese on the subject and, in particular, their quotation of remarks made by Ribbentrop as to the likelihood (but not its place or time) of a big counter-offensive. But he qualified this by pointing out a German tendency to tell the Japanese what they wanted to believe while keeping to the truth, as was compatible with policy. He added that the Japanese were 'indiscriminate reporters, though much valuable information had come from this source'.

Nearer to home were a series of Hut 3 conclusions which should not have been brushed aside. For example, routine Luftwaffe traffic about a concentration near Cologne of fighters and fighter bombers practising low flying; and the training of Ju 88 crews for piloting pathfinders. This might well have been connected with the known existence, also close to Cologne, of a curious command said to be in charge of refitting panzer units. Then there was the abrupt 'disappearance' of major formations and units through the imposition of radio silence, and numerous, significant railway movements. Things such as these demanded synthesis by experts and justified the issue of urgent warnings.

De Grey drew the conclusion that SIGINT had done all that it was called upon to do 'in its unwritten charter' - and possibly more. He seems to imply, however, that some of those who handled daily traffic and knew all the ins and outs of the whole system, failed 'to single out' the necessary evidence that was 'enough to tip the scales'. In other words, 'that little extra' was lacking. On the other hand, the ministries never shirked their responsibilities as the final arbiters upon enemy intentions, and that went for SHAEF.

Nor did Eric Jones, Head of Hut 3, duck the issue when he said (presumably to de Grey) that, although 'We have nothing to reproach ourselves for our dissemination of factual Intelligence ... we made one mistake: we held views which differed from those of heads of sections in ministries on a matter of great strategic importance to our recipients and took no steps to bring them to bear at a higher level.'

But, as many times before in history, the Incredulity Factor interposed against prudence. For although the ministries and High Commands certainly read the signs, they then dismissed them as inconceivable and convinced their commanders accordingly. Field Marshal Montgomery wrote on the eve of the attack that the enemy's situation 'is such that he cannot stage major offensive operations'.

So Watch on the Rhine was launched, achieved complete surprise in weather which prevented flying by both sides, and inflicted considerable damage upon an overwhelmingly strong, invulnerable opponent. The Americans soon recovered and, with the aid of the characteristically profuse tactical SIGINT induced by mobile warfare, rapidly checked and then threw back a battered foe whose fundamentally weak logistics were reduced to fuel and ammunition-starvation as the weather improved to permit crushing attacks from the air that simply could not be warded off by a weak Luftwaffe.

Only when the Ardennes battle was lost did the Luftwaffe intervene on New Year's Day in a manner that neither could be called strategically effective nor in strong, direct support of the Army. For, with relatively few machines available, manned by crews whose training had been neglected through fuel shortage, it, like the Army, was to be thrown into yet another ridiculously sacrificial operation such as the Wehrmacht indulged in during its death throes.

The New Year's Day attack by between 750 and 800 fighter bombers on sixteen Allied airfields certainly, through strict radio silence, achieved complete surprise. Allied SIGINT picked up nothing. Radar detected none of the low-flying machines until it was far too late to warn the ground defences. Many aircraft caught on the ground were destroyed or damaged. But so meticulous were the German security measures that their flight leaders were not given their orders until the previous evening. Therefore insufficient time was available to brief pilots many of whom, consequently, did not find their targets or press home attacks. Additionally there were mid-air collisions. As a measure of Allied surprise, they suffered the loss of 150 machines and 111 damaged with forty-six men killed, including six pilots. But the Luftwaffe lost 270 machines and had forty damaged, with the loss of 260 aircrew when those Allied fighters which did get off the ground caught up with a fleeing enemy.

The Ardennes debacle has been called the death blow of the Luftwaffe. The coming into service in autumn 1944 of rocket-propelled and jet fighters, deadly as they could be, had only a slight impact on the Allied air fleets. As 1945 advanced the Y Service and Air Section at Hut 3 began to lapse into a languor that was foreign to its hard-worked members.

Germany's frontiers shrank from mid-January onward. The renewal of Russian offensive operations along the length of the Eastern Front, commencing on 12 January 1945, saw the overrunning of East Prussia, the remainder of Poland and the arrival of enemy troops on the banks of the Oder by the end of the month. The conquest, almost incidentally in the circumstances, captured several of the great German radio transmitters. Likewise in the south, the Russians thrust deeper into Hungary and the Balkans as Tito's partisans tightened their hold on Yugoslavia and the Allied forces in Italy prepared to launch their final offensive on 9 April. Meanwhile British and American bombers continued, with ever greater ease and negligible losses, to pound the remaining German hinterland prior to their armies crossing the Rhine on 23 March to occupy its western sector.

IT IS THEREFORE astonishing to record that at the beginning of 1945 when the German Army was stretched to breaking point and the Luftwaffe crushed and down to only a few hundred machines, the Navy continued to function with outstanding courage and no little effect. On New Year's Day SIGINT was reporting seventy-five schnorkel U-boats operational – a strength which rose to 110 on 1 April, of which on average more than 50 per cent were at sea. Between 1 January and the war's end, they sank 263,000 tons of merchant shipping. Most of the damage was done by the obsolescent boats, both in home and deep sea waters, and their losses were by no means negligible, amounting to about fifty in this period. Only a few of the latest, fast Walther boats were available but these made their contribution at relatively low cost. New construction was actually increasing, despite heavy bombing of the shipyards.

SIGINT kept track of most redeployments of boats as they were withdrawn from the Baltic ahead of Russian advances. Their voyages were fraught with peril as the German minesweeping organisation collapsed and Enigma indicated where aerial minelaying could best be executed. Decrypts of Japanese traffic from Berlin gave news of Dönitz's intention to launch a major offensive, but events outstripped this over-ambitious boast. Nevertheless the Allied navies were kept on their toes by decrypted reports of wishful thinking that postulated a Norwegian-based U-boat campaign after Germany had capitulated.

Far more worrying, however, was the deadly threat of the new Type XXI and XXIII boats as they completed their working-up and, in small numbers, began to become operational. These would be very difficult to detect and sink. Their detailed radio messages were thus read with great attention and anxiety as they headed for Norway. To raise latent fears, however, came indications that a few boats had put to sea without notifying their presence via radio, their orders assumed by GC and CS as coming by courier or line. It has to be said, however, that worrying as these threats were, their achievements were minimal and did not pay a worthwhile dividend for the enormous outlay expended.

E-boat operations continued on a small scale with little effect and there were several raids by a variety of one-man torpedoes, midget U-boats and explosive motor boats. Usually SIGINT provided, in addition to other sources, a fair share of warnings about these craft. But it failed entirely to detect the development of a long-range midget U-boat called *Seehund*, which came to notice from the Japanese Naval Attaché in December 1944. In the weeks to come this somewhat primitive boat, contrary to expectations, achieved notable successes in coastal operations. They usually evaded SIGINT attention prior to the event but often contributed decrypted, post-action reports that announced results. Ironically, however, the long-term warning of a forthcoming raid by a *Seehund*-landed party in the Channel Islands on 8–9 March was wasted since surprise actually was achieved by the Germans and great damage inflicted.

In proportion to the immense scale of operations in the war's fading weeks, these German naval operations were of little immediate consequence. They dropped any attempt to prolong operations from Norway. Their U-boats surrendered in strict compliance with orders to cease hostilities on 3 May; only one disobeyed to schedule because it had not received the signal. In the longer term, however, they were technologically extremely important. Hence those special naval parties which, guided by GC and CS, entered naval installations with (and sometimes ahead of) advancing army units, were intent on seizing a mass of intelligence which would impact crucially on future naval warfare and the Cold War to come.

British, Canadian and Polish Army Y and American RI units, needless to say, were at their peak in Holland, Germany, Italy and Austria in the closing land campaigns of the war as the German army crumbled. So it was ironic that the quantity of traffic they intercepted got less and less as conditions reduced the quantity of radio transmissions being made. As the armies overran the airfields and Luftwaffe command centres, its organisation collapsed, its machines ceased to fly and its radio stations closed down. Bereft of its best mobile formations and largely reduced to static instead of mobile tactics, the Army had far less demand for radio.

In any case, they went on using line systems so long as they remained intact and manned. Now and again Allied Y units came across their enemy opposite numbers from the Horchdienst and B Dienst, from whom they obtained useful if, at times, academic information that might land in a file at GC and CS.

IT IS THEREFORE fascinating that, in the depths of the German debacle, the Luftwaffe and their Army on 1 February introduced a new method of encoded call signs that, in company with frequencies, changed every three days. Hinsley rated this as 'a greater setback to GC and CS than any it had yet encountered' – including the crisis of twelve months ago, of course, which took ten days to overcome. Once more Hut 6 was hard-pressed to maintain normal service because it was no longer possible in advance to allocate tasks to intercept stations. So these were reduced to searching on a grand scale and trusting to luck in finding wanted enemy stations, thereby causing an average daily cut in decrypted Luftwaffe messages from 1,800 to 1,000 and a drop from an average of 150 keys Enigma keys broken in January to 104 at the beginning of February.

Finding a solution to this highly complicated and threatening problem took six weeks of intensive labour. But find it the British did at a time when the effect on GC and CS output was not nearly so serious as it might once have been at any time during the past five years when the slightest delay or loss of vital intelligence could have been catastrophic. Significantly, de Grey credits the individual Y Service operators, computors and log readers with the victory in this last codebreaking battle. Due to them Hut 6 remained undefeated, and still able to provide a service to Hut 3 that enabled it to supply Commands with all they needed, although once more the latter barely noticed the state of crisis, warned though they had been of its existence.

Of course there were other useful substitutes to hand for acquiring SIGINT if Enigma had become impregnable. The fact was that the low-grade traffic which RAF Y consistently broke not only provided basic intelligence but also, through the skill of three WAAF shifts, each of an officer and five corporals, was of crucial assistance to Hut 6 and SIXTA in identifying call signs and associating them to frequencies. Called Lucifers, these ladies rapidly restored Enigma identifications from 104 to 130 per month.

More important still, at a time when the Germans were using Enigma to a lesser extent, they were employing Fish, non-morse traffic more extensively than ever before. All three services of the Wehrmacht were using it. Delays of up to seven days in its decryption persisted, but the intelligence it contributed was of immense help to the Allies in tracing radical changes in enemy organisation and strategy on the eve of terminal collapse, at a time when, amazingly, the volume of radio traffic actually remained enormous until the beginning of April, when for obvious reasons, it fell sharply into decline.

This also was a moment when the western Allies were becoming slowly aware through SIGINT, and other agencies, of the duplicity of their Russian ally. For example, by listening in to German transmissions it sometimes became apparent that Josef Stalin was not being truthful when, on 1 April, he told General Eisenhower that 'Berlin had lost its former strategic importance' and that he did not intend to start another major offensive until mid-May. In fact, SIGINT already had disclosed from decrypted German and Japanese sources that the Russian intention was to drive on Berlin and the Elbe in mid-April with their best troops.

With this sham, cloaked by radio silence, the Russians persisted until several days after they had advanced on 16 April to encircle Berlin – an event which persuaded the Germans to launch a last local offensive to help the Potsdam garrison to break out and escape on 29 April. Needless to say, this belated effort induced a last flurry of radio transmissions connected with a short-lived mobility.

Twenty-four hours later Hitler committed suicide. There was no announcement of this event for the Y Service to read since none was sent. However, at 0300 hrs 1 May a plain language 'Führer Priority' signal was monitored announcing negotiations for a cease-fire.

At about this time, a member of GC and CS (presumably with nothing better to do) calculated that, at its peak, the number of words for all uses within GC and CS (including multi-copies to various commands) would have amounted 'to an annual output of 79 million words which,

if typed on a single line, would be 625 miles long and reach from Land's
End to John o'Groats'.

Serious thought was now given to what actions might be required
when the Germans formally ceased formal hostilities. Would they continue guerrilla warfare with so-called werewolves? Or set up a redoubt in
the Alps? Or keep going in Norway? If so, how might SIGINT help?
Fortunately none occurred.

What did take place, however, was the despatch into Germany of
Anglo-American raiding parties from SHAEF (in conjunction with GC
and CS) on the heels of the advancing armies, tasked to capture German
SIGINT personnel and the contents of their signal centres. The aim was
twofold: first to discover the extent of B Dienst and Horchdienst penetration of Allied codes and ciphers; second to uncover the amount and nature
of German success against Russian and other foreign communications. The
raiders had many thrilling adventures from which they often had to be
extracted by GC and CS and SHAEF. They captured important machines,
including Field Marshal Kesselring's mobile Geheimschreiber complete, to
add to others found elsewhere, and, with the willing co-operation of the
staff of a signals unit at Rosenheim, brought away five truck-loads of
advanced cryptographic equipment for examination.

But in the event relatively few items of startling importance were
discovered, for the very good reason that through the Y Service and GC
and CS, nearly everything about the operations and achievements of the
excellent German SIGINT organisations already had been uncovered. It was
known, for example, that in 1943 the Germans had been breaking many
British codes, including, of course, the mass of medium and low-grade
kind, and that, mainly through Enigma, the naval convoy code had been
broken long before it was abandoned in June 1943. So maybe it was not a
total surprise when the investigation indicated that, until then, some 80
per cent of *all* British codes were being broken.

The strong suspicion concerning the vulnerability of Russian codes
to German intercept was also confirmed – maybe with a twinge of
chagrin when it was recalled how well the Russians had concealed their
own intentions from their allies! But it was certainly something of a shock

to discover that the Horchdienst had used a very ingenious method of intercept and decoding to break the Russian and, presumably, some British and American book codes. Nevertheless, of greatest satisfaction to the Allies was the discovery that at no time did the Germans break into Typex, nor come really close to thinking that their own Enigma had been broken. This was the crucial difference between the combatant nations which shortened the war in the western Allied favour and, to some extent, economised in the waste of life and material.

When victory in Europe was celebrated on 8 May nearly every German radio transmitter, except those engaged in arranging capitulation, fell silent. The thousands of Y Service searchers and operators took off their headsets and, in company with their many collaborators, relaxed as never before in the knowledge that they had done an outstanding job of shortening the war and reducing the casualty lists. It was an accomplishment which, due to the stringent security demands, they could not share with others and accept the plaudits that were their due.

Now began the redistribution of GC and CS's and its Y Service's talented people to meet the requirements of the ongoing Japanese war and the demands of the Control Commission Germany (sometimes known as Charlie Chaplin's Grenadiers). Those with cryptanalytical abilities either stayed on at Bletchley Park or were sent to South-East Asia Command where their expertise was in great demand. Redundant establishments, such as Cheadle, Kingsdown and their various satellite HDUs and FUs, were run down and soon said goodbye to their German speakers who found their way to Germany. As for the remainder, a contingent of Y Service listeners also were on their way to the Far East. A number stayed at Bletchley Park to fulfil GC and CS's important role in the global intelligence system that had been set up in 1944 with America, India, Australia and Canada (see Chapter 22), and also to keep the wheels turning of what later became known as GCHQ, in readiness for a peace that already looked very uneasy. Some of these would undertake the important task of writing the histories and memoirs of their achievements: a task that, apart from the work of Harry Hinsley and the select official historians, would remain a closed book to the public until the Ultra secret was officially declassified in the 1970s.

CHAPTER TWENTY-TWO

DOGFIGHTS

It will be recalled from Chapter 18 that, towards the end of 1943, there were Japanese authorities who sensed that the war for them already was lost. A stalemated SEAC offensive in Burma at the end of 1943 and the beginning of 1944 (by General Slim) was consuming their resources as the Americans and Australians, under General MacArthur, pursued their attritional campaign in the South-west and South Pacific Areas aimed at New Guinea, Rabaul and the Philippines; and as the Americans, under Admiral Nimitz, in the Central Pacific Area developed their strategy aimed more directly at Japan via the Mariana Islands, where they landed on Saipan on 15 June 1944. Against these converging threats the Japanese would strive with dwindling resources to recapture the initiative and, above all, deny airfields to long-range American B29 heavy bombers that were capable of attacking Japan. Their land offensives would be aimed at India and east China at the same time as they struggled to assemble naval air forces of sufficient strength and quality to check MacArthur and Nimitz as they closed to within B29 range of the homeland.

Naturally both sides depended greatly on radio intercept in support of these strategic operations. Disadvantaged as they were in the crypt-analytical contest, the Japanese searchers found sufficient SIGINT evidence to build up a picture of the looming threat from heavy bombers and even-tual invasion. Essential as the Allied Y Service based on Hawaii and Australia was, those in India and China were equally important because they revealed the strength and strategy of the very large Japanese Army and provided vital intelligence for the forthcoming B29 offensive. Five American experts with intercept equipment (later joined by two cryptol-ogists) had arrived at Chungking, in western China, in the autumn of 1942. Overcoming numerous technical difficulties, they had managed to intercept and send strategically valuable information (based on TA and DF) to Washington via San Diego. Gradually this party was adequately reinforced so that, by 1944, extensive TA surveillance of various Japanese radio nets centred on Tokyo, Shanghai, Hong Kong, Manila, Saigon, Singapore and Rabaul was being carried out.

This information was of widespread use. It helped the Chinese Army and British Fourteenth Army in Burma as well as the American Fourteenth Army Air Force as it geared up for the bombing of Japan. But possibly its most importance contribution came from its tapping of networks dealing with the movement of enemy shipping and convoys – intelligence which, in company with reports from other intercept stations, enabled the American Commander Submarine Pacific at Honolulu (Hawaii) and Fremantle (Australia) to deploy his boats with unerring and deadly effect against the *marus* (merchant and transport vessels).

For further description of these campaigns see below, but never lose sight of the fact that, from 1943 to the end in 1945 as the offensives against Japan developed, radio intercept of Japanese traffic was, to all intents and purposes, total and world-wide. It reached that state, despite many difficulties and crises, as a result of the outstanding collaboration and compromises practised by the British, American, Australian and Canadian authorities involved with SIGINT. The growth of that diplomatic saga must therefore first be tackled here.

IT WILL BE RECALLED that, by the end of 1943, the Allies had moved some way to resolving several of the knotty problems related to the handling of SIGINT throughout the vast Americas (Washington and, to a lesser extent Ottawa)/British (Bletchley Park)/India (Colombo)/Australian (Brisbane) Quadrilateral. Current dissemination of material was improved and foresight directed to what the future would demand. Agreement was also reached over the allocation of work to specified centres on types of codes and ciphers. The chart opposite shows how it would be in April 1944.

This piecemeal approach to meteorology is noteworthy, reflecting as it does the multifaceted problems of a vital subject in a huge portion of the world which by nature could be so violently diverse and threatening to operations. Where such phenomena as monsoons and typhoons posed awesome threats to sea, land and air operations, up-to-the-minute weather forecasts were essential. But this was made far more difficult

Type of Traffic	At GC and CS	Elsewhere
Naval High Grade	Exploited by JAIS	Exploited at Colombo, Melbourne, Washington
Naval Tactical	as above	Exploited by Brisbane and FUs
Army/Air High Grade	Air Section	India
Army Address Cipher	JAIS	India, Canada, US Army
Principal weather	Met Section	Untouched
Naval weather cipher	From Washington	Washington, Brisbane, New Zealand
Army weather cipher	Met Section	Untouched

than in Europe because Japan occupied such a large part of the theatre of operations and also because there was no resemblance between the acquisition and deciphering of German and Japanese data. However, as Dr McVittie (the head of the GC and CS Met Section) belatedly discovered on a visit to Washington in August 1942, the Americans since Pearl Harbor had read the Japanese HEI code (known as JN 36) and were aware of the extremely complicated KOO system (known as JN 37).

JN 37 was then tackled by McVittie and was to prove the most difficulty cryptanalytical problem solved by the Met Section. By July 1943 only about 25 per cent was being read and interception was gradually being handed over by the US Navy to the US Army and to the Canadian Signal Corps in Canada. But by April 1944 65 per cent was yielding, although with difficulty due to poor reception besides cryptanalytic reasons. Interception was best undertaken from the west coast of America or Canada. A large number of machines were required and had to be located for maintenance close to industrial facilities. On 20 December 1943 the Canadian Government, eager to get in on the act, volunteered for this task, backed up by GC and CS.

By the end of February 1944, however, the situation had changed dramatically. The Canadians had run into an internal political jam which took a month to be broken by their Prime Minister. But by then the Americans had captured copies of JN 37 tables which, with the approval of General Marshall and Admiral King, their Navy already was exploiting.

Faced by this fait accompli, Edward Travis, who happened to be in Washington for a conference (see below), abandoned the Canadian scheme, left McVittie's top expert behind to work with the Americans and concentrated on securing adequate distribution of the JN 37 product within the Quadrilateral.

Security, as in Europe, was paramount and there was a prolonged debate which threatened to over-restrict the availability of adequate data where it was most required in time. In Europe it had been relatively easy since main distribution centres, manned by senior officers, were located in fairly close proximity to operational HQs. In the Quadrilateral, however, with its scattered, yet important places where weather was difficult to forecast and where only quite junior officers resided, there was a serious security problem. Acrimony occasionally intruded when the Americans adopted a somewhat rigid approach. Fortunately a British officer with great experience in setting up SLUs was to hand. He drafted regulations known as MANX which, later in 1944, satisfied all concerned.

The allocation of responsibilities listed above was settled in April 1944 when the war was reaching a new climax in Europe and intensifying in the quadrilateral. It was formulated after Washington called another conference for a full-scale examination of all cryptanalytical and TA problems in February. There were several, mostly caused by internecine dissent within the alliance. India, virtually a self-governing Dominion, was in difficulty as SEAC settled to its task and Delhi felt it was being side-lined. CBB, alongside HQ South-West Pacific in Brisbane, also was in an ill-defined position since Australia too was a self-governing Dominion – and proud of it. Misguidedly, the Americans tended to treat these nations as 'commands in the field' which should be sent only the material that Washington deemed essential to them. Meanwhile the American Navy and Army went their customary independent ways and sometimes made unilateral decisions without consulting each other, let alone the British.

The British Chiefs of Staff delegated Edward Travis, the Director of GC and CS, to head the British party at what was framed by the Americans as a purely technical conference. But before attending it he determined to establish the status of India and CBB, and his own position as the speaker for British global policy, before tackling the technical matters of dissemination of intelligence output, questions of security and regulations for their governance. The British wanted the so-called Wireless Experimental Centre (WEC), located at Delhi, to function on the same basis as GC and CS and CBB. In practice WEC was a mere shadow of GC and CS, dealing merely with Japanese signal traffic, yet it controlled two large Wireless Sub-Centres (at Bangalore and Barrackpore) which were fed by Army and RAF FUs attached to formations in General Slim's Fourteenth Army. And, of course, it was linked to SEAC at Kandy.

Therefore, before the Technical Conference opened at Washington, a policy meeting was held with the US Army Signal Branch, at Arlington Hall, between the Travis delegation and the Special Branch of G 2 (US Army Intelligence), among whom there already existed sound and amicable relations. There was no shilly-shally, as de Grey makes clear. The Americans immediately embraced the principle of 'free exchange between cryptanalytical centres of all decrypts and their further dissemination under rules to be agreed between Washington and London'. This, de Grey rightly claimed, was a major achievement since it did more than put Delhi and Brisbane on the same footing as London and create the essential foundation for the Technical Conference. Of far greater importance, it created the foundation of a world-wide organisation for the exchange of intelligence. In fact, this already had been mooted by G 2 in the autumn of 1943 and now was activated by a small party of British TA experts working at Arlington Hall alongside their American counterparts.

During the talks the British put forward their own desire to establish a common pool of intelligence that would embrace the main centres and be radio-linked through a common cipher machine. From these centres information would be re-radiated for further dissemination to commands in the combat areas fast enough to make the system work effectively. Already, of course, the British were doing something very much akin to that. It worked. But although G 2 kept an open mind, it could not accept the proposal, partly because they were not at all signal-minded; but largely because:

1. They were about to use radio-teletype stations with a cipher

machine they were not prepared to share with the British. (In fact, in July 1945, an attempt actually was made to use a machine capable of automatically simplifying double enciphering through a cable teletype link between GC and CS and Arlington Hall.)

2. The long-standing and complicated question of security at every point from GC and CS/Arlington Hall and commands which received Ultra/Magic material. American officers working in Hut 3 were convinced that the British system of strictly regulated security at all levels was the right one. But in Washington suspicions existed between the Army and Navy Departments and between G 2 and the Pentagon because of the latter's affiliation with the State Department. Since the outbreak of war in 1941, for political reasons (among others), these schisms had prevented a full and free exchange of secure SIGINT, thereby inhibiting relations with the British, the Australians and Indian authorities, particularly with regard to Japanese Army and Air SIGINT, but fundamentally delaying the passage of essential information for amphibious operations.

G 2 also harboured reservations about British internal security, although in this instance, during the Washington Conference, Travis managed to convince the Americans that, in respect of India, their fears were groundless. Australia was another matter, however, because in Brisbane General MacArthur ruled and was opposed to any suggestion of G 2 dictating to 'his' GHQ SWPA. An American general was Director of CBB and had under him three Deputy Directors, one American colonel, who dealt chiefly with cryptology, and the others Australian, of whom one worked on technical matters and the Australian FUs who were dependent on them. Working for them were several joint American/Australian branches responsible for typical SIGINT functions, such as Solutions (including traffic sorting); Compilation (including vocabulary and security control); Machine Procedure (including photography, card punching and card files); and Intelligence (which was all Australian and did not serve the Americans).

CBB, like all SIGINT organisations, expanded continuously until the war's end. By 1945 at GHQ it had risen to 3,767 personnel (Army and Air) of whom 772 were American and 558 Australian (including about

140 women). In American field RI units, there were thirty-two officers and 937 ORs; and in Australian Army FUs, twenty-one officers (including a woman) and 499 ORs (89 women). The total of all nations in August 1945 came to 4,339, including 338 Canadians and thirty ex-British linguists from GC and CS.

Multi-national and inter-service as this was, it is therefore astonishing to record deep mutual suspicions between Americans and Australians over SIGINT security that threatened to upset the apple cart early in 1944. Out of the blue, MacArthur high-handedly ordered the American Director of CBB to stop communicating with the British except on technical, cryptanalytical matters. This compelled the senior Australian Deputy Director to appeal to General Blamey (the Australian commander in the field) whose supply of intelligence was about to be cut off. The Australians and British, for their part, objected to lax American security – and with this MacArthur concurred. Politics entered into the diplomatic arena, leading to a suggestion that the Australians should be denied access to military intelligence material!

This was objected to by the British who pointed out that Australia's armed forces were fiercely engaged in defence of their homeland and, from the technical angle, were the main contributors of intercepts of Japanese air and military frequencies through their RAAF WUs. Organised on British lines into small, mobile parties, they accompanied both the American and Australian field and air forces in the field and were controlled by CBB, which contained the TA section; and for the good reason that, as yet, the American RIs were incapable of giving reliable service. It is another astonishing fact that only at this moment did it seem to dawn on the British that security of dissemination to the Americans in Special Branch (as de Grey put it) 'had nothing in common with the locks, bolts, passes and the like which had hitherto been their main preoccupation'.

Strongly pressed by Travis, G 2 acceded to adoption of the British SLU (Special Liaison Unit) system of dissemination of Ultra which had been developed in Europe over the years and which was covered by regulations already in use by the Americans in that theatre of war. In fact the Americans were busy redrafting the British Security Regulations, although it would be July before they were ready for signature by General Marshall for issue not only to formation HQs world-wide but, unlike Europe in some instances, down to FUs: the latter exception being due to geographical difficulties in some regions.

The US Navy was not included in this agreement, although as shown below, that was not a great obstacle to progress. Be that as it may, the new, far more flexible and faster army and air system proved satisfactory. From then onwards the main communication links were:

1. Washington and GC and CS linked by Hydra (the Toronto Y station which in winter months for climatic reasons was unreliable but in summer could relay 120,000 groups a day); by commercial cable through New York; or by air-courier or ship-courier in the two British, fast Queen liners.

2. GC and CS to Delhi, since the end of 1942, through the Y radio network with a peak load of 110,000 groups per day, or by air-courier in ten days.

3. GC and CS to Brisbane through Cable and Wireless Ltd (reaching 4,000 groups per day in December 1944); or via Delhi over a RAAF link at the end of 1943 at 25,000 groups per day; or air-courier across the USA and Pacific Ocean.

4. GC and CS to Kandy via Delhi 140,000 groups per day, or by air-courier; or by Cable and Wireless Ltd from December 1944 at 140,000 groups per day.

5. Washington to CBB and SWPA by special radio-teletype links.

6. Washington to Delhi via GC and CS or air-courier via Africa. All high security British messages were encoded by Typex machines.

The US Navy Department, on the other hand, used the BRUSA Circuit, a far less disjointed system than that of their Army–Air colleagues whose methods were more expensive in man-hours. BRUSA simply connected all its centres in a single network. Only GC and CS was directly excluded, though brought in by side-linking through Colombo. It was guarded by a common cipher system.

The Allied SIGINT systems in the quadrilateral never reached the maturity achieved in Europe. There were unresolved difficulties to the war's end. On the whole, however, they worked sufficiently well to play a central role in winning colossal victories over Japan in 1944 when the war in Europe, which many thought was virtually over, roared on unabated.

THE BATTLE FOR BURMA flared up in December 1943 when General Slim took the offensive in the Arakan and the Japanese fought back in February with a strong counter-attack which was the prelude to their major offensive on 7 March aimed at India. The struggle for air superiority over China lay at the strategic heart of this offensive and also the far larger attack launched from Canton on 7 May. Both were intended to capture the air and logistic bases that supplied China and threatened Japan itself with B29 air raids launched from Chengtu. Tactical air support of the armies took second place in order of priority to the maintenance by the Allies of air supply from Calcutta. Therefore SIGINT was focused principally on these operations, with meteorological information high on the list, beside conventional early warning of Japanese fighter intervention against the transport aircraft fleets.

The inevitability of defeat lay heavily upon the outnumbered and outclassed Japanese Army Air Force as it struggled to fulfil its overbearing tasks. But when their army advanced towards India at the beginning of March and closed in on Kohima and Imphal for prolonged sieges, the achievement of surprise for them was virtually impossible. Battlefield reconnaissance, PR, Y FUs and SIGINT combined to give Slim ample warning. TA as well as radar helped guide the first Spitfire fighters to reach India to a series of victorious dogfights. These guaranteed the safety of the bombers and transports which made feasible the insertion by air and subsequent maintenance of Chindit units which operated behind the Allied lines for nearly four months; as well as supplying the garrisons of Kohima and Imphal and maintaining the airborne build-up of airfields in China.

British SIGINT staffs in India and Burma were hard-pressed to meet all demands from a plethora of sources. Plans at Chief of Staff level were in hand to transfer skilled linguists, computors and intelligence officers to India on the false expectation of an early end to the European war. But although WRNS were reaching Ceylon to ease the 'manning' shortage, ATS and WAAF were still excluded. The Japanese codes remained difficult to crack, although a breakthrough came in May when a copy of Koku Ango 3 (the Japanese Army-Air code book) was captured. This cipher was far simpler than any other and led a senior RAF officer to remark that 'The present situation is more favourable for exploitation than any which has ever before existed for any Japanese Army-Air cipher'.

Nevertheless, exploitation of this cipher was curtailed due to the slow speed of processing in India, which still was at a rate only one-third that of GC and CS. JAIS at Bletchley Park was getting slowly into its stride. The 3366 code, which was in world-wide use, was proving useful. The newly arrived Brigadier Harris's position as Director of Signals in India was improved when he also assumed control of SEAC Signals to become Director of SIGINT SEAC and India. Concurrently he took control of Army and RAF Y Service along with the co-ordination of static and field intercept units, with responsibility for providing SIGINT to all commands.

Yet one receives the impression that India's SIGINT bureaucracy continued to make extremely heavy weather of its task within the over-complicated Allied SIGINT organisation. To some extent this was due to Delhi's isolated position in relation to Kandy, with unavoidable duplication of intelligence staffs, but also related to erratic ionosphere conditions. As de Grey put it in June 1944, however, 'The crux of the matter lay in the fact that the only competent reporting officers available were borne on the establishment of DMI India who was reluctant to forego his hold upon this function.' It would not be overcome until November when communications from WEC were made directly to subordinate commands within SEAC as well as to Army and Air commands.

WEC, of course, stood at the hub of SIGINT in India. Not until

September 1943 had its air and army functions been separated when a fully trained RAF intelligence staff officer joined to impose effective TA procedures with adequately trained operators. But the latter needed protracted training and always were in short supply. So it took another year, in which army officers and the Naval Air Section at Colombo played a major part, to raise standards to an acceptable efficiency, and also to create 'a mobile and independent' radio interception service, reporting to the Tactical Air Intelligence Centre (TAIC) at Comilla, with WUs and DF sets at Imphal, Chittagong and Cox's Bazaar. This delay was exacerbated when an urgent demand in June 1944 for fifty cryptanalyst officers, one hundred WOs and sergeants, seventy airmen, six male typists and 120 women for tabulating at WEC alone, was most coldly received in London where the needs of the war in Europe still stood top of the manpower list.

The big strategic picture was beginning to change as long-standing discussions, concerning who in SIGINT did what and where, continued in the aftermath of the recent Washington conferences. As the combat centre of gravity shifted towards the Philippines, the Marianas and Japan, new players sought more roles. In June, for example, the Canadians were requesting a more active role in the field, and both India and Australia were bidding for reinforcement. This happened in August 1944 when the Americans were on the eve of moving part of CBB, along with GHQ SWPA, to Hollandia in Dutch New Guinea. They suggested that the British might fill their places at Brisbane. But in the event a so-called Advanced Echelon went to Hollandia to conduct local TA, thus leaving CBB intact.

In this atmosphere the British, anxious to retain prestige, became concerned that, in the rush to crush Japan, their efforts would be widely dispersed and their really vital, practical influence on cryptanalytical and intelligence work forfeited in the culminating campaigns of south-east Asia and the Pacific. Reading de Grey in retrospect, when he rightly remarks that the problems of SIGINT in this vast theatre of war were never satisfactorily resolved, one nevertheless can lose sight of the fact that the Allied fighting services rarely were caught by surprise in the Quadrilateral, as they had been at Arnhem and the Ardennes. Strategic mistakes in the coming months there would be by senior commanders who were in full possession of sound intelligence. Slim's delay in moving troops from the Arakan to Imphal and Kohima in March 1944, was one such; as was Admiral William Halsey's abandonment of Leyte Gulf in October in order to go chasing Japanese aircraft carriers instead of defending the American amphibious force against the threat of battleships. But, as will be seen in Chapter 23, setbacks which lengthened the war there were none. Total victory for Slim's Fourteenth Army was within sight. The Japanese Combined Fleet was about to embark on its suicidal charge off the Philippines. For these bounties first-class SIGINT, however incomplete, was very largely responsible and often decisive.

Nowhere else was this factor so pronounced than with the US Navy's blockade of Japan which posed a strategic effect that was far deadly than the Germans and Italians ever managed to impose in the West. For one thing, in the Pacific the Americans, Australian and British (unlike the Germans in the Atlantic) made maximum use of air power to find and sink merchant ships. But it was the American submarines which did the most damage, starting their depredations against the *marus* soon after Pearl Harbor and progressively (despite numerous defective torpedoes) within a year had sunk 142. A year later they had disposed of another 435 when seventy-three boats were operating in the central Pacific and less than thirty from Fremantle: all this for the loss of twenty-five boats against forty-seven Japanese boats sunk.

This equation does more than reflect superior American technology in the shape of radar (which the Japanese lacked) and the information gleaned by aircraft and coastwatchers. It was largely achieved by the radio interception of FU searchers who ringed Japan from Canada, the Aleutians, through China to Australia and via the Solomons to Hawaii and Midway. It was they who plotted not only the courses of convoys and individual vessels but also were aware of, as Ronald Lewin points out in *The Other Ultra*, 'the cargoes carried, the escorts and the noon position for some or all the days of its voyage'. So dependable was the SIGINT that a day dawned when Admiral King felt constrained to stamp on captains' practice of logging sufficient details of engagements as to threaten the security of Ultra.

The calamitous effect on the Japanese war economy of the submarine campaign (in which boats accounted for 70 per cent of Japan's shipping losses) was driven home with such force in 1944 that strategy had fundamentally to be changed by a crippling oil shortage. From January to April submarines sank 179 ships and from then until August another 219, a high percentage of which were tankers. A position therefore was reached in which ship-building yards could replace only a fraction of the losses. Army RI intercepted a signal that blew the gaff when it gave the opinion that 'the present situation is such that the majority of tankers returning to Japan are being lost'. This meant that the Combined Japanese Fleet, to be in possession of adequate fuel supplies, had no option but to base itself on the British-built Singapore dockyard in close proximity to the Borneo and East Indies oil fields. From here it hoped to defend strategically vital Rabaul, New Guinea, the Philippines and, perhaps, Truk, Guam and the Marianas chain against overwhelming forces. But their intelligence was feeble by comparison with that of the Allies; and flawed by the assumption that the Philippines were the main American objective.

On 15 June the big B29s from Chengtu (in western China) flew their first bombing mission against a target in Japan. But four days before that US Navy aircraft had attacked the Marianas almost unopposed as the prelude to an amphibious landing on Saipan – which was 2,000 miles from Brunei where the Japanese Combined Fleet lay at anchor.

As elsewhere in this book, details will be avoided about vastly complex operations. It is sufficient to mention the decisive operations of 1944 which led up to the assault landing on Saipan (also on 15 June) and to the celebrated Great Marianas Turkey Shoot four days later. But it is essential to emphasise the effect of SIGINT on the Japanese who were not nearly so well served as the Americans, whose machine codes remained unbroken. Perhaps the Japanese were not quite so utterly distracted as were the Germans at that moment concerning Allied plans in Normandy. But it was inept intuition and what few grains of intelligence did come their way misled them into assuming that the Philippines were the main objective and that Guam and the Marianas could be defended by shore-based aircraft.

They were disastrously disabused. Over Guam, the ground-based machines were massacred by SIGINT-briefed US carrier fighters which, with perfect timing, caught them forming up in the air. In the approaches to Saipan, where the Combined Fleet put in its appearance on the 19th, the outcome was the same because, thanks to Lt Sims and another Japanese-speaking computor officer on board Admiral Marc Mitscher's flagship, the fighter direction controllers received the same clear warnings of approaching enemy as had controllers in Europe during the invasions of Sicily, Salerno and Anzio; except that on this occasion Sims and his colleague actually heard the Japanese master pilot directing his followers into action. Thus they were able to give real-time predictions to the controllers who could stage-manage the evolving dog-fights. The score of 243 shipborne and fifty-eight land-based Japanese shot down, plus four carriers sunk, when set against fifteen American machines and only four ships damaged, not only pronounced the doom of the Japanese naval arm. It demonstrated the priceless value of tactical SIGINT at its best that was the model for all invasions to come.

CHAPTER TWENTY-THREE

ULTIMATE CLIMAX

In the eyes of many informed Japanese in 1944, the war was lost before the Philippines were invaded on 20 October and their Combined Fleet put to sea for its last great suicidal mission. For by then, despite the exaggerations of their propagandists, news from their several ongoing campaigns added up to a story-book packed with chapters of defeat. Of these the increasing number of effective B29 bomber attacks from China on the homeland were the first to suggest to the prescient what was in store for the future.

Reports from Burma had spoken of heavy fighting at Kohima and Imphal and a check for the Japanese Fifteenth Army which, at the end of June, was converted into a retreat that deteriorated into a rout ill-starred by logistic collapse and outbreaks of disease in the monsoon. Through British and Indian Army FUs the Japanese decay was reported to WEC at Delhi and disseminated along the usual channels to commands and formations. Radio reception was frequently made difficult by climatic conditions, but General Slim and his senior subordinates were rarely short of essential SIGINT. They were thus in a position to press their advantage into Central Burma with confidence, regardless of difficult terrain and the weather, leading to the culminating clash of converging British and Chinese armies with the outnumbered Japanese. This convergence reopened the Burma Road, brought the fall of Mandalay on 20 March 1945 and acted as the prelude to Slim's 'crowning mercy' in the dash for Rangoon, which fell on 3 May as the monsoon broke and virtually put an end to the campaign in Burma.

Meanwhile in the summer of 1944, away to the north, a major Japanese offensive in China, monitored by American and Chinese RI stations, had at first made progress against sporadic resistance (including persistent attacks by American bombers and fighters); but it had then lost momentum and failed to capture five of the twelve B29's airfields which (courtesy of Allied SIGINT) were known to be its principal objectives. This defeat was a crucial turning-point. It released major Chinese forces for the clearing of the vital Burma Road as well as their contribution to the crushing of Fifteenth Army. These operations coincided in October with the bombing of Japan and targets in Formosa by China-based B29s, in support of the forthcoming landings in the Philippines, even though, in August, Japanese pilots had started the premeditated practice of ramming B29s in flight – of which no prior warning was obtained by the Allies, albeit, in 1931, the RAF had foreseen its possibility.

TO THE JAPANESE THE loss of their base and airfield at Hollandia on 22 April to a surprise landing by American troops provided ample proof that the Philippines were the Americans' prime objective. MacArthur received much praise for leap-frogging 500 miles westward along the New Guinea coast to take this strategically important administrative centre. But originally it was his intention to assault Rabaul and it required a direct order from the Chiefs of Staff which compelled him to change plan. For detailed SIGINT of the Japanese immense strengths and dispositions at Rabaul and at Wewak had convinced Marshall and King that these were best bypassed in favour of swiftly and cheaply seizing the only lightly held Hollandia. At a stroke, the entire Eighteenth Japanese Army, along with its air element, was cut off to the east, forcing it to launch costly counterattacks which, in the ensuing months, got nowhere, very largely due to intercepted orders revealing in full detail every impending move. Proudly could CBB claim in the aftermath that 'never has a commander gone into battle knowing so much about the enemy as did the Allied commander at Aitape on 10–11 July'.

The Japanese in New Guinea continued to resist with fanatical zeal and terrible losses. By 25 August they were reduced to impotence, even though isolated elements made nuisances of themselves until May 1945. For MacArthur, however, the victory at Hollandia was uplifting and decisive. It provided him with a splendid logistic base and a suitable location for HQ SWPA, both of which accelerated the launching of his return to the Philippines.

The threat of American invasion of the Philippines in October prompted the Japanese Army feverishly to reinforce its scattered garrisons and air forces there; and their Navy to commit itself to virtual extinction in the vain hope of smashing the enemy's amphibious fleet. As before and in the months to come, SIGINT's quality in timely sufficiency remained top-rate as a matter of course. Here we will deal briefly with each of the mighty, preparatory American operations prior to the landing at Leyte Island on 20 October, before relating the fate of the Combined Fleet as, lacking aircraft carriers, it executed Operation Sho (Victory).

Air power, of course, was at the heart of the preparations and the Americans were perfectly familiar, via SIGINT, with the build-up of Japanese Army and Navy Air Forces in the Philippines, Formosa and Okinawa. Their bombers and fighters from the sixteen carriers of Task Force 38 proceeded to attack enemy airfields from 10 to 16 October. PR and SIGINT had pinpointed those airfields for the bombers, and the fighter controllers, prompted by computor officers, intercepted the inexperienced Japanese airmen as they struggled unavailingly to sink those carriers. The outcome was another turkey shoot. On their own admission, duly intercepted by delighted Navy and Army searchers, they lost over 550 machines. But in return their crews glibly claimed eleven American carriers, two battleships, three destroyers and a destroyer sunk, and another eight carriers and two battleships damaged – figures which Tokyo Radio multiplied and which were celebrated with jubilant public celebrations.

Certainly American losses of aircraft were unusually high – 2.8 per cent from 3,800 sorties. But only two cruisers and one light carrier were damaged and not one sunk. Closer to reality in its exposure of the Japanese outlook, however, was a signal from their Army Chief of Staff soberly confirming ten carriers put down and three damaged. As the US Navy closed on Leyte and prepared to counter Operation Sho, it revelled in the sure knowledge that their enemy was suffering from an excess of hubris that might well prove demoralising in the long run because it showed that the Japanese were underestimating American strength. There is no record of the Japanese reaction to Admiral Nimitz's broadcast communiqué which stated that Admiral Halsey had given 'the comforting assurance that he is now retiring toward the enemy following the salvage of all the Third Fleet ships recently sunk by Radio Tokyo'.

Ronald Lewin made the rather strange comment in *The Other Ultra* that 'SIGINT seems to have made so small a contribution to the enormous naval Battle of Leyte Gulf'. In fact, Admiral Nimitz was in early possession through Ultra of the over-complicated Sho 1 plan. He knew not only that five groups of warships would converge on Leyte Gulf, but also that the most northerly one under Admiral Ozawa, starting from Japan and including the remaining four carriers (embarking only 108 aircraft with inexperienced crews), was a decoy designed to lure away Halsey's Third Fleet. Furthermore, no sooner did the Combined Fleet start to put to sea from Singapore on 18 October, than a breach of radio silence was intercepted by RI in ample time to alert Nimitz.

The rest is history. Reported and successfully attacked by submarines, the two Japanese groups advancing through the Surigao and the San Bernardino Straits were exposed to furious air attacks, against which their own land-based fighters provided little protection. Indeed these were engaged in supporting attacks on American carriers, although without success and at considerable cost. Radar and the shipborne computor officers collaborated efficiently to knock down sixty-six of the 396 aircraft based in the Philippines. Shortly before nightfall it appeared to Admiral Halsey that both Japanese groups had been repulsed and therefore that the main threat had shifted to Ozawa's carriers that were bearing down from the north. SIGINT did nothing to reveal that, in fact, the Japanese facing him had reversed course and again were heading for the straits. And Halsey, who beyond doubt knew through Special Branch that the Ozawa carriers were a decoy, took the bait and raced northward with his entire fleet. This left the Amphibious Force off Leyte under dire threat from battleships, cruisers and destroyers which, as luck would have it, were being most indecisively manoeuvred due to conflicting intelligence which failed positively to confirm Halsey's absence.

SIGINT became almost superfluous once American air reconnaissance and surface vessels had found the approaching Japanese groups. Battleships, cruisers (including one Australian), PT boats and carrier-borne aircraft, most skilfully handled, did all that was necessary to drive off the threat at Surigao Strait with crushing losses; and to keep at arm's length the group which had broken through the San Bernardino Strait. Meanwhile Halsey, charging bull-headed to meet Ozawa some 300 miles to the north, was busy sinking all four enemy carriers by aircraft and yearning for the opportunity to sink the two battleships with overwhelming gunfire. He was denied this treat when brought under pressure by Nimitz to send his battleships to the rescue at the San Bernardino Straits, where the contest already was being won decisively by the defenders of the Amphibious Force, long before Halsey's arrival.

The naval war between fleets, to all intents and purposes, ended at Leyte Gulf, and with it the effective part played in it by conventional Japanese aircraft. In its place there occurred during the final stages of the fight for the San Bernardino Straits a very successful attack by five Zero fighters belonging to the Special Attack Corps – better known as Kamikazi. These machines, carrying bombs, were piloted by young men prepared to sacrifice their lives in almost the only way possible to sink ships with a high degree of certainty. For, as recent experience had demonstrated, the chances of conventional air attacks to hit ships with bombs and torpedoes – above all aircraft carriers – were remote in the extreme.

SIGINT was handicapped in any attempt to give early warning of the approach of kamikazi because they maintained strict radio silence. The best antidote, by day and night, was a blanket of fighters, guided by radar, and intensive gunfire: along with the denial, as much as possible, of the valuable aircraft carriers that were relatively easy targets to identify and hit. Therefore American aircraft, based on recaptured airfields, were crucial in the top priority, anti-kamikazi role to reduce the carnage initially inflicted by these human guided missiles which, unlike conventional bombers, had no need to ask for post-mission, homing signals to their airfields! These were best detected by PR.

The fact remains that kamikazi used by the hundred scored an extremely high percentage of hits and inflicted heavy Allied casualties in the ongoing, island-hopping operations on the route to Japan, via Iwo

Jima and Okinawa, and towards Singapore, via the Philippines and North Borneo. These islands provided bases for a vital screen of RAAF WUs whose intercepts were channelled through CBB to both Nimitz's and MacArthur's widespread forces.

It is, indeed very instructive that, in August 1945, four out of the existing seven Australian stations played a key role from Darwin (3 WU), the San Miguel Islands, in the Sulu Sea (5 and 6 WUs plus a detachment from 4 WU), Luzon (a detachment from 4 WU), Labuan and Morotai (detachments from 4 WU) and Lingayen in the north of Luzon where an RT section was located. The scattering of these parties created all manner of control and administrative difficulties; apart from those of interception, which was hampered by the Japanese practice of transmitting on the lowest power possible to be heard by their control station, making it necessary to locate intercept stations dangerously close to the enemy for audibility reasons.

Like other causes for dissatisfaction, these worries were mainly of the niggle variety, to be viewed in proportion to the rapidly improving, world-wide strategic position that was symbolically underlined by the move of HQ SWPA to Manila in February. Kamikazi might have deterred the Allies – the Americans in particular as they bore the brunt of their depredations – from persisting in their intent of invading Japan. But as sheer mass of material and firepower, mainly from B29s from Saipan (instead of China) from November 1944 onward and from carrier-borne aircraft from16 February 1945, began to lay waste Japanese cities and industry, SIGINT's function, as in the west, tended to revert from a vital operational role to that of a prime reporting agency.

At this very time, any insight into German morale and the people's determination to fight on during the fading stages of the European war was deemed useful, but hardly crucial as an indefensible Reich was overrun. In the east, however, such knowledge was of far greater importance because Japanese fanatical determination to fight on hopelessly was already on record as being something apart, especially since she was in no immediate danger of collapse. Therefore it was of immense importance to gain reliable intelligence about Japan's resources, along with her morale, before deciding how best rapidly and economically in terms of human lives, to compel her surrender.

This is not the place to enter into a detailed discussion on the subject of whether or not the Japanese would have surrendered if two atom bombs had not been dropped in August 1945. It is perhaps sufficient to summarise Ronald Lewin's shrewd analysis of the matter in *The Other Ultra*. Arguably, he stated that the evidence of SIGINT and Magic alone was not enough to provide a firm base upon which President Harry Truman could decide the least costly course open to minimise an unavoidably heavy casualty list (for both sides) in forcing Japan to surrender without delay. The options were either a conventional invasion of Japan, along with unlimited mayhem, or a strike by two atom bombs that would localise destruction and, conceivably, slay fewer people.

Yet SIGINT's prolific contribution from Army RI in July did more than produce a decoded, weekly up-dated, forty-page Estimated Unit Locations statement of Japanese Navy and Army Air Forces, besides an Army Order of Battle giving the locations of fighting formations and their state of training. For it also uncovered an underlying and daunting theme of enemy, doctrinal training focused on suicide attacks which mirrored the hundreds of actual kamikaze actions at sea, in the air and on the ground. There was positive evidence that suicide tactics by numerous self-sacrificial young men, imbued by the Samurai spirit, would be employed extensively to slay and destroy on a considerable scale. Balancing the potential of this threat against the counter-evidence of a genuine peace-seeking mood among some Japanese people and statesmen, Truman was bound to be influenced, as he was by General Marshall, when the Chief of Staff, unanimously backed by Admiral King, Admiral Leahy and General Eisenhower (among others), estimated that an invasion of Japan 'would cost at a minimum one quarter million casualties, and might cost as much as a million, on the American side alone, with an equal number of the enemy'. Truman wrote: 'We sent an ultimatum to Japan. It was rejected. I ordered atomic bombs dropped on the two cities.'

THERE IS SOMETHING weird about Nigel de Grey's treatment of world-wide SIGINT in the last chapter of his draft book. On the one hand he leaves the reader in no doubt that a vast quantity of traffic was being intercepted and huge quantities of documents, along with code books, being captured. But on the other, he seems almost to highlight a long-running catalogue of complaint elaborating the Allied handling of this treasure trove when, in practical terms, the picture of the enemy's position and strategy was clear and the means to destroy him super-abundant: bearing in mind, of course, that the existence and nature of the atomic weapon was known but to a very few and was almost unimaginable in its colossal effects to those who did know.

Niggling laments pervade de Grey's manuscript where it outlines SIGINT performance at the higher levels in the closing months of the war in the Quadrilateral. Many of them are repetitious of old irritations and minor disagreements between colleagues and allies of high intellectual quality and sense of bounden duty. They probably reflect de Grey's own enormous breadth of knowledge, experience and insight; exacerbated by war weariness after nearly six years of ceaseless stress, worry, immense responsibility and travail in developing and holding together such a diverse team of strong personalities, spread world-wide. To expect perfection, as he did, in these circumstances was to ask too much of mankind. The proof of the pudding was in the eating which, for the most part, was good and sufficient in so vast an organisation that had produced war-shortening results of outstanding merit.

In summary, the recurrent complaints centred on discontent with waste caused by lax co-ordination of effort, friction in cryptanalytical affairs, duplication of shared tasks, staff shortages and inferior training of operatives. For example:

1. The belated discovery that the Japanese 3366 code book was enciphered on the same tables as the 6633 book, one of which was used on SEAC's Burma front and the other on SWPA's. As a result of joint action by GC and CS, WEC and CBB no less than 3,000 additional texts became decipherable with relative ease.

2. The continuing paucity of output in India, largely caused by staff

shortage and inefficiency, that induced blatant discrepancies in the performance of certain organisations. In November 1944, for example, one section managed to complete only five pages of a sixty-page document when another had tackled all but fifteen from a 300-page document. As a senior officer remarked, if this was to continue, 'things will get chaotic'.

3. Inflexibility in use of staff had permitted inefficient load sharing and the swamping of some sections while others stood idle elsewhere in the quadrilateral.

This led, for example, to Admiral Lord Mountbatten's complaint to the Head of JAIS (who was on a round-the-world tour) that Army SIGINT, by comparison with Navy and Air, was falling short of his needs. Surprisingly the reason for this turned out to be lack of adequate liaison with G 2 in Washington, a difficulty which was soon ironed out by appointing a British Y officer to G 2 to 'watch out for SEAC's interests'.

Lack of liaison was at the root of many problems at higher levels and many were resolved by personal visits from senior officers. For example, minor who-does-what problems were resolved in March 1945 in Washington at the end of the head of JAIS's tour. This was followed in April by another Washington conference to smooth 'the rumpled surface', including the solution of a trivial matter concerning the transit of Australian raw material through Washington to GC and CS. The most satisfying aspect was that, almost without exception, these matters (which usually stemmed from geographical factors) were sorted in an adult manner with a minimum of friction.

A reorganisation of G 2, initiated in the summer of 1944, was still in progress and inflicting production difficulties in 1945. This led to a request for help from GC and CS, which was most cordially negotiated to the benefit and satisfaction of all concerned. Higher productivity of SIGINT indeed had become such an obsession in mid-1944 that a process of registration of material founded on what was termed 'The Three Rs' was brought into effect to improve matters. For example, the haphazard transit of material from India, which was sent in bundles, more or less as it came from sets; and 'higgledy-piggledy' as sent by the Americans.

The three Rs were:

Routing – the establishment, from coded preamble or call signs by origin, at signal offices and by destination.

Recognition – the acceleration of the time-consuming working out of ciphered discriminants.

Registration – the filing into a form for tabulating machine tape punching that facilitated the quicker, orderly production of essential data for Traffic Analysis purposes; for cryptanalytic runs; and the completion of messages when stripped for decoding and translation.

This was a large-scale scheme, which demanded 200 people for the 3 Rs process alone. But within a month it had reduced the time-lag between key breaker and translator from fourteen to seven days. There was, however, a knock-on effect due to the familiar shortage of capacity that was the result of too few untrained women to operate too few machines, which suffered from punched tape problems, to cope with the increased number of messages from four to five thousand a day. Arrears piling up could barely be kept down even by a so-called 'riot squad' of efficient WAAFs that was introduced in July 1945.

It was a nice irony that, less than a mere month before the war was brought to an abrupt end (quite literally by two flashes from out of the blue) the scope and standards of command and control of intelligence throughout the Quadrilateral reached unprecedented and praiseworthy efficiency in July.

HQ SWPA's move to Manila, after its capture by MacArthur on 10 February, was followed by a significant improvement in strategic radio communications made feasible by American radio teletype and British high-speed sets which already linked GC and CS with Delhi and now Brisbane and Delhi with Manila. This coincided in July with Brisbane taking delivery of a Special Liaison Unit, which enabled it to handle Ultra, and the establishment of complementary high-security American Ultra arrangements with CBB. At the end of the month, CBB set up shop on San Miguel Island alongside 4, 5 and 6 Australian WUs, thus strengthening the Australian presence at this strategic place as well as taking a further consolidation of the world-wide network. Then, on 6 August, the latest security instructions came into force with the publication of so-called Pinup Regulations, governing the use and handling of medium and low-grade signal intelligence, which had been agreed by both the American Navy and Army Departments and the British.

That day Hiroshima was annihilated by an atom bomb. Three days later Nagasaki suffered the same fate. On 14 August Japan surrendered unconditionally, followed piecemeal by a cease-fire on all fronts as orders, monitored by SIGINT, reached and were truculently obeyed by isolated formations, units and detachments.

CHAPTER TWENTY-FOUR

ENDLESS STORY

In March 1944 GC and CS and the Foreign Office began to establish policy with regards to 'Interception in the period immediately following an
armistice with Germany'. Six months later, on 14 September, a draft paper
was written with the 'object to make a reasonable plan'. It visualised the
need for about 500 sets to cover Service and Foreign Office diplomatic
tasks, of which the latter required 140. It was assumed that Japanese
traffic would remain largely unaffected except for German–Japanese messages. Ex-enemy countries would be monitored. Foreign diplomatic 'will
remain constant'. Liberated countries 'should be studied'.

Russia was a prime target. 'The Russians are realists, and they will
intercept our traffic and expect us to intercept theirs. They would make
no bones about it, though they may not be as candid as the French, who
at one time gave us their TA reports complete with "Section Anglais"!
Interception of Russian traffic is normally difficult for us, but owing to
their present advance westwards, the opportunity to do so is good and an
intense study should be made while there is a chance and resources are
available.'

The paper also stated that 'Work on Noise Investigation should
continue.'

After the war was over, and the armed forces began to demobilise,
another one, later called the Cold War, began. Therefore, as it had been
in 1919 after World War One, the monitoring of selected, foreign radio
networks continued world-wide, especially by Britain, Canada, Australia,
New Zealand and the USA, of Russia and those of her satellites on the
other side of what Winston Churchill was to call the Iron Curtain.

Logically, therefore, top men such as Edward Travis, Nigel de Grey,
Eric Jones and Josh Cooper stayed on at GC and CS to contribute to the
writing of secret histories and memoirs of GC and CS's part in World War
Two, and, of higher necessity, to fight coming battles and contribute to
the move in 1952 from Bletchley Park of what, in 1946, became known

as GCHQ (Government Communications Headquarters), to Cheltenham. At the same time, of course, the searchers of Y Service went on listening, computing and learning. Among their earliest discoveries was the sound of Enigma messages from Russian transmitters – traffic encoded on captured machines which, initially, proved fairly difficult to decrypt because their new owners, perhaps helped by German prisoners, had introduced additional safeguards.

It is not the intention to explore the post-war intelligence situation, other than to draw outline conclusions about salient matters and give pointers to developments of fundamental importance. Arguably the basic reasons for the Allies taking so long to catch up with the Axis communicators was their failure to establish adequate intercept facilities and techniques and to recruit a strong cadre of cryptologists and translators prior to 1939. By allowing the Axis experts far too long a lead in SIGINT technology and techniques, gleaned from the war experiences of 1914 to 1918 and from the Spanish Civil War of the 1930s, they put their countries in jeopardy.

Not until mid-1943 had these handicaps been overcome in Europe and, as already mentioned, never wholly solved in the struggle against Japan. League tables of SIGINT prowess can be misleading and invidious, but I would place the US Navy top in Oceania and the Indian authorities (largely because of over-ambition and their incredible failure to utilise the readily available expertise of Wing Commander Laurie and Lt Colonel Vernham) bottom of the list. This left the far more experienced British GC and CS well ahead of them all in security and distribution methods, yet, along with the USA, extremely fortunate against top-class radio interceptors, not to suffer the penalty of having their own encoding machines, such as Typex, Sigaba and Hagelin, broken. Think how much more difficult alone distribution of SIGINT would have been had that been found to have happened; or if, like their enemies, they had remained unaware of the break-in.

Nigel de Grey, however, offers some interesting comments about the Australians, whose effort he praised for its realism based on an independence of spirit, despite the American presence in their area. In the absence of officers trained in high level reporting, they were at a disadvantage because of making negligible calls on Britain for help – and therefore receiving little assistance from that quarter! But, like Britain, they too were defending their own soil.

Setting aside the undeniable failure of the Allies to reach the same level of proficiency in the Far East Quadrilateral as had been achieved in Europe, there was no gainsaying the crucially significant agreements and practices which had been established at the end of July 1945. These laid the foundations of the UKUSA Accord which, in March 1946, formalised a world-wide sharing of intelligence acquisition responsibilities between the USA, Britain, Canada, Australia and New Zealand that did so much to defeat Russia and her allies and satellites in the Cold War. It goes without saying that this might not have been possible but for the excellent relationships forged between 1939 and 1945.

Since then revolutionary strides have been taken in electronics, encoding, decoding, distribution techniques through tabulating machinery and computers, and radio transmissions by such phenomena as tropospheric scatter and the use of space satellite relay stations. But the basic techniques of interception and of TA and DF, which were at the root of early SIGINT activity, remain paramount. Assuredly machines help present-day searchers but, in the final analysis, it is the skills and authority of the experienced, individual expert which makes the final analysis from which intelligence officers, staffs and commanders draw conclusions and select their options. The major difference between today's SIGINT and that of 1904, when the Japanese listened in to the thin morse code signals of the approaching Russian fleet, is that of scale. The sheer volume of material being pumped out can saturate listening stations to such an extent as to prevent them separating the wheat from the chaff in order to find and identify what is vitally needed. This is the reason why the first employment of DF before 1914 and of Traffic Analysis by the French in 1915 were so crucially important then; why they remained the key to SIGINT in World War Two (when at times they were the only reliable source of intelligence to the Americans); and why today, no matter how effective cryptanalytic devices are, TA and DF may at times be the only instruments to detect, identify and locate military organisations and obtain indications of their commanders' intentions.

Of course, since the 1950s, the alternatives to radio communication have been enormously improved. Networks of multi-channel cable systems securely perform numerous duties previously carried out by radio; but these are vulnerable as frequently is demonstrated by penetration of on-line Internet traffic. Far safer are the plethora of revolutionary radio systems which now can enhance security, such as by direct radio beam networks, which have always been difficult to intercept; and by 'frequency agile, hopping' transmitters which are extremely difficult to read. Nevertheless, as the best alternative to radio, stand fibre optic cables which not only carry vast quantities of traffic but also are exceptionally difficult to tap without being detected. Meanwhile the use of supersonic aircraft for couriers has made ocean liners obsolete – provided the former do not inadvertently land intact in hostile terrain.

Unavoidably, however, there will be dependence on interceptable radio traffic along with the security risks attendant on its decryption. For the golden rule remains that no code, except the infallible OTP, can indefinitely resist penetration, as was demonstrated during World War Two, when code breaks often came about due to operators' carelessness, to luck and to hit-and-miss methods; or, as in the case of German and Japanese communicators, in a fatally arrogant belief that some encoding machines were unbreakable. Such a brand of wishful thinking persisted in the minds of some German experts who went on denying that Enigma had been broken other than by hit-and-miss for several years after the Ultra secret was publicised.

Put not your faith in the Internet, for in its confidentiality and privacy there is no security. The author of this book resolutely rejects and avoids dot.com.

BIBLIOGRAPHY

Anon; *The Rise and Fall of the German Air Force*, USA, 1969

Anon MOD (Navy); *The U-Boat War in the Atlantic 1939–1945*, HMSO, London, 1989

Baker, W; *A History of the Marconi Company*, Methuen, London, 1979

Bekker, C; *The Luftwaffe War Diaries*, Macdonald, London, 1966

Brown, D, Shore, C, and Macksey, K; *The Guinness History of Air Warfare*, Guinness, London, 1976

Cave Brown, A; *"C"*, Macmillan, New York, 1987

Clayton, A; *The Enemy is Listening*, Hutchinson, London, 1980

Dyer, G.C; *The Amphibians Came to Conquer*, US Navy, Washington, 1969

Halder, Gen F; *War Diary 1939 –1942*, Presidio, New York, 1988

Hinsley, H. et al; *British Intelligence in the Second World War* (Five Vols), HMSO, London, 1979/90

Hinsley, H and Stripp, A; *The Codebreakers*, Oxford University Press, London, 1993

Howarth, S; *Morning Glory*, Hutchinson, London, 1983

Jones, R V; *Most Secret War*, Hamish Hamilton, London, 1978

Kahn, D; *The Codebreakers*, Weidenfeld and Nicolson, London, 1966

Lewin, R; *Ultra Goes to War*, Hutchinson, London, 1978

— *The Other Ultra*, Hutchinson, London, 1982

— *Slim*, Leo Cooper, London, 1976

Macintyre, D; *The Naval War against Hitler*, Scribner, New York, 1971

Macksey, K; *Military Errors of World War Two*, Cassell, London, 1987

— *Penguin Encyclopedia of Weapons and Technology*, Penguin, London, 1989

— *For Want of a Nail*, Brassey, London, 1989

— *Rommel: Campaigns and Battles*, Arms and Armour, London, 1979

— *Without Enigma*, Ian Allen, London, 2000

Pitt, B. (ed); *Purnell's History of The First World War*, Purnell, London, 1969

Seaton, A; *The Russo-German War 1941–45*, Arthur Barker, London, 1971

Skillen, H; *Spies of the Airways*, privately published, 1989

Slim, William; *Defeat into Victory*, Cassell, London, 1956

Smith, M; *Station X*, Channel 4, London, 1998

Terraine, J; *The Right of the Line*, Hodder and Stoughton, London, 1985

Tuchman, B; *The Zimmermann Telegram 1939–45*, Dell, New York, 1958

Warlimont, W; *Inside Hitler's Headquarters*, Presidio, New York, 1962

Welchman, G; *The Hut Six Story*, Allen Lane, London, 1982

Wildhagen, K. H; *Erich Fellgiebel*, Selbst, Germany, 1970

Winterbotham, F. W; *The Ultra Secret*, Cassell, London, 1974

UNPUBLISHED WORKS

Praun, A; *The Signal Services in the Service of OKH during World War II (MS P-041k)*, Neustadt, 1947

INDEX AND GLOSSARY